NATIONAL INDUSTRIAL POLICIES

FMME

The Fund for Multinational Management Education (FMME) is a non-profit organization that encourages and facilitates a more open dialogue between the managers of multinational enterprises and policy makers in governments and international organizations by means of programs that involve research, publications, and seminars and workshops, and that are practical, immediately useful, and action oriented.

FMME's programs concentrate on subjects relating to the economic and social impact of multinational enterprises around the world, on the organizational aspects of business investment and involvement in host countries, and on programs that aid in the education and technical training of those officials in foreign countries responsible for overseeing the flow of investment into their political systems. Among these subjects are the location of R&D facilities, the transfer of technology, the socioeconomic impact of multinational enterprises, codes of conduct for multinational enterprises, and management of corporate social policies and public affairs.

National Industrial Policies

HD
3611
.N36
1984
West

Edited by

Robert E. Driscoll
and
Jack N. Behrman

A Project sponsored and
administered by the
FMME
Fund for Multinational
Management Education

 Oelgeschlager, Gunn & Hain, Publishers, Inc.
Cambridge, Massachusetts

International Standard Book Number: 0–89946–180–8

Library of Congress Catalog Card Number: 83–25054

Printed in the U.S.A.

Library of Congress Cataloging in Publication Data
Main entry under title:

National Industrial Policy

"A project sponsored and administered by the FMME, Fund for Multinational Management Education."
Bibliography: p.
Includes index.
1. Industry and state – Addresses, essays, lectures. I. Driscoll, Robert E. II. Behrman, Jack N. III. Fund for Multinational Management Education.
HD3611.I445   1984   338.9   83–25054
ISBN 0–89946–180–8

Contents

Chapter 1

Introduction

Robert E. Driscoll* and Jack N. Behrman**

Industrialization has long been seen as one of the quickest, most secure routes to economic development and modernization. Just as Europe and the United States shifted from an agriculture-based economy to one dependent upon industry, developing countries have been urged to industrialize to improve the standards of living of their populations and to join the ranks of the so-called advanced countries. Since the 1950s it has been generally accepted that government intervention into the market would be essential to accomplish this process of industrialization within the very limited time frame envisioned by governments and political leaders.

NATIONAL POLICIES

In the past, government policies to promote industrialization were limited to enticing businesses to locate within their borders—with little concern as to the type of activity as long as it generated jobs and increased the level of industrial activity. In the drive to industrialize, governments promoted investments—by private companies and by state

*Fund for Multinational Management Education
**University of North Carolina at Chapel Hill

enterprises—without much attention to the backward and forward linkages essential to efficient operations. The predominant focus was on growth and employment. As a result, monuments to bad planning, easy credit, and overly ambitious government and private plans abound: turnkey plants that are not operating because the necessary raw materials are not available, or because demand for the product has shifted and the technology is not available to modernize or adjust.

The oil shocks of the 1970s convinced government officials and economic planners that such waste of resources cannot continue. Further, the unbridled pursuit of import substitution has produced imbalances in national economies which are now beginning to constrain national development goals and to hinder the progress of industrialization. Scarce foreign exchange has led many countries to try to increase exports, virtually without regard to the cost. And since most of the import substitution industries have developed behind high tariff barriers, they suffer from technological deficiencies, high production costs, and poor quality relative to competitors in the international markets—and consequently hamper the export drives.

National industrial policies designed to spur investments in specific sectors are a response to the perceived failure of aggregate policies to produce acceptable levels of growth and desirable industrial structures. Governments now attempt to stimulate investments in specific industries with the aim of achieving economic development while balancing industrial structure and assuring domestic production of key materials, products, and services. Governments are not only supporting industries for the domestic market, but also as future export earners. Depending on the country, industrial policies are also designed to assure domestic security through mixture of the basic or heavy industries, specific light manufacturing, critical consumer products, and key service industries.

Partly in response to the growth of manufactured exports from the developing countries, and partly because of their own aging industrial structure, many advanced countries are also implementing industrial policies. These policies are often defensive—intended to retain a certain (sometimes declining) industry within the nation. Increasingly, however, governments are interested in policies that stimulate new, high technology industries. The interests of the French government in informatics is well known. And the debate on U.S. industrial policies—or, more politically, the "reindustrialization" of America—focuses on "picking the winners" in future world competition as well as on protecting existing industrial structures.

Many of the national debates on industrial policies have taken place without reference to the international situation in an industry or to the costs of proposed measures domestically or in other affected nations. Little attention has been paid, even within the United Nations and other intergovernmental bodies, to the implications of these policies for international trade patterns or the flows of capital and technology between countries.

Essentially, governments have decided that the market can no longer be the prime determinant of industrial structures domestically and internationally. They attempt to alter or supplement their comparative advantages to encourage industry to locate within their borders or to retain industries that might otherwise relocate. The policies employed range from tax incentives and tax holidays to promotion of state enterprises and specific credit, technological, and other direct support of industries. Both developing and advanced countries, including those most committed to the free market, have adopted some form of industrial policy.

Seeking short-term advantages and quick solutions to immediate employment and balance-of-payments problems, many policy makers ignore the impacts of these policies on trade relations, investment and technology transfer patterns, the development and modernization of technology, and domestic employment and industrial adjustments. But industrial policies are a significant new force affecting the international economy, which must be recognized by both government policy makers and corporate planners in their investment decisions. The shifts within and among nations will not depend solely on efficiency criteria or to the more market/economic decision criteria of industry. Government equity concerns are a factor in location decisions—and are likely to be increasingly important in the next decade.

Governments' interest in industrial policies also stems in part from a desire to counteract the cyclical shifts in international economic relations and to adjust aggressively for the downturn in the international economy due to the oil shocks of the 1970s and the worldwide recession of the late 1970s and early 1980s. The early manifestation of this drive can be seen in the export expansion policies of both advanced and newly industrialized countries, bolstered by efforts to attract new investments to foster exports of new products.

The rush to adopt industrial policies is taken on scant evidence of the efficacy of these policies. Many point to the "successes" of French and Japanese industrial policies in maintaining economic momentum in spite of worldwide recession. Still others point to the experience of the United Kingdom and lament government interference in private decisionmaking, pointing out that this intervention has decreased the well-being of the British population. Much of this confusion results from lack of knowledge of what governments are doing to promote and implement "industrial policies." This volume is intended to indicate what these policies are in a variety of nations, and to form the basis for further analysis of their impacts on national development and on international trade and investment.

POLICY ORIENTATIONS

The countries surveyed in this volume have chosen policies toward industrialization that range from "hands off" to explicit and extensive intervention.

Industrial Development Strategy

A few governments have adopted no particular policies toward the stimulation of industry or of any given sector but have simply sought to encourage economic growth, trusting that market and other economic factors would result in an appropriate mix of industry, agriculture, and services. These governments have established a general climate that encourages greater local and foreign private investment. The implication of such policies is that any production is acceptable so long as aggregate employment and growth goals are met. The degree and structure of industrialization is determined by the market, the existing technologies, and entrepreneurial responses. Since World War II, only a few countries have taken such a hands-off orientation; Switzerland is perhaps the most notable example.

Industrialization Policies

Most countries have tried to stimulate industrialization in the hope that it would provide diversified employment opportunities for their citizens and raise income levels. Government efforts primarily took the form of aggregate tax, fiscal, and monetary policies; some governments also supported investments in research and development (R&D). The result of such policies was to encourage the development of industry in general, without promoting any particular sectors. The level and structure of industrialization was, by design, left to the choice of companies responding to market signals within the broad industrial growth objectives set by the government. South Korea, Singapore, the United States, and West Germany are among the countries that have relied on this approach.

Industrial (Sectoral) Policies

In current use, the term "industrial policy" denotes the promotion of specific industrial sectors rather than industrialization overall. Industrialization in general can be encouraged through tax policies that provide accelerated depreciation or waivers to companies that comply with certain guidelines. Similarly, interest rates can be reduced to stimulate investment and demand across the board. These policies are considered indirect and macro, as distinct from policies related to price controls of a specific sector or efforts to concentrate companies within a given grouping. Industrial policies are direct, micro, and selective; they are an attempt by government to influence the decision making of companies or to alter market signals; thus they are discriminating.

These discriminatory policies are intended to alter comparative advantages—changing the factor endowments or altering their relative prices to induce investments—and to influence directly the decisions of investors—by offering both incentives and disincentives, inducements and constraints. When such policies have not brought about the desired change in private sources of capital and technology, governments have been more than willing to make such investments themselves; the result is an ever-growing state-enterprise system. In some cases, state enterprises have also been created to provide a national counterbalance to the perceived power of the transnational corporation, in order to assure domestic control of production in the national interest.

Industrial policy has sometimes sought to support the losers, delaying or retarding their decline; in other cases the goal is to succor or catalyze maturing sectors or to stimulate advancing sectors. Countries differ in their emphasis on these three objectives. Some governments have tried to anticipate the decline of mature sectors and to accelerate the economy's shift out of these sectors and into the high technology and advancing sectors. All of these objectives are supported by a variety of techniques that are seen by many as "interfering with the market" or "distorting the efficiency of market decisions."

THE INTERNATIONAL DEBATE

Some governments and organizations consider the present worldwide distribution of industry inequitable and have recommended that national industry sectors be restructured to the benefit of developing countries. The proposal for a "New International Economic Order" (NIEO) contends that the existing pattern of production and investments has resulted more from the international institutions that favored the already advanced countries than from underlying comparative advantages. The United States and the former colonialist powers of Europe, it is argued, dominated the major intergovernmental institutions and led the developing countries into a dependency situation as suppliers of raw materials to feed the industrial structures of the advanced world. In effect, these actions condemned the developing countries to continuing second-class status. The New International Economic Order and the global negotiations called for at the Cancun summit are intended to rectify this situation.

Pursuit of the objectives of the United Nations will entail even more active government intervention in decisions on the location of specific industries. The stated goals of the UN and of the NIEO are the establishment (or transfer if necessary) of 25 percent of the world's industrial production into the developing countries by the year 2000—a goal that even its proponents admit will be unrealistic without a major realignment of investment, trade, and technology transfer patterns. The emphasis within this debate, therefore, is not on the underlying comparative advantages of nations, but on the mechanisms needed to alter these advantages through unilateral and multilateral government intervention.

Such intervention is necessary, according to proponents of the NIEO concept, because most of the inadequacies of the existing structure can be blamed on the workings of the market, which have caused inequities not only in international trade and relations but also within the domestic economies of much of the Third World. Since the market is increasingly not accepted as an appropriate means of determining the location of production, decisions by national governments have intervened. What is not adequately understood as yet, and therefore not taken into account fully in this decision-making process, are the impacts of these interventions on international efficiency and on trade and economic relations among countries. Beggar-thy-neighbor policies could be one result of this plethora of interventions, leading ultimately to increased protectionism and a breakdown of the international system.

No one is currently predicting such a drastic outcome, but significant changes are nevertheless under way both internationally and within countries as they adjust to rapidly changing conditions. At the very least, this process is challenging the classical concepts of the international division of labor and the law of comparative advantage. Comparative advantage is now seen as something dynamic, which can change over time and in response to government intervention. Therefore, some countries are experimenting with processes of industrialization that differ from the patterns of the nineteenth and early twentieth centuries. Yet little is known of the international effects of such interventions on current and future industrial structures, or how to accommodate to these interventions in seeking agreements on national and international goals.

The growing significance of government intervention in investment and trade has given rise to a series of negotiations on nontariff barriers and subsidies sponsored by the General Agreement on Tariffs and Trade (GATT). Further negotiations have been proposed, with the issues of nontariff barriers among the most significant being addressed within the GATT. The GATT, however, tends to focus more on the traditional trade issues than on the effects of industrial policies on the promotion and distortion of trade. In the near future such issues will continue to be considered under the rubrics of "nontariff barriers" to trade, and "performance requirements" for foreign direct investors.

UN ACTIVITIES

The United Nations has determined that the decision making of transnational corporations with regard to trade and investment must be brought under the review of governments and intergovernmental agencies. Broad oversight of these issues is the responsibility of the UN Conference on Trade and Development (UNCTAD). This concern has led to a series of UN sponsored negotiations for codes of conduct: one on foreign direct investment and behavior of parent companies (under the UN Commission on Transnational Corporations), a second on technology transfer that will directly affect companies' decisions on locating business in new environments, and a third on restrictive business practices that will also alter international trade (both promoted by UNCTAD). The first two areas are still in negotiation after seven years of diplomatic effort; agreement has been reached in the third.

The United Nations Industrial Development Organization (UNIDO) is specifically charged with seeking implementation of the NIEO, and the General Assembly itself is currently discussing implementation of the NIEO objectives in the so-called Third Development Decade. Proposals for rebalancing industry in the favor of the developing world would have to be accomplished through either aggregate or sectoral policies; preference is currently being shown for sectoral stimuli, in order to give governments greater control. The advanced countries have generally shown little enthusiasm for outright transfers of industrial capacity, especially in key sectors that are the major foundations of industrial employment (such as the automotive industry) or that are critical to national security interests (such as steel).

These efforts are proceeding without any consensus on a new "ordering principle" for the international economy, which would be the basis for the determination of the international division of labor. Although international specialization has taken place, there is no agreement as to the criteria by which specialization should occur, except that many governments and international organizations would prefer that such specialization not be driven solely by the market decisions of local companies and transnational corporations.

These international efforts are seeking to establish the rules for determining *who* produces *what* and *where*, throughout the world. The problem is complicated by the belief of many that the benefits of industrialization must be more equitably distributed among countries. This problem of equity is coupled further with that of determining the desired nature and extent of international economic integration—as opposed to greater economic autonomy. The intergovernmental organizations are probing the extent to which competition should be allowed within cooperatively established rules that seek greater international integration—rather than within a world economy essentially separated by protectionist policies.

INDIVIDUAL GOVERNMENT POLICIES

The chapters of this volume describe the policies that individual governments are using to promote industrialization or to attract or retain specific industries. The industrial policies and strategies of fifteen developed and newly industrialized countries in Europe, North and South America, and Asia are examined. The authors were asked to describe the policy emphasis on general industrialization or promotion and support of particular industrial sectors, including the content of the rules and regulation of industry, in order to set the stage for later collaborative analyses of the impacts of these policies on specific industries, through shifts in international trade, technology flows, and investment and employment patterns.

Clearly, the fifteen countries surveyed here do not encompass all of the countries implementing industrial policies; indeed, some have shown an aversion to such government intervention. They do represent, however, a cross section of industrialized and newly industrializing countries and the diversity of policies being pursued. Collectively, they are responsible for the bulk of production in a number of key industries.

For a full understanding of the differences among countries, one must examine not only the content of policies, but also their general economic development purposes—that is, whether the policies were intended to induce development, to bring about industrialization in general, or to influence the decisions of specific industries. Figure 1.1 shows a useful schematic approach to analyzing the interests, policies, and techniques of the various countries.

Figure 1.1. Outline of national approaches.

	Industrial Development Strategy	Industrialization Policies	Industrial (Sectoral) Policies
Policy objectives			
Growth			
Employment			
Welfare			
Security			
Policy priorities			
Shifts			
Patterns			
Regional			
Advancing			
Declining			
Techniques			
Government levels			
Macro/micro			
Foreign direct			
investment-inward			
outward			
State-enterprises			
Mechanisms of coordination			
Government agencies			
Companies			
Labor			
Banks			
Evaluation of results			
Competitiveness			
Employment			
Social welfare			
Evaluation of techniques			
Cause/effect			
Cost/benefit			

A country with an "industrial development strategy" has neither a grand design as to industrial development nor a strategy of intervention in corporate decisions; rather it has a strategy of overall development within which industry is included. Countries with "industrialization policies," on the other hand, have adopted specific policies aimed at stimulating the growth of industry, and even its importance relative to agriculture and the services. Governments with "industrial (sectoral) policies" have adopted specific measures for the protection or promotion of individual industries or sectors.

Table 1.1. The Policy Continuum

Switzerland Malaysia	Virtually no direct intervention in industrial development except for some attention to the structure of foreign direct investment.
Philippines United States	Ad hoc intervention in specific sectors coupled with generalized support for industrialization.
United Kingdom	Nonintervention in principle, with protection of a few specific sectors and more support of selected advancing sectors.
Brazil Sweden Germany Canada Mexico	Intervention accepted in principle, but not used extensively across sectors; few sectors given strong support, including state enterprises; with no planning mechanism.
Korea Taiwan	Strong support for industrialization, with some key sectors aided under specific plans.
Singapore Japan	Planning with consensus from industry, leading to guidance of key sectors; some sectors largely unplanned.
France	Repeated attempt at specific sectoral planning under a larger indicative plan, with techniques for guiding sectors to achieve planned goals, including significant state enterprises in key sectors.

An analysis of national policies as described in this book would fill out this matrix by detailing the specific policies, mechanisms, and techniques that an individual government pursues to achieve its overall economic and development objectives. Even among governments with the most interventionist of purposes—i.e., those pursuing sectoral policies—efforts differ as to degree and kind. Moreover, governments will frequently mix purposes as they shift from one stage of economic policy making to another. For example, it is not uncommon for a country to have some sectoral policies within a general industrialization program. One could argue, for example, that in their support of a number of industries, including textiles and shoes, U.S. policies are a hybrid of "interventionist nonintervention."

The countries described in the following chapters could be ranked on a continuum of policy directions, ranging from virtual nonintervention to the highest levels of government intervention, as shown in Table 1.1. The specific policies of these countries are described briefly below.

Brazil

During the 1970s, Brazilian industrial output grew at an average annual rate of 9.4 percent, accounting for about 3.4 percent of total gross domestic product (GDP) in 1980. In that same year, manufactured products accounted for 44.8 percent of total exports, up from 15.2 percent in 1970. This positive performance was largely a result of government efforts to simulate industrial growth and the diversification of exports. A comprehensive analysis of government policy towards the industrial sector would have to deal with a large number of questions at both the aggregate and the sectoral levels. The discussion in Chapter 2 focuses on selected policy topics, particularly those that seem clearly related to an international restructuring of industry.

It is difficult to treat specific features of the recent development of Brazilian industry without reference to an institutional framework. Thus Chapter 2 begins with an account of the institutions involved with industrial policy, followed by an examination of the general lines that seem to guide national industrial policy and of some of the main instruments actually used. On that basis the present problems of implementing a comprehensive and coordinated industrial policy are then analyzed.

Chapter 2 also examines some problems that may arise in the near future. These include the questions of industrial growth and external competitiveness in a context of balance-of-payments constraints, the issue of industrial decentralization, and the process of restructuring industrial production. Finally, the potential role of Brazil in an international restructuring of industry is discussed, taking into account both the operation of foreign corporations in Brazil and the international operation of Brazilian-based firms.

Canada

Historically Canada has not had an industrial policy but rather has promoted industrialization in general to create and maintain a minimum base of industry and to increase Canadian ownership of industry in the face of increased foreign ownership. The nation's policies included formation of crown corporations, tariff protection, and provision of infrastructure for industry.

Since World War II, the government has become more concerned about the extent of foreign direct investment and therefore foreign decision making in Canada. In 1965 a Canadian development corporation was established to promote Canadian firms. It met with some success, but did not reduce the proportion of foreign firms in critical sectors. Consequently, a Foreign Investment Review Agency was established in 1974 to screen foreign direct investment and to encourage Canadian participation in key sectors. No attempt was made to promote specific sectors, simply to control the extent of foreign decision making.

Throughout the 1970s, consideration of industrial policies focused on aggregate and general techniques, stemming from a debate over whether policy should move towards trade liberalization or the achievement of technological sovereignty—meaning the capability of generating new products within Canada. Some argued that trade liberalization could only follow technological sovereignty. Specific sectoral support was offered to the clothing and textile industry in 1971 with the hope of catapulting it into an international competitive status; the plan was to offer similar assistance to other selected sectors as well. But inadequate adjustment measures were adopted, and little structural transformation occurred within the industry. Because results were disappointing, the program was not extended to other sectors.

Some support has been given to energy companies and to manufacturing companies in general, but without a sectoral priority. New programs of industrialization are growth oriented, but not sector specific. They focus on manpower training, capital mobilization, and resource and infrastructure development.

France

France has long been one of the world's leading and least embarrassed practitioners of the art of industrial policy—rivaled only by Japan in the industrial world. The Government of France, in contrast with other countries, was the chief architect and engineer of industrial policy.

Industrial policy in France has its roots in seventeenth century mercantilism, starting with the successful efforts of Colbert, Louis XIV's minister of France, to attract, subsidize, and protect the Venetian glass technicians, initiating industrial production in France.

French policies were sharpened after the second World War by focusing on strengthening French industry to improve its competitiveness with that of other European countries. In the 1950s and 1960s, the focus was on U.S. competition through its direct investments in Europe, and French efforts channeled support to both declining and advancing sectors.

Perhaps the chief tool available to the government was the now famous "indicative plan." The plan, resulting from a top-down approach to national planning, enabled the French government to mobilize capital for industrial expansion through both private companies and through state enterprises.

French abilities to influence the directions of national industrial development have increased with the Socialist government through nationalization of major industries. The chief tool to be utilized by the Mitterand Government, however, will continue to be mobilization of credit through the nationalized banks.

Japan

Japan is a highly developed capitalist country, relying on markets for investment decisions; the role that an industrial policy can play is thereby restricted. The Japanese government has lost most of its tools for controlling industry; thus in terms of policy constraints it is much closer to its Western counterparts than is often recognized.

Japan's postwar industrial policy has undergone a great transformation. Although allocation of foreign exchange was an effective measure for control at an early stage, the Japanese government subsequently lost this tool as a result of a number of deregulations. Today, the measures of Japanese industrial policy are either already adopted or adoptable in the other industrialized democracies.

Japan has relied primarily on the private sector's response to market forces to achieve economic development. After obtaining information from the business and intellectual communities and determining the most likely future shape of industry, the government has declared that this shape was itself the goal of industrial policy. When problems arose, the government generally left the solution to the initiative, creativity, and competition of the private sector.

This policy could be called "the public use of private interest."

Malaysia

Malaysia is predominantly an agricultural economy. The absence of a systematic and well-defined industrial policy is a reflection of both the economic philosophy to which the country is committed and the historical role of manufacturing. Malaysia's industrial development strategies could at best be described as *ad hoc*, dictated mainly by market forces. No great effort has been made to exploit Malaysia's natural comparative advantage. As a result, the country has developed a hodgepodge of import-substituting industries, mainly of the assembly or packaging type; none of these industries has attempted to move up-market. Thus, twenty years after independence, Malaysia has not fully emerged from the classical pattern of industrial development found in most developing economies.

A major objective of the government is to ensure social and political stability in this multiracial society. To achieve this goal, it relies principally on the New Economic Policy (NEP), an attempt to mesh corporate goals and government equity rules. The initial skepticism is now giving way, and corporate strategies are responding to the NEP. Foreign manufacturing companies with well-constructed NEP strategies can effectively match long-term corporate objectives with Malaysia's economic goals. The new administration, recognizing the importance of self-reliant strategies, will emphasize the establishment of capital goods "nucleus" industries, while simultaneously developing small and medium-scale industries to operate as (a) second-round, import-substituting, consumer-goods industries; (b) resource-based, export-oriented industries; or (c) part suppliers and subassemblers to the nucleus industries. As a first step toward building a broad industrial base, the government has set up the Heavy Industries Corporation of Malaysia Berhad. The private sector is also expected to play a role by participating in the various downstream industries.

The principal means of policy implementation are the Malaysian Industrial Development Authority (MIDA) and Bank Negara Malaysia. MIDA is responsible for both promotion of investments, which it carries out through offices in various world capitals, and coordination of industrial development; in the latter capacity it undertakes feasibility studies and broad industry and economic analysis. Bank Negara Malaysia serves as the main government financing tool for industrial growth and diversification.

Mexico

The Mexican economy has achieved remarkable growth rates the last two decades, averaging 6.5 percent in real terms. Rapid growth has been sought as a means of creating new jobs and relieving unemployment. But it has also resulted in an increase in the inflation rate and a devaluation of the peso since 1976 of about 200 percent. Several other problems have accompanied rapid industrialization in Mexico.

First, because Mexican industry has relied mainly on its national market, it has been slow to obtain economies of scale and thereby industrial growth. To encourage exports, Mexico offers several fiscal incentives, including tax credits for expenditures in export activities. It also offers a discount of as much as 30 percent on the price of petrochemicals used as raw materials, and a 30 percent discount on the cost of electric power and natural gas, if a company's exports account for at least 25 percent of the total plant capacity.

Second, industrial development has focused on the three geographic areas in which the Mexican population is concentrated: Mexico City, Guadalajara, and Monterrey. As a result, social overhead costs are very high. For example, Mexico City now has fifteen million inhabitants, and air and noise pollution are beyond acceptable levels. The government has encouraged industry to decentralize, offering fiscal incentives for investments in underdeveloped areas. For example, a company investing in the highest-priority zone, the northeast corner of the country, could receive tax credits of up to 10 percent of the total investment in fixed assets, 20 percent of the annual wage bill on new jobs created, and 5 percent of the purchase of equipment manufactured nationally.

Third, production has been largely oriented to import substitution and consumer goods. To fight inflation, the government has attempted to regulate prices of basic consumer goods, although price controls have caused shortages of these basic goods. During the first stage, the import-substitution model creates an external imbalance (from the import side as well as from the export side), which is financed through foreign capital. Thus it is oriented toward eliminating the savings/investment gap, by stimulating savings through fiscal and monetary policy. In the advanced stage of the model, the strategy is oriented toward eliminating the export/import gap.

Fourth, the Mexican market structure includes both oligopolistic industries, which have sustained the highest growth, and a large number of small industries that barely subsist and contribute marginally to total production and employment.

Fifth, since 1976, Mexico has attempted to maintain its growth through public programs and enterprises. One of the most important ones has been Pemex, the national oil industry.

Finally, efforts to disperse industry from the metropolitan centers have given rise to high priorities for "border" and "in-bond" industries, which will probably remain important in Mexican industrialization.

Philippines

Although the Philippine Government has defined a set of priority industries, its policy orientation is toward overall industrialization rather than the techniques generally characterized as industrial policy. In fact, much of its impact on industry comes through macroeconomic policies stimulating growth. Government manipulates both demand and supply on the domestic as well as the international sectors. Its policies are more oriented toward domestic market development, however, and it seeks to promote industries based on the supply factor of materials inputs.

The government would like to enhance the export orientation of companies but is still operating under import substitution policies for a large segment of industry. In working toward both these objectives, it is concerned about developing natural resources and manpower skills as well as increasing the productivity of the industrial sector.

Eleven major industrial projects are planned which will require significant infrastructure, new capital resources, and substantial materials inputs. If all eleven were attempted simultaneously, they would strain the economy seriously. Many of these projects will be undertaken by public enterprise, with the private sector supported through funds channeled into small and medium companies in other or related sectors.

If the private sector is to play a more effective role, a more liberal trading regime will be required, along with greater international economic cooperation, more effective regional cooperation in the Association of South East Asian Nations (ASEAN), and greater innovation on the part of private enterprises themselves.

Republic of China

The industrial policy of the Republic of China has essentially been to promote development of the private sector, including investments from abroad by overseas Chinese and others. It has specifically promoted selected "strategic" sectors, and continues to alter the list of such sectors in its developmental programs for the 1980s.

The emphasis of industrial policy has shifted toward the higher technology industries, particularly chemical, steel, and nonferrous metals, heavy plant equipment, automotive, electronics, and machine tools. The chosen sectors are much like those emphasized by Japan and other industrialized countries.

Until the mid-1960s, Taiwan's development depended heavily on foreign economic and technical assistance, particularly from the United States. After that time, however, it took off on its own, largely under the stimulation of planning guidelines developed by the government through a central planning agency. The cabinet lays down broad guidelines, which are then spelled out by the planning group, relying on the advice of a number of ministries and dialogues with the private sector. Specific guidelines are then transmitted to the various industrial sectors, which are not compelled to follow them. On the contrary, all sectors are expected to follow market signals, which include many coming from the international market, since Taiwan made an early decision to produce for the world rather than its much smaller national market.

Even so, substantial foreign investment has recently entered the country to serve the national market, which has been considerably expanded by a tenfold increase in per capita income since 1965. Taiwan can expect to emerge from the "newly industrialized" category to join the industrial countries during the 1980s. It will do so by continuing free trade policies, opening its economy to foreign investment and to technology transfers, and educating its workers and preparing them for new industrial assignments, while maintaining an adequate mobility of workers. Taiwan expects further to establish increasingly close relationships with the neighboring countries of Southeast Asia.

Singapore

In 1959 Singapore embarked on a deliberate industrialization policy geared toward expanding and diversifying its economy. Measures used include investment incentives, protection for import-substituting firms, and infrastructure development. In 1965, when the island became independent from Malaysia, government policy emphasized manufacturing for export, led by foreign firms. By the late 1970s, Singaporean policy was encouraging a shift from labor-intensive production into skill- and capital-intensive investments.

Manufacturing has grown at an average annual rate of 20-25 percent since 1965, under Singapore's policies of infrastructure development and maintenance of a climate favorable to investors. Yet the country is also emphasizing expansion in services, including tourism, transport and communications, and financial and business services. The Economic Planning Board was established to provide a wide range of services to investors, including government development and expansion of industrial facilities.

Three sets of policies have been used by the government since 1979 to accelerate the transformation of the economy from labor- to capital-intensive production: wage correction policy, industrial investment incentives, and the expansion of training and educational facilities.

The state plays a highly interventionist role in Singapore's economic development, while still encouraging free enterprise and open competition. As a result, there are few government controls on private investment and few restrictions on trade. Government does seek, however, to influence sectoral allocation of resources and industrial adjustments through its investment incentive programs, which are directed at desired industries. It also provides financing and engages in direct production of goods and services. The government, therefore, clearly has a strong hand in directing industry and labor toward achieving government priorities in the development of the Singaporean economy.

South Korea

The economic progress of South Korea during the last two decades has been phenomenal. The country's rapid economic development has been accompanied by a change in its industrial structure. Outstanding among the tactical factors involved in Korea's remarkable growth has been the key role played by export expansion and an outward-looking strategy.

Recent industrial policy in Korea can be divided into four distinct phases of evolution: (1) 1961-1964, (2) 1965-1973, (3) 1974-1979, and (4) 1980 to the present. The government's policy has oscillated between import substitution and export promotion policy. Since the mid-1970s Korea has begun to move from an industrialization policy to sectoral industrial policy.

Realizing that the recent recession of the economy was structural rather than cyclical, the government has taken a new, longer-term perspective on its industrial policy, with greater emphasis on sectoral policies, R&D, management, and marketing. Since 1980 it has tried to cut back its role in promoting industrial development. Instead, its policy will aim at reducing preferential treatment for selected industries and at exposing domestic producers to foreign competition in order to enhance their international competitiveness.

Top priority in the future will be given to investments in energy conservation, technology, and manpower development to improve the competitiveness of Korean products and to provide a still better qualified labor force for industries. Investment strategies planned for the manufacturing sector will also differ from those of the past. For instance, the emphasis will be on investments that complement existing industrial structures, investments for parts and components for the machinery industry, and investments in quality improvements and the replacement of obsolete facilities for light manufacturing industries.

To sustain long-term growth of exports and of the economy as a whole, the government will further liberalize imports and the inflow of technology and foreign direct investment. In particular, the government will welcome foreign direct investment befitting the "encouraged industries," which will be accorded more favorable tax and ownership treatment. Eventually the government will move from a negative to a positive foreign direct investment screening system; by the late 1980s, all foreign investment applications will be automatically approved except in a few restricted areas.

Sweden

The Royal Swedish Academy of Engineering Sciences has sponsored several studies related to industrial policies. In 1979 it finished a report on Swedish technical and industrial capabilities and competitiveness, which included a comprehensive analysis of the industrially oriented R&D system in Sweden. It is now engaged in two internationally oriented studies concerning energy-related engineering and the building construction sector. A third study examines Swedish international and industrial marketing in technology-intensive products, and a fourth has reviewed national security and industrial policy. These studies have been developed as the background for an extensive public discussion of industrial policies.

Chapter 13 briefly discusses the Swedish orientation toward industrial policies and then makes extensive comments and recommendations based on the earlier studies. The government must support moves in the international market, it is argued, especially because Sweden is tied to international sources of supply as well as to foreign industrial and consumer markets. Recommendations also cover the organization of policy making, the role of labor, and the mix between specific and general policies.

Switzerland

Swiss governments at both the federal and cantonal levels have traditionally pursued policies designed to provide an environment that allows the development of industry, services, and agriculture. It has not, however, pursued industrial policies in the same sense as other Western European countries have. This abstention is due in part to the country's liberal economic tradition, which spurns direct government intervention in decision making of private enterprises.

Broadly speaking, therefore, Swiss industrial strategies are determined primarily by private enterprise reacting to the signals provided by the marketplace—both the domestic and the international markets. Swiss government policies are essentially macroeconomic, emphasizing money, exchange-rate, foreign-trade, labor-market, and fiscal issues.

Nevertheless, Swiss industry is significantly influenced by government interventions in its principal international markets—primarily in bilateral and multilateral negotiations with governments that are more interventionist and therefore influence the terms of trade for Swiss products. Swiss policies are likely to remain in the liberal tradition into the 1980s, with direct government interventions severely limited.

The sectors likely to be most important to Switzerland in the 1980s include chemicals, textiles, insurance, machine tools, other machinery (electric and nonelectric capital goods), consumer products, mechanical industry (watches), and electronics.

Switzerland has a substantial interest in promoting more open trade, since some 60 percent of the sales of the 100 largest Swiss firms is currently generated abroad. For this reason and because the domestic economy has traditionally been open, industrial strategies in Switzerland will be left to the determination of the individual investor and the marketplace.

United Kingdom

Britain's industrial policy measures have been devised and implemented against a backdrop of poor economic performance over a long period of time and an unparalleled decline in industrial jobs. While there has been no shortage of innovations in industrial policy, the wide gulf between the objectives of the two major political parties has meant frequent policy changes. The most controversial aspects of policy have concerned the role of public money in the private sector. Government support for companies in crisis has frequently seemed to be motivated by noneconomic criteria, while the biggest support operation of all, the rescue and restructuring of British Leyland Ltd., has yet to be reflected in corporate profitability.

Since the 1960s, with the establishment of the National Economic Development Council, attempts have been made to plan on a sectoral basis and to encourage high technology industries. In addition, a variety of institutions (most recently the National Enterprise Board) have tried to play a more active and interventionist role in industrial policy. But progress has been hampered by the financial demands of large, failing enterprises. Since 1969, moreover, some sectoral planning activities have been dismantled, and the purview of the National Enterprise Board has been much reduced.

Few links exist between the planning and implementation of domestic and international policy. However, the principle of liberalization of international trade and investment has been generally accepted, and policy in these areas has been less subject to radical shifts of direction with changes in government. There has been considerable concern about the activities of multinationals, both foreign owned and British, and particularly about the large, sustained increase in import penetration in manufacturing. To date these concerns have not found expression in more restrictive policies or indeed in policies to raise the rate of growth of exports.

To a large extent the confused history of industrial policy in Britain merely reflects the frustrated, almost despairing, sense that the country's relative economic decline is irreversible. Furthermore, the prospects for a future policy consensus are not good, as high unemployment increases internal strains and widens the gulf between political parties and between unions and management.

United States

United States policies towards industry run the gamut from aggregate stimulation of industrialization to protection or stimulation of specific sectors. The first element, aggregate stimulation, predominates. The basic principle of U.S. policies is to permit the market to decide which industries are developed within the country, where in the country, and by whom. But exceptions are made: various transport facilities are subsidized, national security industries are subsidized, sectoral protection has been extended, and various regional policies attempt to guide industry into specific locations.

Internationally, the overriding principle is that of freedom of trade and payments—unless the freeing of trade hurts the interests of key sectors. In the main, these interests are expressed in Washington through political influence rather than demonstration of economic destitution.

However, the major thrust of U.S. policies is toward "reindustrialization," which means the stimulation of growth in business and particularly in those sectors that would add substantially to investment in capital equipment, thereby raising productivity and standards of living. This concern results from a decline in international competitiveness, the effects of flows of U.S. technology abroad, the protectionism that has arisen in other countries, and the pressure of developing countries for a larger portion of industrial production worldwide.

The U.S. government has sought to stimulate the leading sectors by encouraging research and development—but again in the aggregate, letting individual companies and sectors determine their responses. It has also tried to protect or ease the decline of other sectors, such as textiles, shipbuilding, shoes, color TV, steel, and autos. Here the chief goal has been to maintain employment in sectors that are politically sensitive.

Internationally, the United States attempts to get other governments to agree to a freeing of trade and investment from impediments and to offer "national treatment" to foreign direct investment.

West Germany

Chapter 17 analyzes the determinants of industrial policy in West Germany, focusing on the interaction between perceived changes in the interindustry structure of international competitiveness and the willingness of policy makers to offer subsidies. The intentions, institutions, and mechanisms of industrial policy are discussed, and the quantitative extent of that policy is estimated. The distribution of benefits reflects an interaction between interest group behavior and the electoral responsiveness of various levels of government. It appears that mechanisms built into the political process to protect industrial policy from interest-group pressures are being circumscribed; as a result old, large, concentrated industries are becoming the net beneficiaries of industrial policy.

LESSONS LEARNED

Little current information is publicly available on the policy positions of governments toward the promotion of industry. The available literature includes a number of somewhat dated studies of industrial policies in various countries; and a few studies have examined the application of industrial policies to specific sectors within a given country. But little comparative work has been done.

Moreover, there are virtually no studies explaining how specific industries have developed internationally, what criteria of location were used, and what effects the new structure has had on trade, capital flows, technology flows, and so forth. Many existing studies are aggregate analyses that pay little or no attention to the causes of industrial mobility or of the existing structure; others have taken the structure and organization of industry as a given in order to assess problems and prospects for the future. Much of the literature is essentially a description of where the industry is and what market changes might be expected; little is said about how the present structure developed and how the industry might relocate itself in the future. There are a few exceptions to these observations, but they are indeed exceptional.

This book has been written as a first step toward an analysis of the causes of international industrial relocation and mobility and of potential problems in a restructuring effort. Using this description of government policies and interventionist proclivities, one can examine the factors that influenced companies' decision making—government policies, technical or economic factors—in specific sectors; on this basis one can begin to understand the structure of industry and the changes that are likely to take place over the next few years.

Clearly governments differ in their selection of sectors to protect or promote. Among countries seeking advantages in the same sector, potential conflicts will arise from oversupply and international economic dislocations within industries. Yet governments are acting with little or no reference to the actions of others.

In many sectors, the transnational corporation (TNC) is a key decision maker. Governments are especially unwilling to cede responsibility for industrial location to the TNC, believing that corporate strategies frequently conflict with national objectives. This perception of conflict, or lack of congruence, between the objectives of TNCs and governments is one of the reasons that governments and intergovernmental organizations are proposing and implementing sectoral policies.

Yet these policies are being developed and pursued without adequate information as to their benefits to the country and their costs in terms of inefficient production, oversupply worldwide, and dislocations among countries in terms of trade, capital, and technology flows. The international organizations that oversee policies relating to trade and investment lack information on the trade-offs required in both government and corporate decisions in order to achieve mutually consistent objectives on industry location.

Given these potential irritants in the system, much better information is needed as to the factors affecting decision making, the cost and benefits of the emerging structure of industry, and of the interventions of governments to affect that structure. These costs and benefits can only be determined on a sectoral basis, precisely because governments are increasingly adopting policies designed to affect only particular sectors. The complexity of some of the major industries is in itself an obstacle even to sectoral analysis, but it is only by such analyses that we can begin to understand the shifting effects of policies on the network of international trade, investment, and production.

The studies reported in this volume demonstrate that governments are determining their own interests and the means of achieving them without feeling constrained by the interests of other countries or by international rules of behavior. Indeed, one of the complaints often heard during debates on codes of behavior for transnationals is that governments would not be bound by the proposed rules. And attempts to influence governments in this regard—for example, the national treatment provisions of the OECD Guidelines—have had indifferent success.

New international rules must therefore recognize the strong concerns of governments as to the international division of labor in particular sectors. In the early postwar period such concerns were presumed to be met by the ordering principle of nondiscriminatory multilateral trade and payments. The reconstruction and expansion of industry itself and the reopening of worldwide opportunities in trade and investment were expected to be equitable for all. The principal institutions created at that time—the GATT, the World Bank, and the International Monetary Fund—were primarily concerned with aggregate policies that provided for free trade and for a currency and monetary system that encouraged greater international integration.

The early experience of the European Economic Community demonstrates that some degree of policy coordination is required among national governments to prevent industrial development from becoming redundant, leading to overcapacity and protectionism. Today, when governments are clearly unwilling to allow the market to determine the totality of industrial structures, the European experience also indicates that some mechanisms of cooperation may be required to ameliorate the international effects of uncoordinated government interventions in decisions as to location and the structure of industry.

This problem is perhaps more crucial now because of the expansion of industrial production in the newly industrialized countries. In the early postwar period, these nations participated in the world economy primarily through exports of raw materials and other commodities, and they were not a significant competitive element in industry. Now, however, in part because of government export expansion policies, these countries are becoming increasingly competitive precisely in those mature industries that have traditionally been major employers in the advanced countries. The problems of adjustment to industrial changes are thus becoming more acute in the advanced countries, and will be particularly excruciating in times of slow economic growth. Given the complex interrelations of industry, economic growth, and national security, several key sectors are considered more important than in the past. Governments will undoubtedly continue to concern themselves with the industrial development of specific sectors, and to undertake further interventions. The past, present, and future influence of these policies on international production, trade, and technology in specific sectors is necessarily the subject of further research.

Chapter 2

Brazilian Industrial Policy and International Restructuring of Industry

Luiz A. Corrêa do Lago*

THE INSTITUTIONAL FRAMEWORK OF NATIONAL INDUSTRIAL POLICY

In Brazil, a large number of institutions active in different fields carry out industrial policy in a rather decentralized fashion that hinders an appropriately coordinated action. Therefore, strictly speaking, there is not yet a global industrial policy, in the sense of a consistent set of well-defined objectives, institutional arrangements, and economic policy instruments oriented to the development of the industrial sector. The purpose of this section is to illustrate the complexity of the institutional framework of industrial policy in Brazil.

At the top of the hierarchy of institutions dealing with the industrial sector is the Council for Economic Development (CDE), whose members include all the ministers in the economic area and the president of the republic. In theory, at least, the CDE establishes the general directives for the formulation and implementation of the country's overall economic policy, not just industrial policy. Its resolutions regarding the industrial sector should condition policy decisions by institutions at lower levels.

Since 1964, the executive agency in charge of implementing industrial policy has been the Industrial Development Commission (CDI), although recently its autonomy has been limited by its subordination to the Ministry for Industry and Commerce (MIC). Since 1978, the CDI formally "orients" the policy to be carried on by the MIC. Therefore, in

*Instituto Brasileiro de Economia (IBRE) Fundação Getulio Vargas

recent years, the CDI's main role has been to grant fiscal incentives (basically the reduction of import duties on imported equipment) to industrial projects, which it approves subject to the fulfillment of various requirements. This approval is particularly important because it may be a requirement for the concession of incentives by other agencies, and also because the firms that benefit from the CDI's incentives are likely to be more competitive. Paradoxically, to the extent that domestic firms purchase more of their machinery and equipment in Brazil, a tendency encouraged by the CDI, the agency will become gradually less important, unless it is given additional responsibilities.

At the sectoral level, several agencies are active in appraising expansion plans and in supplying the CDI with information so that it may grant the necessary fiscal incentives to specific projects. These include, among others, the SUNAMAN for shipbuilding, the CONSIDER for steel production and nonferrous metals, the GEICOM for the industry of equipment for communications, and the GEIMI for the mining industry. Some of these institutions, like SUNAMAN, may also be involved in the financing of production and exports.

Several agencies at the regional level may grant fiscal incentives, such as exemption from state taxes (independent of the approval of a specific project by the CDI), using different criteria for project approval. These agencies include the SUDENE for the Northeast (which dates from 1959), the SUDAM for the Amazon Region, the SUFRAMA for the free trade zone of Manaus, the SUDESUL for the South, and the SUDECO for the Center West.

Finally, various other institutions play a part in industrial policy. The National Bank for Economic Development (BNDE) and its subsidiaries (FINAME, EMBRAMEC, FIBASE, IBRASA) are particularly important in the financing of industrial projects and, more specifically, in helping the capital goods industry expand its sales. Their action is complemented by Financiadora de Estudos e Projetos S. A. (FINEP), which gives financial support to technological development and R&D. For the construction industry, two public institutions are of special importance. The National Housing Bank (BNH) acts on the supply side, financing building activities, while the Caixa Econômica Federal (CEF), a federal savings and loan institution, finances the purchase of housing.

With respect to foreign trade, CACEX, the foreign trade department of the Banco do Brasil, which in theory acts on behalf of the CONCEX, the Council for Foreign Trade, has some control over imports of capital goods since it is responsible for determining whether similar machinery and equipment is produced in Brazil before projects are approved by the CDI. CACEX may forbid the importation of specific equipment on grounds of "similarity" with domestic products, even though the "similarity" may be quite ambiguous and subjective. CACEX also approves so-called "agreements of participation" of domestic firms in the supply of equipment to industrial and infrastructure projects. These agreements try to reconcile the interests of domestic producers with those of the private or government corporations or agencies involved in these projects. Finally CACEX executes the policy of export promotion (which is regulated by Comissão de Incentivos as Exportacoes (CIEX) and occasionally participates in the financing of exports of goods and services, which are also financed with subsidized credit granted by Fundo de Financiamento as Exportacoes (FINEX).

The Commission for Tariff Policy (CPA) may grant reductions of import duties on specific industrial products, though one of its main tasks is to examine changes in tariff rates that may have protectionist effects. By contrast, the Beneficios Fiscaies a Programas Especiais de Exportacao (BEFIEX) grants fiscal incentives (which may also include reductions of import duties on equipment) to firms that formally pledge to export manufactured products up to a certain value in a given period. These incentives, in certain cases, clearly contradict the goal of promoting the domestic production of capital goods and are not scrutinized for "similarity" by CACEX.

Other important institutions include the Interministry Council for Price Control (CIP), which may control prices of industrial products, granting price increases only on the basis of detailed evidence on cost increases. CIP has been less active recently, as price controls on products of several industrial branches have been eliminated. Besides implementing exchange, financial, and monetary policies that affect the industrial sector, the Central Bank is also more directly involved with industrial policy, as it executes the decisions of the National Monetary Council (CMN), which establishes policy regarding foreign capital.

Industrial policy is also affected by several other agencies dealing with technology, the control of pollution, abuses of economic power, mergers of corporations, purchases of equipment by the public sector, and specific branches of industrial production (such as the production of equipment for data processing). One could also cite some large public corporations such as Petrobrás, whose expansion plans involve large orders with detailed specifications to the industrial sector. However, this long enumeration of agencies and institutions was not meant to be comprehensive but rather to illustrate that the institutional framework in which industrial policy is implemented is sufficiently complex to allow for inconsistent measures by different institutions. Even when agencies clearly articulate their activities, coordination is difficult because they are subordinate to different ministries. As Suzigan put it, "There is an overlapping of functions (with respect to project approval, for instance, between sectoral, regional, financing, and sometimes even more specific, institutions) and conflicts and inconsistencies with respect to criteria and objectives. These in turn, involve costs, represented by an inadequate allocation of financial resources and fiscal incentives."[1]

Because of its limited formal responsibility, the CDI cannot perform the necessary coordinating role, nor can the Ministry for Industry and Commerce (MIC), since several agencies are subordinate to other ministries. On the other hand, the CDE, which is charged with implementation of a coordinated industrial policy, is not an executive institution and must concentrate on issues related to general economic policy. Therefore, up to the present, it has limited itself to establishing goals for specific industrial branches—no doubt an important task, but still incomplete from a point of view of a global industrial policy.

Despite the inconsistencies and possible insufficiencies noted, various incentives at the sectoral or even firm level have had quite positive results. Between 1970 and 1980, in spite of two oil shocks, the performance of the Brazilian industrial sector as a whole was very satisfactory. In the next section, we examine specific instruments of industrial policy that have contributed to that performance and try to identify their objectives through inference from the criteria for concession of economic incentives.

INSTRUMENTS AND OBJECTIVES OF INDUSTRIAL POLICY IN BRAZIL

It was only in the 1960s that the idea of general economic planning took root in Brazil, as the country passed through a period of economic stagnation. The CDI was created in 1964 to absorb the existing "executive groups" that had been created in the 1950s to implement specific industrial programs, and to grant incentives to investments in the industrial sector. The CDI acquired special importance after 1966, when it was effectively entrusted with the administration of fiscal incentives to be granted to industrial projects.[2]

At that point, industrial policy remained undefined, though a general goal of inducing investment in the industrial sector was widely accepted. Several policy instruments, most of which still exist in a somewhat modified form, were then used with this purpose.[4] These included:

1. Fiscal incentives to encourage imports of capital goods (these were subsequently substantially reduced to favor the development of domestic industry).

2. Fiscal and credit incentives to encourage exports of manufactures, reinforced after 1968 by a more active exchange policy of frequent small devaluations.
3. More numerous regional fiscal incentives and creation of sectoral incentives (notably to shipbuilding, the petrochemical industry, and steel making).
4. A more abundant provision of internal and external funds to the industrial sector (in which the BNDE and its subsidiaries, notably FINAME, preserve an important role).
5. Implementation of sectoral programs and of government investments in economic infrastructure (especially in the energy, transportation, and communication fields) with important "linkage effects" on other sectors.
6. Expansion of the direct entrepreneurial action of the public sector in industrial production, notably in the areas of mining, metallurgy, and chemicals.

These instruments were complemented by the creation of some of the specific sectoral institutions mentioned earlier. Nonetheless, government action in the industrial sphere continued to be "characterized by an absence of selective criteria. Given the absence of clear priorities, incentives were granted indiscriminately."[4] This state of affairs generated imbalances and delayed investments in the production of basic inputs and capital goods. It was only toward the mid-1970s that industrial policy goals were gradually established, though not always very clearly, in the face of a changing economic situation and a balance-of-payments problem.

The CDI became more selective, attempting to induce purchases of domestic capital equipment while giving incentives to certain priority sectors. In 1974, without a well-defined industrial policy set by a coordinating institution such as the CDE, the CDI established several conditions for the approval of projects and the concession of incentives that, at least implicitly, corresponded to more specific objectives. Thus, each industrial project had to:

be destined to substitute for imports;
be linked to an export commitment, if existing supply was considered sufficient;
contribute to industrial decentralization or reduction of regional imbalances;
be supported by an adequate financial structure, in terms of owned equity capital as opposed to capital of third parties;

present a quantification of fixed and working capital sufficient to provide for the specific conditions of the project;

induce a more intensive use of domestic inputs;

permit the adoption of technological processes appropriate to sectoral and regional development;

present a scale of production compatible with competitive costs;

fulfill certain antipollution requirements.[5]

Other guidelines, showing greater selectivity, were adopted for specific sectors. In certain cases the incentives granted by the CDI depend on a previous approval of the projects by sectoral institutions.[6]

Several criteria adopted by the CDI in practice were not explicitly acknowledged in writing. For instance, projects of foreign corporations are more thoroughly examined; there must be a positive balance of payments at the company (not project) level, and special requirements are imposed governing the import of equipment and the long-term financing of these imports. Criteria of a more general application include the existence of a domestic market compatible with a minimum scale of production; a priority to purchases of equipment in the domestic market; and the requirement of a "nationalization program" to increase local content. By contrast, less emphasis is often given to the questions of location and pollution, as these would not be sufficient to cause the refusal of a project.

Thus, although the CDI has not explicitly identified its economic policy objectives, they can be inferred from the internal regulations and informal criteria used by the agency. There is an effort to improve the balance of trade, through import substitution and export promotion, and to absorb modern technology. The CDI has also shown concern with the actual dimensions of the domestic market (which are difficult to establish with precision) and their compatibility with the scale of the projects; it attempts to orient the demand for capital goods and engineering services to domestic firms, with some priority to private Brazilian firms. On the other hand, the explicit and implicit criteria of the CDI are not always consistent, so that the explicit objectives of decentralization of industry through the relocation of projects to new areas and the control of pollution are often neglected in practice.[7]

In any event, these implicit objectives are in many respects more comprehensive than those initially set forward by the CDE, whose most important measure remains its Resolution 9 of 1977. In essence, Resolution 9 defined general objectives for industrial policy by laying down a strategy for supporting national private enterprise, proposing a policy for the mining and basic inputs sectors, and establishing a policy for the capital goods industry. It includes the following directives:

1. Support will be offered to encourage the participation of national private enterprise in the development of dynamic sectors (capital goods, basic inputs, and mining).
2. When an investment opportunity is identified, federal financial institutions and those that administer fiscal incentives will try to increase the probability that the national private sector will participate.
3. Priority will be given to projects under control of national private enterprise; this will apply to the BNDE system (including FINAME, EMBRAMEC, FIBASE, IBRASA) or any other institution involved in advancing financial resources.
4. Brazil will follow the "model of the tripod" (with various improvements) for the association between national private capital, foreign capital, and the government in investments in the sector of basic inputs and mining.
5. Government participation will only be predominant when absolutely necessary and mainly in the sectors of petrochemicals and fertilizers, and in basic-products projects that require large investments.
6. Policy for the capital goods sector will promote domestic prodution to meet national needs.[8]

In a country where both government and foreign corporations are very active in several branches of the industrial sector, the explicit support to national private enterprise was welcomed by Brazilian entrepreneurs. While the CDE acknowledges the contribution of public and foreign corporations, its policy emphasizes the importance of an effective absorption of technology by Brazilian firms involved as partners in projects involving the "model of the tripod." Finally, the CDE also deals with such important questions as the standardization of machinery and equipment and the definition of "indices of nationalization" for capital equipment used in industrial projects.

Resolution 9 has not been completely implemented through appropriate regulations, although other measures of support were subsequently adopted. Thus in January 1979, Resolution 9 was reinforced by Resolution 003 of the CDE, which established global ceilings for the imports of equipment and components eligible for incentives from the CDI and certain regional and sectoral agencies. It also entrusted CACEX with the control of such imports. Additionally Decree 83,053 of the federal government established similar ceilings for the imports of ministries and other units of the government, and determined that public corporations will only be allowed to import equipment after verification by CACEX that no "similar" domestic product exists.[9]

One of the most frequent complaints of the capital goods industry remains the lack of a medium- or long-term policy of purchases of equipment by the public sector, which would permit a better planning of capacity expansion in the industry. Although certain public corporations such as Eletrobrás forecast future demand of energy, and Petrobrás has tried to direct its purchases to domestic suppliers, future public sector demand for equipment is highly uncertain. Moreover, the questions of a "reserved market" for Brazilian firms in the capital goods industry, as opposed to foreign and government corporations, and of a technological policy toward specific sectors are still left undefined (in spite of specific measures, for instance, with respect to the computer industry).

The strategy of the CDE emphasizes the short and medium terms, for it is predominantly concerned with the disequilibrium of the Brazilian balance of payments, to the detriment of a long-term, comprehensive industrial policy. The problems of pollution and the excessive concentration of industry in a few metropolitan areas have been the object of recent resolutions, as have specific sectors such as cement. So far, however, the resolutions of the CDE do not add up to a comprehensive and consistent policy.[10]

In summary, the main policy objectives that can be inferred from the resolutions of the CDE are import substitution in the area of capital goods and basic inputs and a preferential support to Brazilian private firms.[11] These objectives are not inconsistent with those implicitly adopted by the CDI and with several measures recently proposed to promote technological development.[12] However, the approach to industrial policy is centered on specific cases, with sectoral or even more specific objectives, and there are certain inconsistencies between rules and criteria actually implemented.

The need to formulate a unified industrial policy remains. Several government institutions continue to participate in decision making with respect to various aspects of industrial policy, inevitably creating inefficiencies that might be avoided through a centralized orientation. A council of industrial policy—with real power to make decisions and to govern all institutions involved with industrial matters, including technology—seems much needed. A strengthened CDI might be able to perform that role.[13] In the meantime, there is also a need to define a global and coordinated industrial policy, with clearly specified objectives and priorities, and consistent sectoral and regional goals (including the planning of government purchases of equipment). Such a policy should take into account such important issues as industrial decentralization, pollution control, the participation of national, foreign, and government corporations in specific sectors, and technological development (including regulation of standards, quality of products, and industrial norms).[14] Such a unified policy might also permit an easier adaptation to problems arising in the world economy and to a changing international environment for multinational corporations.

PROBLEMS IN THE INTERNATIONAL ARENA

Balance of Payments Constraints on Industrial Growth and External Competitiveness

The balance of payments will remain a basic constraint on Brazilian industrial growth in the near future. Problems in that area lead to policy actions that are inconsistent with the implicit or explicit goals of industrial policy listed in the previous section. For example, foreign loans have often been linked to a commitment to accept suppliers' credits for the purchase of equipment abroad. Since similar equipment frequently can be obtained in the domestic market, this practice clearly contradicts the objective of stimulating the Brazilian capital goods industry by maximizing its participation in industrial projects.

Bilateral trade agreements, notably with Eastern European countries, often have a similar effect, as only certain types of equipment can be offered in exchange for Brazilian products. Imports resulting from these agreements have recently aggravated the problem of idle capacity in the domestic railway equipment industry.

On the export side, a basic issue with respect to successful competition in world markets remains the quality of Brazilian products. In recent years Brazil has exported quite sophisticated manufactured products,[15] but these are often produced by multinational corporations. In the automobile industry, for example, one multinational firm exports thousands of cars from Brazil to Italy. Problems with standardization and industrial norms often preclude the penetration of Brazilian firms in world markets, but these problems have sometimes been successfully circumvented, as in the case of exports of airplanes by EMBRAER. If Brazilian manufactured products are to perform well in world markets, a well-implemented technological policy, including industrial norms, will be an essential part of an overall industrial policy.

Apart from quality, another obstacle to successful exports may be the unit cost of production of specific products. The emphasis of the CDE and the CDI on an adequate scale of plant, consistent with the size of the domestic market, thus acquires special importance. The idle capacity currently observed in the capital goods industry is partly due to the industrial recession and a stagnation of government orders. To some extent, however, the problem has a more permanent character, and is a result of inadequate signaling on the part of the government during the 1970s. Unrealistic goals were set for several sectors in which public corporations are predominant;[16] consequently, expectations as to the growth of demand for machinery and equipment were also inaccurate. Once again, the need for a unified and comprehensive industrial policy is underscored.

Finally, exports of manufactured products have recently depended on a series of credit and fiscal incentives, which have prompted some importing countries (notably the United States and the European Economic Community) to threaten (and in some cases to impose) retaliatory duties. A basic feature of the system of incentives, which was temporarily abolished in 1979 but reestablished in April 1981, is the so-called "premium credit" of the IPI (tax on industrial products). That incentive corresponds to 15 percent of the value exported and is paid in cruzeiros to the exporter after the transaction has actually taken place. It may be viewed as an exchange rate premium or as a subsidy to the exporter of industrialized products. Under international pressure, Brazil agreed to reduce that premium gradually during 1982 and to abolish it completely in 1983. To avoid more serious retaliations, Brazil has already been forced to establish an export tax on certain manufactured products destined for specific countries.

Other important instruments of support to exports of industrial products are subsidized credits to both the exporters and the importers of Brazilian products. Credits to customers have been notably directed to Eastern European countries, and are now far from negligible. (These may account for about 10 percent of Brazilian total exports in 1982 and therefore for almost 20 percent of exports of manufactures).

It is clear, then, that Brazilian competitiveness in foreign markets is due in part to specific incentives whose suppression might seriously retard the future growth of Brazilian exports of manufactures.

Toward a Restructuring of the Industrial Sector

The need to reduce oil imports and to substitute domestic sources of energy has forced changes in processes of production in certain sectors; these changes may later require a significant adjustment in the Brazilian industrial structure. Though there are limits to the substitution of various types of energy, and notably of electric power, for petroleum, some opportunity remains for the substitution of domestic sources of energy (including coal) for imported fuel. In the longer term, if the real price of imported oil rises significantly again, the sectors that use that input less intensively will probably receive greater priority and attract new investments. The national program for alcohol production, Proalcool, has been receiving great emphasis and abundant government funds, for both its agricultural and for its industrial phases, resulting in a large increase in capacity. In 1981, Brazil produced about 4 billion liters of alcohol.

In view of the government's revision of some sectoral goals in manufacturing and its recent emphasis on energy and agriculture—both related to reduction of imports—some reconversion in the capital goods industry may also become necessary. Thus, certain lines of production could be reoriented to supply equipment for large-scale irrigation of the Cerrados region; for a better infrastructure for the commercialization and storage of agricultural production; for the industrialization of agricultural products; or for a more intensive program of rural electrification, to help supply the basic needs of the poorer segments of the population.

BRAZIL AND THE INTERNATIONAL RESTRUCTURING OF INDUSTRY

Brazil has a potential role in an international restructuring of industry, both as a host country for foreign firms and through the operation of Brazilian-based firms abroad.

The Operation of Foreign Firms in Brazil

In recent decades, Brazil has provided a quite stable environment for the operation of multinational corporations. In the 1950s, special incentives were granted to the entry of foreign companies. The basic legislation, which covers the question of profit remittances, was established in the early 1960s and has not been significantly changed since. There is no official hostility toward the activities of foreign corporations in the country; indeed, in many cases they have access to credit and fiscal incentives. A continuous inflow of direct investment, mostly directed to the industrial sector, suggests that Brazil continues to attract foreign investors.

By December 31, 1981, total direct foreign investment in Brazil reached $19,247 million, of which $13,533 million represented direct investments and $5,714 million reinvestments. Data on the distribution of foreign direct investment for December 31, 1980, show that manufacturing accounted for 74.4 percent and mining for 2.8 percent of the total; these shares changed very little in 1981. Virtually no foreign capital is involved in the building industry or in the production of electrical energy. The presence of foreign firms in the manufacturing sector is very significant. According to a survey of the 1,000 largest firms in manufacturing, the average share of foreign corporations in total sales in the 1978-1980 period was 40.8 percent, as opposed to 41.8 percent for private Brazilian corporations and 17.4 percent for public corporations. Foreign firms probably account for at least one-fourth of total sales in mining.

As mentioned earlier, the objectives of industrial policy that can be inferred from recent government resolutions include a preferential support to private firms with Brazilian control. Given Brazil's recent balance-of-payments problems, the attraction of direct foreign investment acquires special importance. Yet success in this attempt may mean greater competition between foreign and Brazilian firms in the industrial sector, particularly in manufacturing, and might create conflicts with the explicit objectives of the CDE's Resolution 9.[17] On the other hand, the government explicitly acknowledges that there is still room for foreign capital in many sectors; in fact it has supported the so-called "model of the tripod" for specific sectors, notably mining and basic inputs. Since the government's attitude is favorable and since legislation relating to foreign capital seems satisfactory to foreign firms, Brazil should continue to be an important option as a location for the operation of foreign firms. Thus the country could play an important role in an international restructuring of industry.

The International Operation of Brazilian Firms

Direct investments abroad by Brazilian-based manufacturing firms are practically nonexistent. The few exceptions, such as the takeover by a Brazilian firm of a famous British stereo equipment producer, remain mere curiosities.

Brazilian-based firms have been increasingly active, however, in the exportation of services in general and particularly in the execution of engineering projects, whose importance is growing. Such projects have a clear impact on domestic industry, for they often imply subsequent exports of equipment and of manufactured products in general.[18] These projects have received active support from government agencies or corporations in the area of marketing and financing. Their market consists exclusively of less developed countries.

Some public corporations are also contracting projects abroad. In the technological sphere, PETROBRAS Distribuidora S.A. has signed a contract for the transfer of the technology of mixing alcohol with gasoline to Costa Rica. And Brazilian expertise is winning recognition in prospecting for oil, through the action of BRASPETRO (Petrobras Internacional).

In summary, the international operation of Brazilian-based firms has not yet involved significant direct investments in industrial activities abroad. Only in mining, and more specifically in oil extraction, do there seem to be more promising prospects for the near future. But if Brazilian firms gain a reputation for efficiency in the provision of services to less developed countries, the country's balance of payments may be improved, reflecting both payments for the services provided and the additional manufactured-product exports these services may generate. In the longer term, direct investments by Brazilian firms in industrial plants overseas should not be ruled out.

NOTES

1. W. Suzigan, "Politica Industrial no Brasil," in W. Suzigan (ed.), *Indústria: Política, Instituicões e Desenvolvimento* (Rio de Janeiro: IPEA/INPES, 1978), p. 52. This chapter's description of the institutional framework of industrial policy in Brazil draws heavily on that study and on L. A. Correa do Lago, F. L. Almeida, and B. M. F. de Lima, *A Indústria Brasileira de Bens de Capital: Origens, Situacão Recente e Perspectivas,* (Rio de Janeiro: Editora de Fundacão Getulio Vargas, 1979), especially Chapter VI.
2. Data on projects approved by the CDI between 1964 and 1967 and other details on its operation in its early stages, are presented in Correa do Lago et al., Section 4-3-1.
3. See Suzigan, p. 48.
4. Suzigan, p. 48. See also p. 54.
5. See Suzigan, pp. 61–62.
6. See Suzigan, pp. 62–63 and Correa do Lago et al., pp. 376–80.
7. See Suzigan, pp. 64–65, from which the last two paragraphs draw heavily. On the growing share of domestically produced equipment in the value of total investment in projects approved by the CDI, see Correa do Lago et al., Table VI.I, p. 379. Between 1973 and 1978 this share doubled reaching 72 percent in the latter year. In the "agreements of participation" approved by CACEX, such a share reached 76.8 percent of a total of $1,592.7 million (see p. 255).
8. See Suzigan, pp. 58–59, where part of Resolution 9 is reproduced. For details on the policy for the capital goods industry, see Correa do Lago et al., pp. 380–81.
9. See Correa do Lago et al., p. 381.
10. See Suzigan, pp. 59–60. On the cement industry, see p. 83.
11. See Suzigan, pp. 65–66.
12. On the "technological policy" of the government, see Correa do Lago et al., Chapter VII.
13. See Correa do Lago et al., pp. 482–89 on possible lines of action for a comprehensive industrial policy and for a policy toward the capital goods industry in particular.
14. Such a need is clearly perceived by the government, particularly in view of certain objectives laid down in the third National Development Plan (III PND). The Ministry for Industry and Commerce and the CDI are currently discussing written proposals for a precise definition of policy objectives for industrial development. These have not yet been made public but may result in actual measures in the near future.
15. In 1981, Brazil exported $2.1 billion of transport equipment, including trucks, buses, and automobiles. Exports of boilers, machinery, and mechanical instruments reached $1.5 billion, and those of electrical machines, $566 million. Other less sophisticated

but important manufactured export items included steel products ($801 million), orange juice ($659 million), and shoes ($586 million). See Banco Central do Brasil, *Informativo Mensal*, February 1982, p. 7.

16. For instance, a target for steel production of more than 30 million tons for 1980 was subsequently revised to 24 million tons, which is now the target for 1985. On these problems, see Correa do Lago et al., especially Chapter V.

17. From 1976 to 1980, direct foreign investment (net of reinvestments) has averged only $1,160 million, while total investment and reinvestments in 1981 reached $1,767 million. For additional foreign direct investment to have a significant impact on the balance of payments, it would have to increase considerably in absolute terms. See Banco Central do Brasil, *Boletim Mensal*, Separata, April 1981, p. 19, and Banco Central do Brasil, *Informativo Mensal*, February 1982, p. 9.

18. We abstract here from the financial operations of Brazilian banks abroad, notably of the Banco do Brasil and BANESPA, which are particularly active in chaneling loans to Brazil.

Chapter 3

Industrial Policy in Canada: An Overview

*Wendy A. Dobson**

INTRODUCTION

For the purpose of this paper, the term industrial policy will be used to denote policies intended to alter a country's industrial structure. Industrial structure can be viewed cross-sectionally (in terms of each sector's contribution to employment and output) or dynamically (in terms of the interaction between the different subsectors that leads to the satisfaction of new demands for goods and services, and hence to a continual reallocation of factors of production). From either point of view, industrial policy represents an intervention designed to alter the shares of the various sectors and the results of their interaction.

Today, virtually all countries pursue industrial policies. The planned and unplanned consequences of these policies affect each country's trading partners and in turn their industrial policies. Thus we must be concerned not only with the content of industrial policy—the measures a country uses to try to improve its industrial structure—but also with the country's underlying objectives, the strength of its commitment to industrial policy, and its effectiveness in pursuing this commitment.

Industrial policies can be explicit or implicit, systematic or piecemeal. Canadian industrial policy has always been more explicit and systematic than that of the United States, but less articulated and coherent than that of some well-known models in post-World War II Europe. Because

*C. D. Howe Institute, Montreal

its "National Policy" adopted in 1897 was, in fact, an industrial policy, Canada provides a 100-year case study of a country that has been groping to adapt an explicit, if weak, policy framework to a changing economic environment.

This chapter first reviews the reasons underlying Canadians' desire for an industrial policy and explains the constraints under which Canadian policy makers labor; these general needs and constraints were present, at least in an embryonic form, in the nineteenth century and are still with us today. A second section describes Canada's experience with industrial policy, from the adoption of that National Policy to the attempts to replace it in the 1970s. The final section examines the outlook for Canadian industrial policy in the 1980s.

THE BACKGROUND: NEEDS, OBJECTIVES, AND CONSTRAINTS

Geopolitical Realities

Geopolitical realities have played an unusually important role in Canada's economic development. Some 90 percent of the country's 24 million people live in a strip of land about 100 miles wide and 3,000 miles long, just north of the U.S. border. Mineral, forest, agricultural, fishery, and water resources have been abundant, although much of this wealth is located in remote areas. Canadian manufacturing activities thus have always had to face the obstacles of small markets, heavy transportation costs, and competition from high wages and from profit opportunities in the resource sectors. Sharing a common culture and language with the Americans, English-speaking Canadians could have satisfied most of their needs south of the border in the absence of tariffs. At the same time, the more densely populated U.S. cities offered Canadian management and labor diverse opportunities.

Under these circumstances, one option for Canada was a complete dependence on resource extraction, forestry, and agriculture, with the addition of a few resource-based industries such as sawmills, pulp mills, and, before World War II, steel mills. The arguments against this option were the volatility of natural-resource-based earnings and the need to provide a larger number and range of job opportunities than agriculture, forestry, and mining could offer. The establishment of a manufacturing sector appeared to be necessary to ensure a minimum of economic stability and to maintain the critical population mass necessary for the transition from colonial to independent status.

The decision to create a country distinct from the United States, one that would extend along its entire northern frontier, thus entailed a commitment to the establishment of secondary industry as well as to major infrastructural investment. As we shall see later, a large part of Canada's manufacturing activity began as the result of explicit government policies, principally tariff policies. Because Canadian unit costs have historically been higher than those in the United States, Canadian plants have relied on tariff protection; as demand grew in Canada, U.S. firms set up tariff-jumping plants to tap the Canadian market.

While tariff protection has not been essential to all manufacturing in Canada, the dominant role played by the "tariff crutch" has led to a perception that the existence of Canadian manufacturing—its nature and weight in the economy—is dependent on policy decisions. Canadian policy makers have appeared to be responsible for maintaining a desired level of manufacturing. Not surprisingly, they have rarely attempted to defy that level.

Concerns and Objectives

The peculiarities of the Canadian economy have given rise to three interrelated concerns about the country's industrial structure: (1) the unsatisfactory sectoral distribution of output, exports, and employment; (2) the chronic weakness of the manufacturing sector; and (3) the undesirably large proportion of decisions affecting the Canadian economy that are taken by foreigners. These problems had created anxiety even before World War I, and that anxiety has found increasingly sophisticated expression ever since. The response has been the adoption of objectives, which, although their formulation may change, are also recurrent in Canadian policy. But the process of responding has given rise to a fourth, more recent concern: Canadians' apparent sluggishness in adjusting to changing market conditions. It is therefore useful for us to review these concerns and objectives before examining particular industrial policies.

First, Canada is extremely dependent on the sale of nonrenewable, often nonfabricated, raw materials as a means of balancing its international payments. While employment growth has been strongest in services, as shown in Table 3.1, the external service sector, including business services as well as interest and dividends paid abroad, has recorded massive and growing deficits. Table 3.2 illustrates the contributions made by the different sectors to the international account. Canadian governments have often tried to upgrade the processing of raw materials, both to reduce the country's vulnerability to commodity swings and to increase the market differentiation and value added of Canadian goods.

Second, Canadian manufacturing has been chronically uncompetitive. Canadian plants tend to produce high-cost, standard-technology goods. The combination of a small market of consumers and heavy exposure to U.S. advertising has led to the inefficient proliferation of products, models, and production processes within a plant that, in a larger market, would specialize in a smaller range of products and a shorter segment of the production process. Improving the competitiveness of the manufacturing sector is thus a perennial objective. How it should be done remains a key question in Canadian industrial policy.

Third, an exceptionally large proportion of economic decisions affecting Canada are taken by foreigners. This situation is caused by the geographical concentration of three-quarters of Canada's foreign trade south of the border, the extensive foreign ownership and hence control of strategic decisions, and the continued reliance on short-term capital inflows to balance deficits on international trade. Canadian industrial policy can only be understood in the light of a constant anxiety concerning foreign ownership and a general desire to reduce it—a desire that waxes and wanes according to the country's economic prosperity.

Finally, it is generally agreed that Canada has been slow in adapting to changing market conditions. This apparent lack of flexibility has been variously attributed to the ease with which Canadians can rely on their resource endowments, the inhibiting influence of foreign ownership, the constraints imposed by regional interests, and the labor market rigidities arising from collective agreements and relatively generous unemployment insurance benefits. Because it does not belong to any one of the large trade blocs, Canada is isolated in the contemporary world economy. Its survival is likely to depend on its ability to respond to changing demand. Increasing the Canadian economy's flexibility has therefore come to be an important industrial policy objective.

Constraints

Despite Canadians' generally favorable attitude toward explicit industrial policies, the nation's governments have faced some serious constraints in trying to adopt and implement such policies. The two major difficulties have been the openness of the Canadian economy and the commitment to regional economic development. As a small, very open economy, Canada has little market power and must bear any long-run costs of market intervention. In addition, as a long-time importer of foreign capital, Canada is dependent on the decisions of foreign owners operating in Canada, as well as on other foreigners' current investment decisions. There is always the danger that industrial measures too far out of line with those of other countries will deter new investors and

Table 3.1. Employment Growth by Industry in Canada, 1961–1981 (Average Compound Annual Growth Rate)

	1961–1971	*1971–1981*
Forestry	−2.28%	−0.80%
Mining	1.39	2.56
Manufacturing	1.98	0.66
Construction	1.45	−1.56
Transportation, communication and utilities	1.37	2.04
Trade	3.45	2.85
Finance, insurance and real estate	3.85	3.97
Services	6.43	4.93

Source: Statistics Canada, Employment Indices, CANSIM.

Table 3.2. Selected International Trade Account Balances (in Millions of Current Canadian Dollars)

	1975	*1978*	*1979*	*1980*	*1981*
Food and raw materials[a]	4,234	4,327	6,596	6,692	7,215
Fabricated materials[a]	3,842	10,113	12,303	16,633	16,006
End products[a]	−10,206	−12,434	−17,102	−17,800	−20,662
Overall merchandise trade[a]	−2,167	2,157	1,456	5,666	2,624
Interest and dividends	−1,953	−4,696	−5,241	−5,544	−6,982
Overall service account	−4,686	−8,992	−9,734	−10,995	−14,814

Source: Statistics Canada, *Summary of External Trade,* Ottawa, various years, and *Quarterly Estimates of the Canadian Balance of International Payments,* Ottawa, various years.
[a]Customs basis.

drive away foreign owners. Because these foreign owners and investors are principally U.S. citizens, and because nearly two-thirds of Canada's manufactured exports consist of intrafirm sales to U.S. companies, too great a policy divergence between the two countries is risky. Canadians have to remember the traditional U.S. aversion to explicit industrial policies.

The second major constraint on the successful implementation of industrial policies is the Canadian commitment to regional development. For historical and cultural reasons Canadians have not only attempted to redistribute wealth from the more to the less prosperous regions of the country but have also tried to influence the location of productive activities so as to reduce regional economic disparities. This policy has been summed up as moving jobs to people rather than people to jobs. Although infant-industry arguments may occasionally justify subsidies to encourage the location of manufacturing or processing plants in areas of high unemployment, such a regional development policy often imposes heavy costs and conflicts with the goals of an industrial policy.

This regional constraint has been shaped and strengthened by political considerations. Provincial governments in Canada control major economic policy levers, particularly in taxation, regulation, public procurement, and manpower training. Dissatisfied with the results of regional specialization—which has obliged resource-rich regions exposed to the swings of international supply and demand to purchase protected, high-cost manufactured goods from central Canada—provincial electorates have welcomed their respective governments' economic ambitions. These ambitions have been summed up as "province building," or wealth maximization on a regional basis. Province building competes with country building by the use of provincial procurement policies, regulation, and competitive subsidies—all of which may lead, and in some cases have already led, to nontariff barriers within the Canadian economic union.

CANADA'S EXPERIENCE WITH INDUSTRIAL POLICY

There have been three stages in the evolution of Canadian industrial policy: the National Policy introduced in 1897 by Canada's first prime minister, John A. Macdonald; the attempts to modify this policy in response to new demands in the post-World War II period; and the search in the 1970s for a new industrial policy based on trade liberalization or on technological sovereignty. First, however, we should look at the various types of policy instruments favored by Canadian governments.

Policy Instruments

Canadian governments tend to use public participation, protection, and regulation rather than direct subsidies to private-sector firms as a means of furthering their policies. Thus, in addition to assuming responsibility for the extensive Canadian transportation infrastructure, governments do business via crown corporations and public enterprises in a very wide range of commercial activities.[1] This role contrasts sharply with that of government in the United States.

Canada has a long tradition of using regulation to protect its citizens. Thus chartered banks must be Canadian owned, agricultural marketing boards prevent unacceptably large swings in farmers' incomes, the Canadian Radio and Television Commission assures Canadian content in the electronic media, and so on.

Support for such areas as transportation, communications, agriculture, and fisheries has figured large in the federal budget, while manufacturing assistance, research and development subsidies, and export financing have been relatively less important than in other industrialized countries. Canadians nonetheless pay, of course, for the support of the manufacturing sector through the direct and indirect costs of tariff protection. This option, which can be partly attributed to the difficulty of providing highly visible support for firms that are often predominantly foreign owned, may be changing.

The National Policy

The National Policy's goal was to create a single economically viable country from the Atlantic to the Pacific. The three main thrusts of the policy were tariff protection; the encouragement of immigration from Europe as a way of building a population base, particularly in western Canada; and the linking up of the different parts of the country by means of a continental Canadian railroad.

Transportation has always been a crucial element in Canadian political and economic life. The creation of the Canadian Confederation depended upon the completion of the railroad, and the federal government ultimately accepted responsibility for getting the job done at whatever cost—in this case, heavy indebtedness and the alienation of large tracts of Canadian land to the Canadian Pacific Railway, which was then a multinational corporation. Federal responsibility for transportation infrastructure, usually without any planned user-pay cost recovery, is a constant element in Canadian industrial policy.

The first element of the National Policy, a comprehensive set of tariff barriers designed to protect and stimulate manufacturing activity in central Canada, has also had long-lasting effects. Because the Canadian market was too small for the scale of much best-practice technology, even in the 1880s, and because the United States had recently closed its market by revoking the 1854 Reciprocity Treaty, Canada adopted across-the-board protection for its infant manufactures. Tariff protection is only now being reduced or phased out following the Tokyo Round of Multinational Trade Negotiations, and some sectors, such as textiles and clothing, remain highly protected.

While protecting manufacturing and assuming responsibility for infrastructure, Canadian governments have tended to pursue a noninterventionist policy toward resource exploitation and foreign investment. There have been some notable exceptions, such as the Ontario and Quebec embargoes on the export of pulpwood in 1900 and 1910 and their founding in 1920 of the Newsprint Institute to force the U.S.

market to buy Canadian forest products in a more processed form. In general, however, Canadian governments in the early part of the century did not attempt to make foreign- or Canadian-owned resource developers process their raw materials before shipping them out of the country. Until the late 1960s, Canada was one of the countries that put fewest restrictions on direct investment by foreigners.

The consequences of the National Policy can be seen in the very large influx of immigrants, particularly before World War I; in the massive investment, both public and private but largely foreign, in the economy; and in the creation of a substantial manufacturing sector employing about 22 percent of the population and contributing over 25 percent of gross national product in 1960. The 1950s were a period of very heavy foreign investment, and by the mid-1960s foreigners owned over 60 percent of the petroleum and natural gas industry, 60 percent of the mining and smelting industry, and 58 percent of the manufacturing sector. Within manufacturing, foreigners owned more than 80 percent of the assets of the tobacco, rubber, automobile, and chemical industries.

Such extensive foreign ownership inevitably gave rise to anxiety. In the resource sector, for instance, doubts were expressed about the compatibility of the interests of multinationals and Canadians. The National Energy Program, discussed below, was an attempt to address this long-standing concern. In the manufacturing sector foreign ownership has been the subject of repeated criticism and some analysis.[2] Although it has been difficult to substantiate accusations that foreign-owned firms are relatively weak in export, profit, or investment performance, current research suggests that product design and development activities, which are essential to the long-term health of manufacturing enterprises, will not normally be located in foreign-owned branch plants, particularly if these have been established to jump tariffs. Moreover, because Canadian-owned firms have to compete with such firms, they will not carry the costs of these activities if they can purchase them from abroad. At the same time, the combined influence of branch plants and U.S. continental advertising will lead to the proliferation of standard-technology products in a small branch plant economy.

Modifying the National Policy

During the 1960s and the early 1970s, Canadian governments invested in two sets of policies—one governing the special relationship with the United States, the other designed to reestablish control over economic decision making. These strategies, which were to a certain extent contradictory, represented attempts to update the National Policy, which was by then over ninety years old.

Special Relationship with the United States. During the Cold War period, U.S. governments relied on Canadian defense capabilities and tacitly integrated Canada into their defense strategy for North America. In this context, the United States agreed to a series of special deals with Canada, including the Defense Production Sharing Agreement, the Canadian-U.S. Automobile Pact, the mutual elimination of tariffs on farm machinery, exemptions from borrowing restrictions in the New York market in the 1960s, and an unofficial exemption of regional subsidies from the imposition of countervailing duties.

The value of each of these agreements has been much debated in both countries. Whatever the conclusions on a case-by-case basis, it seems obvious that such arrangements will only increase the smaller country's vulnerability to termination, unless it can use the opportunity to build up an internationally competitive activity. Unfortunately, Canada has not done so in either farm machinery or automobiles, and although the country may be internationally competitive in a few branches of aerospace instrumentation, it is not clear whether this position is the result of the Defense Sharing Production Agreement.

Canada's vulnerability was revealed in 1972 when the U.S. administration decided to impose countervailing duties on the exports of the Nova Scotia Michelin tire plant, which had received regional development assistance. In earlier cases, Washington had turned a blind eye to such assistance, as it again did subsequently. A recently negotiated international code on Subsidies and Countervailing Duties should prevent such surprises in the future. They are likely to recur in other forms, however, whenever a small country relies on an unofficial, discretionary "special relationship" with a larger neighbor.

Controlling Foreign Ownership. The significant inflow of foreign investment in the 1950s and the resulting anxiety about foreign ownership led to a series of major reports on the effects of foreign ownership on Canadian industry. Public opinion appeared to be ready for government action. Two policy measures followed: the creation of the Canada Development Corporation (CDC) and the establishment of the Foreign Investment Review Agency (FIRA). In addition, a number of measures to strengthen Canadian control of telecommunications, transportation, and financial institutions were adopted. During this period it was also decided that the cost of Canadian advertisements placed in U.S. news magazines and weeklies, which held a dominant share of the Canadian magazine market, would no longer be tax deductible. This decision provoked extensive controversy and high-level U.S. involvement; but the ensuing "cause célèbre" did little to increase understanding of Canadian concerns.

The creation of the CDC in 1965 was intended to reduce Canada's dependence on foreign equity capital. It was thought that the domestic capital markets could not pool sufficient amounts of equity for large projects, with the result that Canadians were missing out on new development opportunities. Despite widespread initial skepticism, the CDC has succeeded fairly well in refusing demands to bail out failing Canadian firms—an activity that would have prevented it from performing its primary role. Although the CDC has been operating as a crown corporation with 49 percent government ownership, a government spokesman recently announced Ottawa's intention to sell that federal share to the public.

In 1974 the federal government established FIRA with a mandate to screen investments that entailed the acquisition by foreigners of a Canadian business unrelated to their existing Canadian activities. This agency assesses the impact of a transaction by weighing a long list of benefits, often nonquantifiable and not necessarily complementary, against the fact of foreign ownership, which is automatically assumed to be a cost. Among the agency's criteria are job creation, increased resource processing, increased Canadian ownership, increased export volume, product innovation, and compatibility of corporate plans with federal and provincial industrial policies. The agency's screening has now been extended to include takeovers of Canadian assets within the range of a foreign firm's existing activities.

FIRA can block transactions that do not pass its tests. Although its powers are no greater than those of analogous agencies in other countries, the discretionary manner in which it operates has been the subject of much criticism. The benefits it claims to have produced cannot easily be demonstrated, while its costs, in terms of discouraging investment and lowering the returns to retiring Canadian businessmen who wish to sell their businesses, may be very high. But despite the opposition of the Canadian business community, many sections of public opinion support the existence of FIRA and are unconcerned about its mode of operation.

The Search for a New Industrial Policy

During the 1970s, policy makers, academics, and individual members of government advisory bodies and industrial associations all participated actively in an attempt to refurbish the Canadian industrial policy. The downgrading of the special relationship with the United States and the realization that Canada was the only industrialized country that lacked tariff-free access to a market of at least a hundred million consumers heightened Canadians' awareness of the need for new initiatives. This awareness coincided with the disturbing climate following the 1973 oil crisis and the realization that macroeconomic stabilization policies were unable to produce price stability, full employment, and a satisfactory level of economic growth.

Federal and provincial governments experimented with such measures as sectoral policies, targeted incentive programs, pressure to increase resource upgrading, and large-scale consultation. At the same time, a fundamental reappraisal of Canadian industrial policy was undertaken. Two opposing approaches emerged from the reappraisal: organized trade liberalization (supported by the Economic Council of Canada) and technological sovereignty (supported by the Science Council).[3]

The trade liberalization strategy suggested that Canada lower its tariff barriers, if necessary unilaterally. Such a move could be expected to reduce the cost of intermediate inputs, streamline manufacturing, and increase consumer spending power. Since most of Canada's trade is with the United States, this strategy was often presented in terms of a Canada-U.S. free trade agreement. Although the overall thrust was aimed at strengthening market signals in Canada, the strategy nevertheless provided for a major governmental role in the industrial, manpower, and regional transition to a more competitive economy. For example, FIRA was to continue its monitoring of foreign takeovers.

The technological-sovereignty approach was based on the premise that an economy dominated by foreign-owned multinationals can at best achieve growth at the expense of sustainable economic development. Even though trade barriers were responsible for inefficient manufacturing and a high level of foreign ownership in Canada, it was argued, removing them before Canadian manufacturing had developed a sophisticated innovative capability in technology would result in the demise of Canadian manufacturing, not its competitive rebirth. This strategy therefore called for the development of a Canadian-controlled technological capacity before trade barriers were removed. The role of government was to provide direct support for technological development and indirect support by means of public purchasing and export marketing assistance.

While debate continued on the respective merits of these two strategies, the Canadian government attempted to implement an industrial policy for the textile and clothing sector.[4] The Textile and Clothing Act, adopted in 1971, promised to replace ad hoc protective measures with systematic procedures for reviewing claims of injury from imports, implementing adjustment measures when Canadian production had no long-term chance of becoming competitive, and adopting transitory special protective measures when they appeared warranted by the long-term feasibility of Canadian production. However, since no effective adjustment measures were adopted, the Textile and Clothing Board found it difficult to refuse special protective measures in cases of injury, even when the long-term competitiveness of Canadian producers was in doubt. The Textile and Clothing Act certainly increased the visibility and the consistency of special import measures, but it did little to bring about structural transformation in the industry. It was the first and the last of a proposed series of sectoral industrial policies.

A second key policy area that received attention in the 1970s was resource upgrading in Canada. Several provincial governments, particularly the Progressive Conservatives of Ontario and the National Democratic Party of British Columbia, attempted in different ways to persuade resource exporters, both Canadian and foreign, to increase the Canadian value added of their sales. At the same time, the federal government made a considerable effort to reduce tariff escalation by level of processing on a sectoral basis within the Tokyo Round negotiations.[5]

In some industries, such as asbestos, efficiency criteria pointed to market-located rather than resource-based processing. In other sectors, some progress was made toward the objective of increasing Canadian value added. But in general, Canadians were not prepared to take the risks that would result from imposing serious constraints on resource exporters or from participating fully in export cartels such as the Intergovernmental Council of Copper Exporting Countries.

Program support to manufacturing firms also assumed increasing importance in the 1970s. The federal and some provincial governments offered support for research and development, technology, improved productivity, fashion design, exports, and so on, to eligible firms, both Canadian- and foreign-owned. Assistance took the form of grants, guaranteed loans, and tax expenditures.

The resources devoted to these programs were limited in comparison with similar programs elsewhere, and many firms felt that the paperwork required made them unattractive. Furthermore, a proliferation of programs led to user and taxpayer skepticism. Many of these programs have now been consolidated, and the federal government has attempted to provide assistance on a "one-stop shopping" basis.

A final noteworthy element concerning the industrial policy in this period was the federal government's attempt to bring labor and management together with policy makers to take stock of Canada's industrial situation and to work out joint plans of action. Unlike other countries that pursue an active industrial policy, Canada has no national social and economic council through which policy objectives and programs can be adopted and implemented. Tripartite sectoral task forces were set up in 1978 under the Liberal government, and the short-lived Conservative government of 1979 had planned to hold a national economic conference but was defeated before it could take place. Investment in consultative activities of this kind improved the understanding between government and the private sector and helped open up channels of communication between labor and management groups. The centrifugal forces in Canada are too strong, however, and the labor and management organizations too weak for consultation to lead to the adoption of an overall industrial policy, even if there were consensus as to its objectives and strategy.[6]

As the 1970s came to an end, therefore, Canadians had not succeeded in replacing the National Policy of 1897 with a set of policies adapted to the late twentieth century.

INDUSTRIAL DEVELOPMENT POLICY FOR THE 1980s

The federal government recently took two major industrial policy initiatives, which may serve as pointers for subsequent decisions in this decade. In the fall of 1980 it announced the long-awaited National Energy Program (NEP), followed little more than a year later by a major policy paper on economic development.

The National Energy Program

The three central objectives of the NEP are to develop security of oil supply and eventual energy self-sufficiency; to increase the opportunities for Canadian participation in energy industries, particularly in the petroleum industry, and to set petroleum prices and intergovernmental revenue sharing so as to distribute energy wealth equitably across the country.

Increased Canadian participation is to be achieved through measures that encourage the takeover of foreign firms by private Canadian firms and through takeovers by PetroCanada, the government-owned oil and gas corporation. Much of the land with exploration potential, called the Canada Lands, is owned by the federal government. Canadian-controlled firms and PetroCanada will be favored in agreements governing exploration on these lands.

The NEP has proved costly in both political and economic terms. A year's haggling between Ottawa and the western provinces over rent sharing has discouraged investment and lowered Canadian credit. Meanwhile, the severity of the North American recession has increased the risks of alienating investors both at home and abroad. The Canadian government has been under pressure to reverse the negative effects of this program by canceling some of the Canadianization measures or by eliminating other perceived deterrents to investment in Canada, such as FIRA. As a result, it seems unlikely that similar programs will be adopted in the next few years.

The Federal Government's Development Paper

A year after the NEP was announced, the federal finance minister issued a paper entitled *Economic Development for Canada in the 1980s*[7] to accompany the government's second budget. This document incorporates elements of both the market-oriented and technological-sovereignty approaches to industrial policy. Perhaps the most significant aspect of the paper is the proposed major resource development projects to be undertaken in Canada over the next nineteen years. These projects, which were identified by a private-sector task force composed of labor and management representatives,[8] are estimated to cost $440 billion in 1981. Implementation of the projects is expected to provide Canadian suppliers of equipment and services with opportunities to become internationally competitive. Both the need to strengthen market signals and the need to assure Canadian suppliers of preferential treatment are strongly expressed in this document.

The policy explicitly rejects the option of direct governmental intervention in favor of a substantial supportive and regulatory role. In federal-provincial relations the guiding principle is increased cooperation and consultation between governments, to avoid unproductive program duplication and to resist the tendency toward balkanization. In addition to preferential treatment of Canadian suppliers, the instruments to be employed include increased regulation, assistance geared to the goal of long-run competitive viability, direct government subsidies, and public sector investment. The mix of instruments will be differentiated to meet the needs of four priority areas: industrial development, resource development, transportation, and human resources.

Industrial Development. The policy thrust here is to make sure that Canadian benefits from the resource activities are optimized while the necessary complementary measures to facilitate adjustment in other sectors are being adopted. Even if the resource projects are undertaken in the manner envisaged by the policy document, a major challenge remains: to ensure that Canadians and Canadian-owned firms derive maximum benefits from supplying the machinery, equipment, and labor force for these projects, and in a manner that supports aspirations for regional diversification. To address this challenge, an Office of Industrial and Regional Benefits (OIRB) has been established to advise the government on matters of industrial policy, to coordinate its policy efforts, and to provide a focal point for consultation with the private sector. In a series of complementary measures, the federal government has committed itself to an increase in the level of research and development activity in Canada and has set target levels for the private and public sectors. Paralleling this commitment is the new Industrial Opportunities Program (IOP), set up to coordinate existing programs with the goal of achieving a more effective resource utilization.

Recognizing that permanent protection from change is impossible, the government has created several new adjustment programs. The Canadian Industrial Renewal Board (CIRB), for instance, has been established to facilitate restructuring in the clothing, textiles, and footwear industries, all areas that have long been internationally noncompetitive. Unlike previous boards of this type, the CIRB is composed of members of the private sector drawn from noninvolved industries, and it has been invited to take a hard look at the firms' claims of long-term viability.

The seriousness of the government's intentions was indicated by its recent refusal to renew import quota protection for leather footwear. The footwear sector is small, however, relative to the clothing and textile industries, which continue to command a considerable amount of special protection. The adjustment process for these industries is complicated by their concentration in two provinces and by the fact that they constitute the economic backbone of certain regions within these provinces.

Resource Development. Five key resource areas are identified: petroleum and natural gas, agriculture, fisheries, resource-based industries, and mining. Although the NEP continues to be applied in the petroleum and gas sectors, its options have not been extended to other resource areas. Instead, the government is studying the different resources' potential in conjunction with the private sector and provincial governments, as a first step toward developing more specific programs.

Transportation Development. Although the transportation network in Canada is already highly developed, substantial improvements will be needed to handle the volume of shipping expected to arise from resource-based expansion. The federal government has committed funds for grain terminals, roads, and major port projects. One significant transportation issue is the expansion and financing of the western railroad system. The issue is potentially divisive, with roots in the regional specialization and tariff issues of the National Policy. A five-year plan was scheduled to start in 1982.

Human Resources. The federal government recently announced a National Training Program, which will bring about a major reallocation of existing training resources. The centerpiece of this new program is the identification of national priority occupations that will be needed to support the development of the resource-based expansion and manufacturing spin-offs.

Potential Trade-offs among Policy Objectives. The thrust of the new policy is toward growth. However, the pursuit of other objectives expressed in the policy document is not necessarily consistent with that emphasis on growth. Three requirements must be met if industrial diversification is to succeed. First, spin-off effects must be realized that will benefit secondary manufacturing and high technology industries operating in Canada. Second, Canadian as well as foreign-owned firms must be able to benefit from the spin-offs. Third, the spin-offs must lead to the creation of internationally marketable outputs that can continue to be sold profitably once the resource project is completed. A major unknown is the way in which the policy of maximizing industrial benefits will be implemented. If resource developers are forced (or encouraged) to purchase inputs from less efficient Canadian firms, there is a risk of reducing the growth impetus itself and of creating industries that will not be able to sell in international markets. The policy can not be effective unless Canadian firms' disadvantages are only temporary ones that can be overcome by the "learning by doing" process involved in obtaining a major contract. In other words, the strategy still depends on the validity of the infant-industry argument, albeit in a milder form.

The potential resource projects are well distributed among the various regions of the country, with the exception of Ontario, which is expected to be the main beneficiary of spin-off manufacturing activity. Nonetheless, the OIRB will be keeping a close eye on the actual regional distribution of the projects. If political objectives dominate the regional distribution and the preference given to suppliers, the growth potential of the economy may be undermined, making it impossible to reach the goal of long-run competitiveness for Canadian manufacturing.

Major Economic Constraints. The major projects are capital intensive and will require large quantities of savings. Although gross savings as a percentage of GNP averaged 24 percent during 1974–1980 period and the personal savings rate was slightly less than 10 percent, the main source of future savings is likely to be in the public sector unless Canadians borrow more abroad. Canada's capital requirements are greater than those of other Western countries, not only because of the requirements of the major projects, but also because the country must undertake new capital formation to restructure the manufacturing sector, replace obsolete capital stock, and ensure a high level of economic activity distributed among all regions of the country.

Another major constraint is the need for skilled labor. At present there is a mismatch between labor supply and demand in Canada. If the country is to develop an import-substitution capacity in order to supply machinery for natural resource projects, it will need more skilled workers. Yet the National Training Program is encountering provincial opposition because training is a field of provincial jurisdiction. An additional problem is that if workers migrate to more profitable opportunities once they have been trained, the benefits of the program may be reaped in other countries, particularly the United States, which has just announced major training cutbacks. Canadians are well aware of the migration problem, for Canada has long benefited from the same phenomenon at the expense of Europe.

Short-term disinflation policy priorities constitute a third constraint. Whatever the long-run effect of restrictive monetary and fiscal policy, the immediate impact is a downturn in economic activity that will increase the costs of the adjustment process and thereby slow it down. The desire to control government budgetary deficits and not increase public indebtedness makes it particularly difficult to find the resources to improve the transportation infrastructure and human resources. Up to this point, there has not been any major movement to find such resources by cutting social programs, but health and education expenditures have been tightened at the provincial level.

The Outlook

It is still too early to say whether the economic policy document of 1981 will be a turning point in Canadian industrial policy. The current recession and the fall in real energy prices, however, are making it difficult for the new policy orientations to get off the ground, and there is widespread skepticism about a development strategy built on major resource projects, most of which are predicated on a strong and growing demand for energy.

Several elements in the policy provide pointers for the future, regardless of the near-term fluctuations in energy supply and demand. First is the acknowledgment that Canadian industrial growth and development must be built on linkages to the country's resource endowment. Second, there is a commitment to strengthening market signals to improve flexibility. Third, the budgetary estimates show a planned reallocation of federal spending toward industrial incentives at the expense of constant growth in social expenditures. Fourth, it is recognized that federal-provincial cooperation is essential to achieving industrial policy objectives. Refusal on both sides to face up to this necessity has seriously undermined industrial policy over the last ten years. Canadians are beginning to realize that they cannot afford to attempt high-risk industrial policies while serious internal divisions remain unresolved.

The industrial policy that emerges from the recessionary years of the early 1980s is likely to be less ambitious than that proposed by the government's development paper. That document, however, has played an important role in going beyond the mutually exclusive proposals of the 1970s, thereby inviting Canadians to take stock of their place in the world economy.

NOTES

1. See Marsha Gordon, *Government in Business* (Montreal: C. D. Howe Institute, 1981).
2. A task force under the direction of Herb Gray, currently minister of industry, trade and regional development, synthesized the information and concerns about the "branch plant economy" in a major study entitled *Foreign Direct Investment in Canada* (Ottawa: Government of Canada, 1972). A brief critical review of the debate in the 1970s, with references, is contained in *Canadian Public Policy*, vol. 3, Summer 1979.
3. For a useful summary of the two approaches and appropriate references, see "The Bold Alternatives" in Richard D. French, *How Ottawa Decides* (Ottawa: Canadian Institute for Economic Policy, 1980), pp. 96–105.
4. For a discussion of this policy, see Caroline Pestieau, *The Canadian Textile Policy: A Sectoral Trade Adjustment Strategy?* (Montreal: Canadian Economic Policy Committee, 1976).
5. See Caroline Pestieau, *The Sector Approach to Trade Negotiations: Canadian and U.S. Interests* (Montreal: Canadian Economic Policy Committee, 1976).
6. See Douglas Brown and Julia Eastman, *The Limits of Consultation* (Ottawa: Science Council, 1981).
7. Government of Canada, Ottawa, 1981.
8. Consultative Task Force on Industrial and Regional Benefits from Major Canadian Projects, *Major Canadian Projects, Major Canadian Opportunities* (Ottawa, 1981), often referred to as the "Megaprojects Task Force Report."

Chapter 4

Industrial Policy in France

Lawrence G. Franko* and Jack N. Behrman**

France has long been one of the world's leading and least embarrassed practitioners of the art of industrial policy—rivaled only by Japan in the developed world. Much is therefore known about what French industrial policy is and is not, about what it has been, and about how it has developed.

The history of industrial policy in France contrasts markedly with that of Japan and Germany. There are similarities in objectives, tools, and processes. But while in Japan and Germany industrial policy grew "from below," out of doing what came naturally, in France it was engineered by the government.

In Japan, the industrial policy process grew out of consensus-oriented, cooperative social traditions. In Germany, similar traditions, with the addition of novel postwar social structures such as codetermination, substantially attenuated the need for a highly visible government role. France after World War II was in a sense continuing an historical development policy whose roots extended back at least as far as the successful effort made in the 1600s by Colbert, Louis XVI's minister of France, to attract, subsidize, and protect the Venetian glass techinicians from whose skills sprang today's Compagnie de Saint Gobain. Indeed,

*Fletcher School of Law and Diplomacy
**University of North Carolina at Chapel Hill

the postwar core of French industrial policy until 1975 – indicative planning – served as one means of creating a business-government-labor-social consensus in what had become a highly divided society.

"PLANNING" IN THE POSTWAR REVIVAL

Partly because of historical accident, the postwar French state found itself owning a large portion of the French banking system, as well as a number of key enterprises. Thus, Renault, nationalized because of its founder's wartime collaboration, could be told by its new owner to stop concentrating on wealthy, big-car customers and produce a small "people's car" (the 4-CV). Nevertheless, it was realized that coercion would not bulid consensus, so "indicative planning" was adopted. Ironically it was the antiplanning United States that provided the catalyst. Jean Monnet produced the first plan in 1946 to convince the United States that it could give France money (under the Marshall Plan in 1948) for reconstruction because the money would be well spent!

The "indicative" part of indicative planning was unique to the French, creating tripartite government, business, and labor "modernization commissions" in the poisoned social atmosphere of the late 1940s. Each major sector had its "modernization" and later "planning" commission, and although government and business dominated (because of the school and university ties shared by many business and government leaders in France, as well as the importance of state-owned enterprise), the process kept labor (even Communist organized labor) informed and, particularly during reconstruction, involved.

The agenda of these commission meetings was partly set by the sectoral projections generated by the government economists in the planning agency. These indicative projections, and the "discussed projections" that followed, were only indicators: they could be totally ignored (and often were, especially by small firms). Nevertheless, investor confidence grew, the unknown void of the future seemed less risky, and when most firms felt reassured and invested, investment and growth became a self-fulfilling prophecy.

The basic philosophy of France's planning was similar to Japan's: break supply-side bottlenecks – especially of imported goods or exportables – rather than reduce growth as the primary means of controlling inflation and keeping external accounts in balance. As in Japan, a very large assortment of tools was used, with perhaps even greater use of credit-market interventions to steer resources to priority bottleneck sectors. State enterprises, especially in the energy sector, were also used as entrepreneurial resource allocation tools. As in Japan, market sanctions were hardly ever eliminated (two partly state-owned oil firms competed with each other—and foreign competitors) but "limited competition" was sometimes imposed.

Indicative planning produced real investment and growth. And the process involved an unusual amount of communication between public and business policy makers. That communication alone reduced the propensity, so noticeable in other countries, for different government ministries and agencies to set conflicting standards and targets for firms and industries, and to adopt macro and micro policies that were in conflict.

At the time indicative planning was first introduced, France was a rather closed, not highly industrialized economy. As the nation opened to the European Economic Community (EEC) and the world (in a "planned" way: firms were told they had only so many years to get into internationally competitive shape), as the sheer number of firms grew, and as a few sectoral commissions threatened to turn into rather too cozy clubs prone to investment errors, the sectoral detail of the plans diminished. The Eighth Plan (1981-1985) spoke at length about the general need to increase R&D and investment, and in only general terms of priority sectors. In French terms, moreover, the Giscard-Barre team leaned toward a more "German concertation" approach.

During the 1960s, the French sometimes made the "British mistake" of attempting to pick single national-champion firms, creating monopolies for them, and pumping money into them. The result was typically a technological success, but a market failure, like the Concorde. During the 1970s, however, French practice moved much more in the direction of "Japanese horsebreeding" for high-value-added, high-income, resource-saving sectors through the creation of multiple-firm, competitive industries, often with foreign joint venture partners.

Nevertheless, the concern with the structure of industry remains, especially with respect to reducing dependence on imported energy and creating a world position for France in telecommunications and electronics. The Ministry of Industry has traditionally been quite specific about sectoral priorities (see Table 4.1). And the business-government-labor communication process that takes place while the Plan is being debated appears well enough established in French mores to obviate the need for the highly formalized consultations of the 1950s and 1960s.

The most interesting questions about French industrial policy at this time turn not only on achieving a better understanding of what France has done in the past, but also, since a major political change occurred during 1982, on obtaining a sense of what it will be in the future. Accordingly, the next section discusses the tools and broad structural approach used during the 1960s and 1970s. Then sectoral priorities under

Table 4.1. Major Industrial Policy Measure Applied by France in the Mid 1970s.

Sector	R&D Grants	Direct Subsidies or Grants	Credits or Tax Relief	State Guarantees	State Equity Capital	Export Promotion	National Procurement Preferences	Merger Promotion	Rationalization Agreements, Cartels or Trade Protection	Promotion of Inward Foreign Investment
Textiles & clothing				*				*	*	
Shipbuilding		*		*						
Steel		*		*	*				*	
Automobiles & trucks		*	*	*	*	*		*		* (2)
Machine tools		*	*	*						
Vehicle components				*				*		
Food products				*				*		
Chemicals				*				*		
Aircraft	*	*	*	*	*	*	*	* (1)		
Computers	*	*	*	*	*		*	*		
Electronic components	*	*		*			*			
Nuclear power	*			*	*	*	*	*		*
Telecommunications				*	*		*	*		
Energy Conservation	*			*						
Raw materials conservation	*			*	*					
Space and ocean mining	*			*						

(1) Early 1970s

(2) Unsuccessful

Source: Lawrence G. Franko, "European Industrial Policy: Past, Present and Future," European Research Report (Brussels: The Conference Board in Europe, 1980), p. 27.

the Gaullist and Giscardian governments are compared with those of the new Mitterand administration.

THE 1960s AND 1970s

French industrial policies shifted significantly during the 1970s, as shown in Table 4.2. Before the mid-1970s, French industrial policy was aimed at preventing the takeover of French industry by foreign firms and strengthening it through consolidation, in order to compete more effectively with European firms in anticipation of further European integration. Even during the 1950s and early 1960s, the French government used a wide variety of techniques to stimulate industry — encompassing virtually all that are used currently. It selected certain sectors for encouragement, through R&D assistance, suport of mergers and consolidation, creation of investment-banking facilities to provide risk capital, and protection of industry from international competition. Some sectors it deliberately exposed to international and domestic competition to force efficiency and competitiveness, encouraging them to cut their losses when competitive forces were overwhelming. In others, it allowed cartel-like groupings of industry to achieve competitiveness. Its policy has been highly selective, pragmatically shifting between market and nonmarket approaches to meet whatever pressures seemed to need countering.

In addition, France tried to promote high-technology industries through government investment in "national champions" (sometimes a state-owned company) in various key projects, and in the selective admittance of foreign firms that could accelerate technological innovation in cooperation with French companies.

During the late 1970s, crises in steel, oil refining, and petrochemicals led to government support for cartels in these sectors, followed by a partial nationalization of the steel industry. Efforts were also made to maintain employment in steel, shipbuilding, autos, and machine tool sectors through subsidies and low-interest loans as well as export-promotion efforts, such as loan guarantees, export credits to foreign customers, and direct assistance in sales of aircraft and nuclear power units to foreign governments. Under the regime of Raymond Barre, industries were left more to the free market, with price controls removed so as to stimulate investment; bankruptcies were permitted to eliminate marginal firms; mergers were slowed and competition encouraged, and subsidies were reduced. Even so, promotion efforts were directed at high-technology sectors including nuclear energy, aircraft and aerospace, energy conservation, electronic data processing, and telecommunications, through

Table 4.2. Shifts in French Industrial Policy

Pre-1974	1974–1978	1979–1980
Encourage concentration and mergers of national firms, often with the intention of blocking foreign takovers. Promote high technology industries by: • Government investments in "national champions" • Prestige projects • Gradually reversing the Guaiist policy of excluding foreign firms.	Maintain employment by subsides and low-interest loans to steel, shipbuilding, auto and machine tool companies. Push for EEC crisis cartels in steel, oil refining and petrochemicals. Parital nationalization of steel industry. Major export promotion effort, via: • Loan guarantees • Low interest credits, for export sales and for capacity enlargement in export oriented industries (10 billion FF in 1976; 3 billion in 1977). • Foreign policy support, especially for aircraft and nuclear power sales. The oil price effect on the balance of payments is seen as a major constraint on French growth; energy policy is placed in the industry ministry headed by a former atomic energy chief. Establishment of CIASI to rescue ailing firms.	Remove price controls to permit firms to have larger investable surpluses. Allow bankruptcies (to eliminate inefficient management). Legislate to control merger and promote competition. Reduce current subsidies. Promote "Sectors of the Future," e.g. nuclear energy, aircraft, energy conservation electronic data processing, telecommunications by: • State investments • Government purchasing • Low interest loans • Subsidies and tax incentives to users • Soliciting and giving tax incentives to foreign (especially U.S.) firms to form joint ventures. • Establishment of special funds for employment creation in troubled regions • Employment creation by rebates of social charges to hiring firms. Reorient savings toward industry by tax deductions for share purchases. Increased consultation with labor. "Hard line" energy conservation. Emphasize public R & D support for industrial needs and small business creation.

Source: Lawrence Franko, "European Industry Policy: Past, Present, and Future," *European Research Report* (Brussels: The Conference Board in Europe, 1980), p. 6.

Table 4.3. French Mechanisms of Coordination

Planning Mechanisms

Commisariate du Plan . . . Interministeral Planning Agency of Federal Government; selects priority sectors, determines techniques of stimulation; selects national champions, provides directives to ministries for application of techniques.

Plan Calcul . . . . Planning for the mainframe computer sector.

Plan Composants . . . . Planning for micro-electric components.

Plan Peripherique . . . . For EDP peripheral equipment.

Plan Software . . . . Assistance for a creation of appropriate software.

Plan Electronic Civile . . . . For the civilian electronic sector.

Plan Mechanic . . . . For the entire mechanical industry.

Ministry of Industry—Bureaus and Divisions Realted Specifically to industries (as Under Japanese MITI) in Continuing Dialogue with Specific Sectors.

Caisse des Dépôts et des Consignantions—Largest French bank, state-owned but "independent". It dominates the bond market, utilizing all small postal savings and funds in savings banks, holding pension funds of state-enterprises and municipalities, as well as government accounts and and other funds. With Treasury and Fonds de Development Economique et Social (FDES), it has responsiblity for financing large projects in the Plan.

Banks—Channels for capital provided by the state for priority sectors and national champions.

Nationalized Firms—Both leaders in specific sectors and purchasers of equipment on a preferential basis.

Patronat—National Association of Industry Associations, coordinating representation to the Federal Government; (French industry has a larger number of weaker firms in each sector, though it has attempted to merge and concentrate them for easier coordination, without much success).

a variety of techniques including government purchasing, R&D support, tax incentives and direct financial assistance, and special funds for distressed regions. (See Table 4.2.) In addition, consultations between companies and labor were encouraged, and capital markets were bolstered.

To accomplish these objectives, the French government employed virtually all the measures we recognize as constituting industrial policy. They included:

1. Government or joint government-business identification of high- and low-growth industries and technologies.
2. Support of long-term sectoral strategies through governmental education, research, and social policies.
3. Credit-market interventions to channel capital to investment in growth or defense-related sectors, or to tide declining industries over sudden demand drops or competitive shocks.

4. Technology, science, and education policies aimed at supporting high-growth, defense, and advanced-technology sectors, including the encouragement of the importation of foreign technology and know-how through:
   - acquiring licenses,
   - accepting joint ventures,
   - accepting foreign subsidiaries,
   - sending nationals abroad for specific technical or business studies, and
   - providing government financing, insurance, or other encouragement for the acquisition of foreign firms and their technology.
5. Encouragement of mergers (a) among firms in related industries, on the theory that structural adjustments within diversified companies would be less socially and politically disruptive; (b) to obtain production, R&D, and marketing economies of scale to match foreign competition.
6. Ownership policies aimed at keeping some national ownership and legal control in sectors such as nuclear energy, electronics, and materials, to offset foreign economic or political monopoly power.
7. Creation of public investment banking corporations to supplement government loans with risk capital for entrepreneurial ventures.
8. Protection of industry from international competition through tariff barriers or, after the EEC and Kennedy Round tariff cuts, through nontariff barriers, subsidies, tax measures, and national preferences in public purchasing.
9. Deliberate exposure of industry to international or domestic competition on a selective basis, to promote efficiency and competitiveness through legal or administrative means.
10. Subsidies and tax concessions.

A major difference in policy after 1976 was that the criterion of success became achieving international competitiveness—preferably without, but if necessary with, technological assistance from abroad, even accepting joint ventures with foreign firms. In addition, the techniques used shifted somewhat from direct guidance by the government to specific sectors and firms toward greater reliance on market signals, enterprise strategy, and government stimulus to growing enterprises, so as to hasten market processes. These moves brought French policy closer to both German and Japanese practice.

The planning structure for guidance of a sector may be fairly simple or complex. In the case of computers, there are four separate plans: the Plan Calcul, for the mainframe computer; the Plan Composants, for micro-electronic components; Plan Peripherique, for EDP peripheral equipment; and the Plan Software. In addition, there is a Plan Electronic Civile and a Plan Mechanique for the entire mechanical industry. All of these are formulated in close cooperation with industry. (See Table 4.3.)

French financial assistance for industrial objectives is channeled through government-controlled institutions—namely the Caisse and postal savings, which are the savings and loans institutions that mobilize individual and small-company savings of the economy. These funds are agglomerated and passed out through the Bank of France and the now state-owned banks. The control of the government over the access to credit has restricted the commercial banks' ability to lend and has permitted the government to determine the ultimate recipients of loan funds. The French banks are not, however, tied in any direct way to private companies as they are in Japan and Germany. In addition, the government has created state-owned, venture-capital institutions.

Coordination in France is made easier by the fact that the leaders of government and industry are largely members of an elite, having graduated from one or more of the country's *grands écoles*. The top graduates go into the top ministries or companies and maintain their old school ties throughout life—on retirement a government official will join a company as a board member or top official. Personal requests for information, consultation or even cooperation thus get a more cordial response than in the United States or Germany.

Despite these efforts, France has not been able to gain a strong position in electronics; its policy has shifted several times, but market share has not increased, and it remains dependent on foreign technology. This sector is the focus of more recent policy, as discussed below.

In 1974, the French government embarked on the industrialized world's most ambitious nuclear power program. It acted through the instrument of equipment purchases by Electricité de France, as well as gradual acquisition of Westinghouse's French nuclear equipment interests by Framatome. Unlike many countries in the West, France was able to maintain a social consensus in favor of nuclear plant construction, and will generate some 55 percent of its electricity through nuclear power by 1985. An investment of some $6 billion per year is being made in this program. In 1979, the French Minister of Industry noted that the French nuclear industry already employed as many people as did the French steel industry.

The government directly supported Peugeut's takeover of Critroën and its renovation of Critroën's management. The French auto industry has now become the world's third largest—after the U.S. and Japan— apparently validating the government's efforts in that sector. R&D

grants, government purchasing, and state-supplied risk capital helped the French aircraft industry regain commercial aircraft markets (witness the relative success of Airbus Industries). Exports in many sectors were substantially increased—more than might have been expected given relative price movements between France and its major customers.

In the declining industries, France continued the sectoral investment programs in steel and obtained sanction for a crisis cartel in steel and trade protection from EEC members. It was also a strong proponent of the tightening of the Multi-Fiber Agreement on textiles during 1977, and it retarded the shrinking of the clothing industry. French policy toward textiles illustrates its reluctance to accept adjustments that cause severe unemployment. It has not cut its facilities in this sector as much as have Germany or Britain—partly because of the structure of the industry, which is greatly fragmented and therefore difficult to guide. Sweeping policies of admitting foreign competition would damage too many areas of the country and make assistance difficult, in the government's view. An interministerial committee established to restructure of industry gave direct assistance to a number of firms about to collapse; recently, however, it has allowed some bankruptcies in declining sectors.

Although much of the publicity given to French industrial policy between 1973 and 1978 concerned efforts to protect employment in the declining clothing, shipbuilding, and steel industries, the center of gravity of French industrial policy was actually elsewhere. Considerably more steps were taken to promote investment, efficiency, and French independence in high technology, knowledge-intensive sectors than went to defend sick industries (Table 4.3).

French policy is also critically dependent on the existence of state enterprises in key sectors—particularly petroleum, computers, and aerospace. These enterprises are used to subsidize customer companies (through lower prices) and supplier companies (through preferential orders). Five of the ten largest corporations in France are state owned, including Electricité de France and Renault—each employing more than 100,000 workers. The French government holds monopolies in telecommunications, electricity, gas, railroads, sea ports and airports, potash, lignite and coal, banking, and aerospace. It holds more than 40 percent of the sectors of shipping, shipbuilding, insurance, and trucking and over 20 percent of the machine tools, automotive, and petrochemical sectors. In such state-owned enterprises, purchases take on the coloration of government purchasing and therefore are potentially politically guided.

In steel, the government controls private companies through price and investment guidance, supplies coal to the industry through its monopoly companies, and is the major customer. In aircraft, the government has a majority ownership position, sometimes nearly 100 percent, in the major companies. In addition, it is a joint-venture partner in a number of companies manufacturing specialized aircraft equipment. All of these activities give it a strong influence, if not complete control, over the relevant sectors.

Paradoxically, these interventionist practices coincided with a general opening of the French economy to international competition in the mid-1970s. French policy did not often attempt a complete defiance of long-term market forces, however.

The emphasis on international competitiveness brought another contrast with Gaullist insistence on purely French solutions in high technology sectors. Giscardian France invited selected foreign companies to participate in joint ventures with French firms as a way to achieve competitiveness as well as technological excellence.

There was yet a third difference: French industrial policy became notably less oriented toward individual projects and *dirigiste* involvement in particular firms, and leaned more toward providing risk capital, purchasing support, and stimulants to growing enterprises in the context of sectorial programs and objectives. The prod of competition was thereby maintained. These moves actually brought French industrial policy much closer to Japanese practice than it had been in the past. In 1978, for example, France decided to provide grants and incentives to three electronic components firms, each of which had taken a United States joint venture partner, and then to support success with purchase orders and additional funding. This decision closely resembled the Japanese practice of promoting high technology sectors much in the manner of a horse breeder.

More than some other countries, France was willing to cut its losses when particular approaches were revealed as clearly uneconomic, and it learned from past mistakes. French industrial policy pragmatically followed no rigid market versus nonmarket approaches to economic management, but rather tended to support, strengthen, salvage, and promote industry on a selective basis.

RECENT CHANGES

Despite the liberal measures adopted in the latter part of the 1970s, France has not given up its historical orientation of state intervention. Only France and Japan have publicly announced the selection of target industries for government support in the 1980s, and the lists are virtually identical.

To encourage competitive efforts in these sectors, tax deductions have been offered to individuals who purchase shares on the stock exchange,

Table 4.4. French Industrial Policy Priorities, 1979

Industries of the Future
  Energy Conservation devices
  Nuclear energy ("which employs already in France as many people as the steel
    industry")
  Solar energy
  Data processing, equipment and utilization ("three times the employ of steel in
    France")
  Aerospace
  Ocean farming and exploration
  Microelectronics, microprocessors and semiconductor devices
  Telecommunications
  Biotechnology
Classical Industries That Must Be Renovated
  Automobiles ("but the enterprises are sufficiently healthy not to require state
    aid")
  Machine tools ("to aide adaptation to numerical control and microcircuitry")
  Textiles and clothing
Industries To Exploit French Resources (principally through public infrastructure investments)
  Agribusiness and food
  Wood, pulp, paper, and leather
Industries Needing Complete Restructuring (Including Capacity Shrinkage) With Massive State Help
  Steel
  Shipbuilding

Source: Interview with M. André Giraud, French Mininster of Industry, "La technologie
contre le chomage," *Le Nouvel Èconomiste* no. 189, June 25, 1979.

and mergers are being restricted. Renewed emphasis has been given
to business-government discussions focused on raw material and energy
needs. And a five-year, five-billion-franc support program for electronic
data processing and telecommunications equipment is in place. Most
recently, President Mitterrand announced a 33 percent increase in
spending by the Ministry of Research and Technology; total research
spending is expected to rise from 1.8 percent of GNP to 2.5 percent by
1985. These moves are intended to assist French business in achieving
greater international competitiveness, especially in the selected
industries.

The difference between Mitterrand's policies and those of his
predecessors can be seen by contrasting the key sectors identified by
former Industry Minister Giraud in 1979 (Table 4.4) with the approach
summarized by Industry Minister Dreyfus in mid-1982 (Table 4.5). Three
policy shifts appear most salient. First, the Giscard government's emphasis on indirect and general financial measures for promoting industry

Table 4.5. Major Industrial Policy Initiatives of Socialist France, 1982

Research and Development

> Massive government budget increase for civilian research: 17.8 percent annual increases projected to 1985.

> More than twenty regional, consensus-building colloquia on R&D and R&D priorities, including government officials, scientists, technicians, and businessmen.

> Appointment of a highly visible socialist politician as technology ministry head and elevation of the ministry to "ministry of state" level.

Reconquering the Domestic Market

> Moral suasion and guidance of national firms.

> Some additional restrictions on Japanese imports (but largely symbolic, apparently as bargaining counters in trade negotiations).

> Selective approval / disapproval of Japanese direct investments in France (blockage of Thomson/JVC joint venture in video cameras, acceptance of Pioneer in high fidelity equipment and Citizen in watches.)

> (Potential) guidance through credit terms and allocation by nationalized banking network.

Development and Strategic Plans Based on Vertical Chains (Politique de filières)

> Investment, R&D, and financial resources allocation analyses and decisions to be based on broad "related technology / related market" perspectives, rather than firm-by-firm decisions.

Nationalization of (Most) Credite Institutions and Several Leading Companies

> An end in itself, as part of the class warfare ideology of much of the French left, but also

> A means to redirect the attention of firms and banks to production, R&D, and other value-added activities within France. Many pre-election socialist and communist case studies and documents supporting nationalization criticized the export of jobs, capital, and technological activity by rapidly multinationalizing French firms.

> Tools in a neo-Keynesian policy of stimulating countercyclical investment spending. Some $5 billion of new government equity is to be injected into the nationalized firms over the next three years.

Prompting Inward Foreign Investment

> To give France continued access to foreign high technology activities.

> To serve as a confidence-building example for French enterprises, which have been reluctant to increase their investment.

and short-term financial criteria for evaluating firm performance has been considerably downgraded. While most prices remain uncontrolled, and tax exemptions for share purchases are still in place, technological and "strategic control" instruments and criteria have come to the fore. Market sanctions remain, but the state has equipped itself to guide or determine the behavior of major market participants.

Not only is there greater concentration of state ownership in key sectors but the government has set aside some ten billion francs (over U.S. $1.5 billion) for investment in capital equipment in four key sectors over the next two years. The purpose is to permit management to concentrate on longer-run positioning of the companies in the chosen industries. Although short-term profitability is not stressed, longer-run profits must be sufficient to "ensure the development of the company," Minister Dreyfus insisted.

Second, a relatively narrow concern with high technology specialty niches and sectors of unavoidable salvage or reconversion has seemingly given way to a broader orientation, which retains technology as its main pillar, but in which the state concerns itself with a considerably wider spectrum of industrial activity. Underlying this new orientation, particularly in the "filière" concept, is the belief that broad categories of industry have such positive externalities for other related activities that "niches" alone are not a sufficiently viable strategic base for a large nation's industry. The *filière* concept refers to vertical lines of production in a sector that are linked together in a mutually supporting fashion. This mutual support extends quite broadly, and explains the shift from sectoral niches to the wide-ranging restructuring of industry projected by the Mitterrand government. Specific government officials are responsible for the major industrial sectors, and each will seek to make his sector the "lead industry" for French revitalization and international competitiveness.

Four sectors are key: chemicals, electronics, health (pharmaceuticals), and materials. In chemicals, the uncoordinated mixture of companies has still not provided a significant competitor to German industry. Here state enterprises will be given incentives to merge with others or engage in cooperative activities to form three strong groups that will be "stronger, better integrated in terms of raw materials, and with more effective control over their markets" (M. Dreyfus, quoted in the *Financial Times,* February 26, 1982). In electronics, the state-owned enterprises dominate already and will be relied upon to create new strength in components, computers, industrial electronics, and consumer electronics. In pharmaceuticals, nationalized companies will again lead the way, drawing on governmental R&D support funds. Similarly, in materials, the newly nationalized companies will be relied upon to provide necessary glass, fibers, aluminum, ceramics, and building materials. All of these efforts are directed first at regaining the French market and then moving strongly overseas.

The intellectual origins of this concept appear related to French judgments about the efficacy of Japanese companies' business strategies, which frequently emphasize related, "organic" diversification and vertical integration among firms and within Japanese *keiretsu* groups.

French officials seem to have arrived at—and decided to act upon—a view now widely discussed in management consulting and business school circles. The hypothesis is that Western corporations' tendency toward either overspecialization (e.g., in TV sets only) or conglomeration (TV sets plus car rentals) has been a significant weakness in competing against Japanese firms whose related product lines (e.g., TV sets, tubes, electronic components and other electronic products) or group-related companies made possible the sharing of experience, facilities, or R&D results, which led to lower unit costs and/or technological synergies.

A third noteworthy observation about the new French regime is that comprehensive, sectoral indicative planning has not been revived as an industrial policy tool. If anything, The Plan has been downgraded further still.

Indeed, the dominant philosophy of the administration in industrial matters appears to derive less from economics and economists, left or right, capitalist or socialist, defunct or not, than from notions of strategic management akin to those of the Boston Consulting Group and the Harvard Business School.

Chapter 5

Public Use of Private Interests:
Japan's Industrial Policy

*Kiyohiko Fukushima**

INTRODUCTION

Japan is often seen as something of an "out-of-this world" country, in which things can be done that would be impossible in the other countries. Foreign views of Japanese policy are consequently not always reflective of what actually takes place.

One reason for these misperceptions could be that the Japanese have overemphasized their country's special situation, and Japan experts in the United States have often been influenced by such remarks. The universal principles that prevail in Japan's economy have too often been disregarded. If Japan had explained itself by using widely accepted principles and concepts, a truer understanding of its policies could have been achieved, confirming a commonality based on universal laws.

THE ROLE AND THE LIMITS
OF INDUSTRIAL POLICY

Japan's industrial policy has undoubtedly been a success, but not necessarily in the ways or for the reasons perceived by foreign observers. Therefore caution is required in applying such perceptions

*Nomura Research Institute

elsewhere. In particular, it is important to give fresh consideration to the limits of government, the limits of industrial policy, and Japan's loss of tools for control.

The Limits of Government

If Japan performs well in allocating scarce resources properly and raising its national income, homage should be paid to the gods of the market and to each successful participant in the marketplace. Capitalism is run by millions of spontaneous decisions on buying and selling, and savings and investment by innumerable companies and individuals. However well organized a government may be, and however capable its bureaucrats, they can never successfully dictate where the economy should be going. The sheer size of Japan's economy (a gross national product of more than $1 trillion in 1980) makes it impossible for a central authority to control at will. If Japan's economy is doing better than some other market economies, the major factor must be favorable market conditions, both inside and outside the country, and a proper response by industry. No single policy or apparatus of policies can claim credit for Japan's success.

Private corporations that produce goods and services have been continuously aiming at increasing their profits, and their behavioral patterns will not change, whatever policies the government adopts. Japan's economic success is ultimately the accumulation of the success of every company that gropes its way toward maximizing profit. Needless to say, the government has sometimes, rightly or wrongly, tried to affect industrial development in Japan. In 1956, for instance, the law of ad hoc measures for the promotion of machinery industry was instituted; but in 1965 the Diet rejected the bill proposed by the Ministry of International Trade and Industry (MITI) for the promotion of certain industries. On the whole, the Japanese experience is one of private initiatives in a market economy, with government support and urging.

Limits of Industrial Policy

Among the economic policies that governments seek to implement, industrial policy is fairly limited in its efficacy. In fiscal policy, the government is the main player and can decide the level of expenditure and the rate of tax. In monetary policy, the central bank is the decisive factor and can decide the discount rate and influence the financial market as the lender of last resort. The government or the central bank can decide on the quantity of spending or the price of money and implement the decision singlehandedly; the other participants in the market have no alternative but to follow.

In the case of an industrial policy, however, the main players are private corporations. The government can only try to influence the industrial activities of the private sector. Even if government tries to guide the industrial activity in a certain direction, the private corporations will behave in the desired way only if that behavior seems to be consistent with its motive of profit making. For industrial policy to succeed, therefore, the goals and techniques must be mutually acceptable to both companies and governments. This is a limitation certainly greater than in other fields of economic policy.

Loss of Tools for Control

In the last ten years the Japanese government has abandoned most of the control techniques it once used. As a result, the measures that the Japanese government can rely on in the implementation of an industrial policy are no longer peculiar to that country. The other industrialized democracies have either already adopted the measures now used in Japan or could readily do so.

Hence, Japan's industrial policy has moved increasingly from an exceptional case based on Japan's special postwar conditions toward a normal case based on global principles. As others have adopted Japanese techniques and Japan has eliminated more direct controls, its industrial policy has recently taken on something of a universally acceptable character.

POSTWAR INDUSTRIAL POLICY

A book would be required to describe in detail the history of Japan's trade and investment regulations, its later trade liberalization, the deregulation of capital transactions and foreign exchange, and the development of industrial policies. Figure 5.1 briefly summarizes the development of Japan's postwar industrial policy.

In general, the less powerful and the less influential the government became in the implementation of industrial policies, the stronger and the more competitive the private corporations became. As the government gradually loosened its control over the allocation of resources, its goals of industrial policy grew closer to those of the private sector and were more effectively attained.

Table 5.1. Japan's Postwar Industrial Policy.

	Events	Goals of Trade Policy	Goals of Industrial Policy	Tools For Policy	Sunshine Industry	Sunset Industry	U.S.–Japan Frictions
1945	Surrender			Allocation of Foreign Exchange	Coal		
		To overcome balance-of-payments deficit	Reconstruction and stabilization		Steel		
1955		Export promotion	To achieve international competitiveness	Import Restrictions	Textiles		
	High economic growth		Heavy industrialization	Deregulations	Steel Automobile Petrochemicals Electronics Shipbuilding	Coal mining	
1971	"Nixon shocks"		"Knowledge-intensification"	"Long-term vision"			Textiles
1973	First oil crisis	Import promotion			Integrated circuits Computers Telecommunications Dataprocessing Office automation	Shipbuilding Nonferrous metals Textiles Fertilizers	Color TV Steel
1979	Second oil crisis		Opening domestic market				Integrated circuits Automobiles Overal Japan market Service industry
1981							

This is an irony but not a miracle, for the government's goals were, on the whole, little different from the aggregated goals of major private companies in each industrial sector, with a word of philosophical generalization on the directions where the industries are already going—that is, "heavy industrialization" in the 1960s, "knowledge intensification" for the 1970s, and the recently proclaimed "knowledge vitalization" for the 1980s.

As Japan rebuilt its economy after the destruction of the war, it emphasized coal mining and steel making, since coal provided the energy for development and steel was an essential basic material for reconstruction. The nation's balance of payments was chronically in deficit in those years, and foreign exchange was scarce. Therefore, imports were restricted and exports were encouraged. To earn the terribly needed foreign currency through exports, priority was given to imports of those raw materials that would enable Japan to manufacture exportable goods in a relatively short time. For instance, imports of raw cotton were given easier access to foreign exchange reserves than were consumer durables, because Japan could expect to export cotton yarn and fibers, but could hope for no such result from imported automobiles.

In the first decade after World War II, Japan's economy was reconstructed and the groundwork laid for rapid economic growth. From 1955 to 1965, the Index of Industrial Production grew at an average annual rate of 13.2 percent; from 1965 to 1973, at 11.9 percent. Japan acquired comparative advantages in several industries such as steel, shipbuilding, textiles, and electric appliances. This line of development was called "heavy industrialization."

Around the end of the 1960s, it became increasingly clear that Japan had become competitive in major industries. Moreover, the balance of payments crises that had afflicted the country periodically during these years of rapid growth were over. Policy makers and business managers realized that Japan was becoming a capital surplus country. The government's former tools of industrial policy, such as regulations on foreign exchange and restrictions on imports, were no longer effective. Restrictions and regulations were lifted gradually during the 1960s; by the early '70s, the liberalizations on direct investments and foreign exchange were almost completed.

In 1971 the yen was revalued, and agreement was reached on the "voluntary" restraint of textile exports from Japan to the United States. There was a general feeling in Japan that the economy had succeeded in gaining comparative advantages in major industries, but at the same time had entered into dangerous, uncharted waters. The overwhelming superiority of the U.S. economy was diminishing, and no one was sure where the world economy was going. As uncertainty about the future became widespread, opinion leaders initiated serious discussions about appropriate directions for Japan's economy. In that same year, MITI issued its first "Long-term Vision of Industrial Structures," which concluded that Japan had caught up with the developed countries of the West in major industries and should begin moving toward high value added, high technology industries.

With the oil crisis of 1973, the era of high economic growth was gone forever. In 1974 Japan experienced rampant inflation, huge wage increases, and negative growth. Amid this sudden stagflation, the feeling of uncertainty about the future grew in Japan's business and policy communities.

To challenge the underlying uncertainties, the government issued another "Long-term Vision" in 1974 and each successive year until 1978. In 1980 another "Long-term Vision" was issued, titled "The Industrial Structure of Japan in the 1980's—Future Outlook and Tasks."

LONG-TERM VISION: THE CORE OF JAPAN'S INDUSTRIAL POLICY

Why did the Japanese government begin issuing its "Long-term Visions" after it had ceded control over the industrial activities through deregulation? Although it may have had ideas about where particular industries should be going, it lacks coercive means to direct them.

Industrial policy represents the government's efforts to guide sectoral activities in appropriate directions. It may include a wide range of policies, such as environmental regulations, factory location, direct subsidies, financing, trade policy, competition policy, and so on. Here I will focus on the Japanese government's policy of making a future prospect and on that basis trying to guide specific industries in a certain direction.

How the Future Prospect Is Formulated

MITI has followed a four-step process in formulating its annual "Long-term Visions." The steps could be described as (a) getting together; (b) defining the problem; (c) starting the discussion; and (d) synthesizing a vision of the future.

Getting Together. Every relevant person is invited to an informal discussion on future prospects—not only representatives of the particular industry, but scholars and experts knowledgeable about the problems. The discussion forum may be defined as a study group on certain problems, or a subcommittee of an industry council. Members join quite voluntarily and express their own views in the discussions on their own responsibility.

Defining the Problem. The discussion begins by defining what is to be discussed; what is to be clarified, and what approaches might be possible. Each member sees the problem differently, reflecting his or her background; tremendous efforts are made and much time is spent in synthesizing various views and finding congruent words to let the divergent views coexist in the discussion forum.

Starting the Discussion—Empirical Approach and Econometrics. As the subject for discussion becomes increasingly clear, members contribute all their relevant data about the subject. The group then begins discussing the steps by which the problems should be approached, and the likely evolution of present problems in the future.

For example, suppose the subject is the tasks of the steel industry in the 1980s. The study group will gather each steel maker's informal, private estimates of future demand. People in the steel manufacturing companies, through their long experience of actually making and selling those products, will also have a hunch about how much the sales of this particular product will rise. Accumulating the data item by item, the group will develop a vague perspective on the plausible shape of the industry in the future.

At the same time, help will be sought from economists both inside and outside the group. Relying on their academic expertise, economists will come up with a growth rate prediction for the world economy in the 1980s; given the elasticity of steel demand in relation to economic growth, they will then estimate the growth rate of the steel industry. As for Japan's steel industry, its growth rate would be in this range, therefore, Japan's share in global production will rise or fall.

Because of the different approaches taken, the predictions submitted to the discussion group will vary widely. But by exploring the causes of those discrepancies, the members will come to realize that the differences in views are much slighter than it first appears. A slight change in the assumptions could alter the future prospect almost completely. A series of such discussions and analyses naturally narrows the divergence of views about the future, though total agreement in these matters is virtually impossible to achieve.

Government bureaucrats—in this hypothetical example, the basic industry bureau of MITI—participate in each session as the secretariat of the study group. They are well aware, when writing up the report, that a certain phrasing would be acceptable to everybody, that controversial issues should be mentioned without any conclusive judgment, and so forth. Thus there is typically little difficulty in winning all participants' endorsement of the report.

The study group will probably discuss many other subjects besides the size of the future market. In the case of the steel industry, other topics might be possible—new methods of steel production, improvements on the existing technology of production, implications of the changes in the world market, means of securing the supply of raw materials needed for production, effects of environmental regulations, enhancement in the conservation of energy, upgrading the utilization rate of the raw materials, and so on. Each of these subjects would be thoroughly discussed; if necessary, a subgroup might be organized to investigate in detail some specific problems requiring technical knowledge. In every study group, all the relevant data available would be gathered and analyzed from various aspects and by different methods; in this way, the whole group gropes for the most plausible scenario on the future course of Japan's steel industry.

It should be stressed that the study group does not attempt to reach a unanimous consensus on the future goal of the steel industry with specific numbers and details. Rather the goal is to clarify the problems facing the industry. Through the discussions it becomes increasingly clear what problems must be settled if the industry is to stay viable in the future. The nature of the problems will also come to be commonly understood. Some could be settled through an industrywide cooperation, others only through close international cooperation; for some, no solution may be possible in the foreseeable future. This sharing of views about the future may well be a more important outcome of the group's effort than the official final product reported in the press.

Synthesizing a Vision of the Future. Through their deliberations, participants in the study group naturally come to share views on the path the industry is most likely to follow in the ensuing years. They will realize that, whether one likes it or not, the main directions of the future course cannot be altered; yet some room exists for selection among alternatives in the course of future developments. To a certain extent, therefore, it is up to people participating in the economic game to choose between the wished-for scenario and the unwelcome one. They will recognize what type of effort and policy is needed to enable the wished-for scenario to come true.

Thereupon, the secretariat of the study group will write down a wished-for scenario for the industry based on more or less concrete grounds of realization. Meanwhile similar efforts to envisage the future have been going on in the other industrial sectors. Further work is needed to coordinate the various working groups, trying to find a coherent explanation of where Japan's economy is going. The impending tasks and the nature of the problems are generalized and further articulated.

When vague prospects about the future have been aggregated in this way, they are given a somewhat plausible philosophical interpretation, such as knowledge intensification. This is the long-term vision of Japan's industries.

The Role and the Limits of "Long-term Vision"

In some respects, MITI's "Vision" seems a useless paper made for the aggrandizement of government's influence. Close examination will reveal ambiguities in details that were required to win political acceptance and to avoid inconsistency with other governmental policies. In a country built on democracy and a market economy, it is impossible to have a solid, elaborate, coherent scheme for the future, free of any internal contradictions. And no governmental agency has the authority or is held responsible for the implementation of that vision.

Furthermore, those chapters in the "Vision" that describe the tasks of each industry contain nothing new for major corporations in that sector. It was the people in those companies who contributed to the making of the future prospect, and numerous formal and informal consultations have been held with big businesses in that industry and other major interests involved. Thus, most of the private interests know well beforehand the contents of the "Vision" that might be related to their business. Indeed, there would be little chance of success for any "Vision" that emerged from the desk of bureaucrats without ever having been discussed with the businessmen.

I must reiterate that the extensive discussion that takes place has some meaning in itself. The Special Subcommittee on Policies for the 1980s, a substructure of the MITI's Industrial Council, which authorized the issuance of the "Vision for the 1980s," includes two representatives from the trade unions and two from consumer groups, as well as businessmen, scholars, and experts. Of course, the role played by these representatives in formulating the "Vision" is not clear. What counts is the fact that efforts have been made to reach the maximum degree of consensus among a wide range of people from various backgrounds.

And for the businessmen, the reconfirmation of the likely future course, which was all too evident for them, may have some meaning. The same future prospect is now placed in a global and historical perspective, and the role of that industry in the nation's economy will be appropriately weighted. This will provide a basic ground for the general public's understanding of business activities.

The Possibility of Attaining the Goal

It goes without saying that the behavior of businesses does not change a bit after the issuance of the "Vision." Companies keep on doing business as usual, and make new investments only when they see a chance of reaping a handsome profit from them. The same holds true for the government, which does not have any specific new tool to guide the economy in the directions described in the "Vision."

However, since the "Vision" is built on business reality rather than wishful thinking, the actual economy of Japan is likely to fulfill its predictions, unless government regulatory policies distort the natural development or all the participants in the study made serious mistakes in formulating the future prospect. In other words, the "Vision" has an inherently high probability of success. Japan's postwar experience with its "Long-term Visions" seems, on the whole, to verify this point.

Japanese bureaucrats have thus been able to make a case that they were responsible for Japan's success. They claim to have planned the whole grand design, employing administrative guidance, using scientific analysis, informal discussions, legislation, and so on. Some of their remarks may be intentional official braggadocio to foreigners, but to a certain extent they may believe what they say, reflecting their genuine faith and devotion as public servants. However, the paradigm of economics tells us that such an exaggeration of the role of the public sector cannot be anything but an overstatement.

Even the Japanese businessmen have sometimes made such statements, indicating that they owe their success to the government's industrial policy and the close cooperation of business and government, which is rooted in Japan's cultural tradition. Successful businessmen are not necessarily good economists in any country, and Japan is no exception. It is naive to believe that either the government's policy or a cultural factor was the key to an economic success as phenomenal as Japan's. The firms' sensitivity to competition, both domestically and worldwide, was the more salient factor—and so concluded the U.S.—Japan Economic Relations Group in January 1981:

> Both the United States and Japan have relied primarily on the private sector responding to market forces to achieve economic growth and development. A significant exception in the 1950's and 1960's for Japan, however, was the targeting of some "key" industries. In these decades the Japanese government, in consultation with industrial leaders, designated certain sectors as target industries to receive priority in allocation of foreign exchange, direct and indirect governmental loans and loan guarantees, and tax incentives. These target industries were also protected by trade barriers and restrictions on foreign investments, as were virtually all industries.

Specific target industry measures involving trade and investment barriers as well as tax incentives and research and development aid were also used in the 1970's for promoting some high technology sectors. Although these policies were important, probably a more important factor in Japan's industrial growth was the highly competitive domestic market, encouraging firms to adopt more productive technologies and processes. Another major factor was that Japanese firms were oriented towards exporting, forcing constant awareness of international competition when making pricing, product, and production decisions. (Wiseman Paper, pp. 71-72).

Public Use of Private Interest: the Principle of an Economic Policy

The experience of Japan's industrial policy could be generalized as follows: Government should try to identify the impending basic problems of an industry, and should then propose a solution honoring the initiative, creativity, and competition of the private sector. A privately incorporated company struggles each day for profit maximization and growth. No more efficient way of combining, organizing, and distributing economic resources needed for production and sales of a product has yet been found. Thus, public policy has no choice but to use the resiliency of the private corporations, with all the social wastes and costs that sometimes accompany them. This seems to be the core of Japan's industrial policy.

Japan's industrial policy is multifaceted and has gone through many transformations since World War II. It has met with both success and failures. The government more often succeeded in attaining its goals when it intentionally made use of the market forces for policy purposes (as in the cases of the semiconductor and shipbuilding industries) rather than trying to stem the fundamental conditions of the market (as in textiles and agriculture). A necessary precondition for this policy to work is that all participants in the economic game share some prospect about the future of the industry, when left to itself under the "invisible hand." The government's policy goals were reached when it tried to minimize the loss and maximize the benefit to the society of the changes that accompany the market forces in the long run. In this fashion the Japanese government has been a good by-stander at best.

IMPLICATIONS FOR OTHER COUNTRIES

Two aspects of Japan's industrial policies are particularly noteworthy for other developed countries. First, Japan has tended, on the whole, to honor the market principles and initiatives of the private corporations. Second, Japan has employed a distinctive method of policy formulation, in which bureaucrats, experts, and industrialists expend considerable time and effort in deliberation until they can reach an acceptable consensus on the shape of the future.

Each country has its special history and culture. Thus the Japanese experience should be emulated only in a way that is workable in a particular society. Industrial policy may look quite different in other countries, because of cultural differences. (The American cowboy spirit, for example, is quite opposed to the Japanese ethic of harmony.)

Therefore, each country should look back to its history to discover the social framework for the implementation of an industrial policy. And the policy should be formulated in a way that does not resist, but takes advantage of the fundamental market forces; moreover, policy should aim at long-term growth, rather than short-term profit maximization. We should try to use the private interest for public purposes, in a manner consistent with the historical and social fabric of each country. This could well be the most important lesson of Japan's experience.

Chapter 6

Japanese Industrial Policy: A View from Outside

*J. N. Behrman**

In the late 1950s, Japan had established a list of priority sectors—including textiles, shipbuilding, steel, autos, and chemicals—in which it restricted imports, prohibited foreign investment (except as minority partners), and encouraged imports of foreign technology. The automotive sector had been supported even in the 1930s, but it began its postwar expansion with a boost from the Korean war; parts manufacturers were consolidated and modernized. Electronics, telecommunications, and other sectors were encouraged by government policy.

Today, Japan periodically constructs a national industrial plan (really a vision of the future), which identifies the sectors considered to have the best prospects for technological advance and international competitiveness, and then adopts supporting techniques. At the same time, companies are encouraged to shift workers out of declining industries into advancing sectors. This process is conducted under a consensus approach that involves several stages of consultation between the government and all other interested parties, particularly private enterprise.

*University of North Carolina

Sources for this chapter are principally: OECD, The Industrial Policy of Japan, Paris 1972; Magaziner, I. C., and Hout, T. N. *Japanese Industrial Policy,* London: Policy Studies Institute, No. 585, January 1980 and Diebold, Jr., William, Industrial Policy As An International Issue, New York: McGraw-Hill, 1980.

Table 6.1. Japanese Mechanisms of Coordination

Organization	Function
Ministry of International Trade and Industry (MITI)	Tax incentives, antitrust, lending, price and capacity controls, export–import measures, environmental regulations, raw material price setting and procurement, technology subsidies, dislocation subsidies, and regional policies—*anything* affecting the sector or firm—judged on a differential basis according to priorities.
Ministry of Finance	Tax incentives, low-cost loans, subsidies, tariffs, foreign exhange rate changes.
Research Development Corporation	Subsidy for R&D, join private/government research, licensing of technology.
Ministry of Post and Telecommunications	Guidance to telecommunications sector.
Ministry of Health and Welfare	Guidance to pharmaceutical sector
Keidanren (Federation of Economic Organizations)	Coordination of industry views on industry policies.
Shoko Kaigesho (Chamber of Commerce and Industry)	Coordination of the views of industry, including medium-sized and small companies, commerce, and banking.
Keizai Doyukai (Committe on Economic Devlopment)	Position papers on economic and industrial policies by companies.
Nikkeiren (Federation of Employers Association)	Coordination of industrial relations among industries and companies.
Zaikai (Friday Club)	Small group of CEOs close to prime minister and parties.
Industry associations	Coordination with MITI on specific sectoral policies and formation of industry cartels as desired.
City banks	Linked with keiretsu (conglomerate enterprises) as financial sources and directors; linked with Bank of Japan and other government banks, Industrial Bank Development Bank.

The plan of the government is part of an overall document entitled "Industrial Policy Vision of the 1980s," which was published by the Ministry of International Trade and Industry (MITI) in April 1980. This vision sets priorities, and industry sectors are expected to respond as each company deems appropriate. Each major company belongs to an advisory board (the Industrial Structure Council) composed of more than fifty representatives of government, business, and academia. The Council meets frequently, and because its members are personally known to each other in many other contexts, they are able and willing to make compromises.

Japanese business-government cooperation began in the mid-nineteenth century with the Meiji revolution to industrialize the country. The government sold state enterprises to the private sector, which was made up of merchants and samurai who felt a responsibility for the growth and security of the country. Although the zaibatsu were broken up after World War II, the companies formerly associated regrouped into keiretsu (groups *not* under a holding company but managed under a coordinated policy). This concentration and the connection of each keiretsu with one of the major banks facilitates coordination with the government. The network of cooperative institutions is shown in Table 6.1.

Government industrial responsibilities are centered in divisions of MITI, and company interests are represented by industry associations through committees often attended by labor officials as well. The concern of all parties is to achieve consensus, if feasible, without endangering company survival. Agreement is not always reached, and some companies simply refuse to follow if the cost to their interests is deemed too high; but the process of accommodation is a continuing one.

ADVANCING SECTORS

The objective of industrial policy in the growing sectors is to anticipate and accelerate signals from the market. Consequently, the Japanese government supports R&D activities, capital expenditures, and export efforts; it does not restrain competition for market share among the companies within the domestic market. Financing assistance is provided by both MITI and the Ministry of Finance, through the Japan Development Bank, the Industrial Bank of Japan, and indirectly through commercial banks. In addition, MITI often supports a selected group of R&D projects and technologies proposed by key companies in these sectors; it is currently funding (in whole or in part) nine group projects for the development of high technology breakthroughs in steel, jet engines, robotics, and various energy sources. A given project may receive hundreds of millions of dollars in support over a several-year period. Participating companies share in the development work and in the rights to innovation. The Japanese government also provides tax incentives and low-cost financing, plus accelerated depreciation to encourage R&D activities of any qualifying firms. Japan has had more success than European countries and the United States in supporting the sectors of autos and trucks, vehicle components, industrial machinery, computers, electronics and components, and telecommunications. The success is reflected in greater industrial concentration and economies of scale, in greater market share worldwide, in employment, and in technologies used.

The sectors Japan will emphasize in the 1980s are the "knowledge-intensive" industries. The newly designated industry sectors include ultra-high-speed computers, oceanic and space development, aircraft, optical fibers, ceramics, amorphous materials, high-efficiency resins, and a group of energy producers (coal liquification and gasification, nuclear and solar energy, and deep geothermal generation of energy). Adding these twelve to those already selected for the 1970s makes a total of two dozen specific sectors to be supported by the government.

For example, the government has helped move the industrial machinery sector from the mere production of mechanical components and machine assembly in the 1950s to the construction of entire plants, with all the components of machinery and assembly therein. As its companies have become more competitive, the government has shifted from offering financial aid and specific guidance to a looser form of support, responding to strategic initiatives of different companies. The government has assisted this sector with a wide range of techniques in over 100 programs during the past three decades, including funds for modernization and development, rationalization cartels, establishment of standards, preferential tax rates, consolidation of enterprises, and the establishment of joint ventures. The emphasis has shifted from the improvement of individual company efficiency in the late 1950s to a consolidation of the sector during the early 1960s, and, in the late 1960s and 1970s, to the encouragement of greater specialization and economies of scale.

In the early 1970s, policy directions shifted towards R&D assistance and financing of sales of entire plants abroad. Some 60 percent of Export-Import Bank loans are now directed to exports of entire plants. A number of Japanese institutions work together to promote these exports. MITI has published a 400-page book on how to make such sales in particular markets overseas; industry associations and trading companies cooperate; the banks cooperate with all three groups in support of the cartels that have been formed under MITI guidance.

Japanese financial support for industrial policies comes through the Ministry of Finance, the Bank of Japan, several specialized government banks, and the City banks. The budget procedure of the Ministry of Finance sets the limits of the scope of industrial policy and approves the financial packages. Senior officials examine industrial policy proposals at several stages and at several levels within the Ministry. Each of its seven bureaus—Budget, Tax, Financial, Banking, International

Finance, Customs and Tariffs, and Securities—has a role to play. The Financial Bureau manages the Fiscal Investment and Loan Plan (FILP), through which trust funds are channeled into specific sectors via public financial corporations such as the Japan Development Bank, the Export-Import Bank, Japan Industrial Bank, and others; this trust fund is equal to one-half of the government's general-account budget. Thus, resources of the FILP are a major stimulus (or constraint) on cash flows to specific sectors. In addition, the International Finance Bureau employs exchange-rate changes as an instrument of industrial policy by altering comparative advantages at the margin and thereby forcing specific industrial restructuring.

Thirteen City banks together are large enough to extend one-quarter of all loans and discounts made by financial institutions (both public and private) in Japan. They are principally tied to large corporations (keiretsu). Each keiretsu has a principal bank on which it relies for funding advice on investment and operating positions. This principal bank is not the only source of funding, but it is the one to which the company turns in time of expansion or need. This relationship is so important that one keiretsu, which refused to adopt such a close relationship, lost significant market position when it got into difficulties and could not secure adequate financing.

Traditionally, the keiretsu have relied on loans rather than equity, increasing the ties to the banks; today this pattern is shifting somewhat, with increasing self-financing by the companies. Government ministries and the banks discuss industrial objectives together, setting up ad hoc committees to examine specific proposals and issues. These banks are linked with the Bank of Japan (supervised by the Ministry of Finance), which lends to the thirteen City banks for industrial expansion. Further, they can be encouraged to lend funds to industrial sectors as guided by the Ministry of Finance. Finally, these City banks have officers sitting on the boards of directors of various companies of the keiretsu and are therefore able to help in the balancing of operations or shifting of emphasis among the companies of the keiretsu or of a sector.

Direct government R&D activities are small in Japan; rather, the major effort is made under contracts with the keiretsu, usually formed into consortia for large-scale projects. MITI has formed sixteen associated research institutes for such long-range, large-scale projects, developing systems for commercial use. They are engaged in projects on very large scale integration (VLSI) semiconductors, high-performance jet engines for aircraft, water desalination, and natural-resource recycling. In addition, R&D support is provided in tax credits, grants, low-cost loans, accelerated depreciation, and sponsorship of R&D consortia for both large and small companies.

Information electronics is supported through substantial R&D subsidies such as the VLSI circuit development project and the special
assistance given to software development. MITI has used government
funds to create consortia among firms to conduct joint R&D activities.
But it has been unsuccessful in consolidating companies to achieve
greater economies. The companies continue to be independent in production and sales of the resulting products and systems.

On the marketing side, the government has aided companies purchasing computers, expanding the national market. It offers financial
assistance and established a joint venture with private enterprise to
lease computers. The government also reserves about 90 percent of its
purchases of computers for Japanese producers. In semiconductors, much
of the private market is closed to foreigners; telecommunications has
only slowly been opened up to foreign bidders. Nippon Telephone and
Telegraph Corporation has not only given a preference to Japanese suppliers, but has directly supported R&D of the major telecommunications
equipment suppliers and helped to finance their exports.

As a result of these trilateral cooperative efforts among the government, private enterprises, and financing institutions, the Japanese companies have a high degree of flexibility in pricing and in competitive
efforts, both domestically and internationally.

DECLINING INDUSTRIES

MITI has classified aluminum, fertilizers, ferro-alloys, plywood,
sugar refining, synthetic textile fibers, shipbuilding, and other sectors
as "declining" (increasingly less competitive internationally). If the sector
is declared "structurally depressed," it will receive reconstruction
measures; to be so classified, an industry must have substantial overcapacity and must be in serious financial difficulty; moreover two-thirds
of its firms must sign a petition for such designation. MITI then develops
a stabilization plan, forecasting supply and demand; it calculates ex-
cess capacity, and it identifies marginal plants and ones to be cut back
or eliminated. During this process MITI consults with the industry, and
labor unions are given a voice. A workable plan is agreed upon, and
measures are then put into effect. To date some forty industries have
been so classified; these industries have accepted MITI guidance so that
the government approves the process it is funding. This assistance is
given regardless of the origin of the difficulty; that is, it is not dependent on injury from imports, as in the United States.

In one of the declining sectors, aluminum smelting, the industry and
the government have not been able to agree on a plan. The companies

do not wish to rationalize or regroup or even to cut capacity significantly on any permanent basis; but MITI is seeking a permanent structural shift and does not want to provide any protection to sustain existing capacity.

The government has also supported and guided the shipbuilding industry over its rise and decline within the past three decades. In the first decade, the Ministry of Transport and the Ministry of Finance assisted the introduction of new technology and encouraged rationalization, providing tax benefits, financing, price subsidies and consumer financing. Government assistance virtually disappeared in the late 1960s and early 1970s, but after the tanker boom faded in the mid-1970s, Japan's launchings fell to less than 50 percent of earlier levels. As the industry has progressively shifted to lower-wage countries, an advisory commission has recommended significant cutbacks in capacity. Again, however, not all of the firms in the industry have agreed as to the specific rationalization measures to be taken, not wanting to cut capacity permanently and looking for strong temporary financial support. The stand-off was considered so intractable that the prime minister issued a direct order that a solution be found. Even so, no final agreement has been reached on how the cutbacks are to be distributed among the producers.

The Japanese experience indicates how much more difficult it is to gain consensus on measures to adjust a declining sector than to distribute benefits in a growing sector. Japan has been successful, however, in easing adjustment in employment and product changes in the textile and shipbuilding sectors, principally through concentration of facilities in a few companies. It has also succeeded in cutting losses in steel through concentration. All three of these sectors received government support after consensus decision making.

Despite the apparent overall success of industrial policy in Japan, there have been some significant failures in its efforts to provide industrial support or stimulation. Strategies for construction equipment, chain saws, plate heat exchangers, and marine engines have been frustrated by aggressive responses of U.S. and European producers to Japanese competition both in the world and in Japan itself. And in aluminum smelting, plywood, sugar refining, ferro-alloys, and synthetic textile fibers, a lack of agreement between business and government has thwarted the development of sectoral policies.

Chapter 7

Why Malaysia Needs an Industrial Policy

*V. Kanapathy**

INTRODUCTION

Malaysia's industrial policies cannot be referred to as a course of action deliberately adopted after a review of possible alternatives. The government's firm commitment to free enterprise principles left industrial development to be dictated by market forces and underlying comparative advantages. No firm policies were developed to organize and, where appropriate, to dictate mechanisms for promoting specific industrial sectors that could help lay an industrial base. Decisions were taken on the basis of vague ideas of general progress, and often somewhat haphazardly. Therefore, the policy-making process was not an even one, and probably quite a good deal of misplaced energy and effort went into overinvestment. Some, for example, have held this state of affairs responsible for the fragmentation of Malaysia's automobile industry and the stifling influence it has had on the development of a viable indigenous ancillary industry.[1]

The good times of the 1950s and 1960s facilitated pursuit of the sort of industrial policy described above, increased the overall standard of living of most Malaysians, and essentially hypnotized the country by this prosperity. It was taken for granted that the economy would continue to grow at a real rate of 8 percent—a calculation based on the fact that the nation is a net exporter of oil and a major producer of vital industrial raw materials—and that the global economic environment would be relatively stable.

*United Malayan Banking Corporation

Unfortunately, the 1970s have not been a particularly good period for the industrial countries. The recession continues to deepen amidst global political uncertainties. The industrial countries, anxious to keep inflation under control, have been pursuing financial policies that have slowed economic recovery in most cases; this in turn has had an adverse impact on world trade and commodity prices. Recent experience has also shown that, in today's world, the notion of free trade is purely an illusion. Protectionism, mercantilism, and autarky are the realities that have divided the world we live in.

In this type of economic scenario, the general consensus is that Malaysia needs to strengthen the techno-economic base of the economy to generate autonomous industrialization. Most of the investments made so far are of the assembly or packaging types, which do not give much opportunity for forward or backward linkages. Consequently, despite twenty-five years of industrialization, Malaysia has not yet cultivated her own industrial elite and developed her own industrial culture. Only very recently has the nation addressed such questions as what type of industries are most beneficial to its long-term industrial development, and what techniques of production should be encouraged. The indications are that emphasis will now be placed on capital or producer goods "nucleus" industries. The fact that the Heavy Industries Corporation of Malaysia Berhad (HICOM), which is responsible for the development of such industries, will come directly under the supervision of the prime minister reflects the significance attributed to this sector. Simultaneously, measures will also be taken to accelerate the development of small to medium-scale industries, which will operate essentially as second-round import-substituting consumer goods industries, resource-based export-oriented industries, or parts suppliers, subassemblers, and the like to the "nucleus" industries. Additionally, the government will continue to encourage industries that could be integrated with and support existing industries. In other words, the government hopes to generate backward integration into the supporting industries not only to meet the needs of the existing industrial sector but also the proposed heavy industries, with a view to establishing a firm foundation for future growth.

ISSUES AND POLICIES IN INDUSTRIAL DEVELOPMENT

Industrial Policy Content

Malaysia is neither an industrialized nor a semi-industrialized country. It could be classified as an industrializing country.[2] Production of primary products still forms the main sphere of economic activity, contributing 26 percent of the gross domestic product, though the contribution of the manufacturing sector has been steadily increasing in recent times. Malaysia is still the world's largest producer of natural rubber and tin, as well as the largest exporter of palm oil and timber. With other mineral exports, especially crude petroleum, the country still enjoys a relatively healthy economic situation. The authorities, however, have long felt the need to avoid depending on primary products as the chief source of sustenance because of instability in their prices. In 1958 the Pioneer Industries (Relief from Income Tax) Ordinance was enacted to encourage manufacturing industries. Government policy then, and to some extent even now, has been to permit industrial development to be determined by market forces and underlying comparative advantages, and not to attempt to alter market signals. Though tariffs, quotas, and the like have been introduced to encourage industrial investment, they have been kept on a smaller scale than in many developing economies and even such developed countries as Japan.

The initiative for industrial development was left in the hands of the private sector, both local and foreign. In the early stages, it was easier to attract foreigners than domestic entrepreneurs to invest in manufacturing industries. As in most developing countries, industrial entrepreneurship was thin, partly because local investors were accustomed to the safer and more lucrative investments such as retail trade, extractive or plantation industries, or real estate development. The first opportunties were therefore seized by foreign investors.

An important motivating force for foreign investments was defensive in character—firms that had been exporting to Malaysia wanted to protect their share of the market. By taking advantage of the tariffs that were introduced and establishing a preemptive position, they tried to prevent competitors from setting up plants. The tire, pharmaceuticals, electronics, fertilizer, chemical and petroleum industries fell in this category. Some came to carve out a new market for themselves by taking advantage of nonprice factors, such as funds and availability of servicing in the Malaysian market, and others (tobacco, textiles, food and beverages, shoes, toiletries, sewing machines) took advantage of cost factors and legal restrictions. During the first twenty-five years of independence, Malaysia concentrated on light industries—mainly import-substituting industries—as they were thought to bring with them powerful development stimuli.

Because industrial policies were not clearly defined, a hodgepodge of import-substituting industries were established. Most were of the assembly or packaging type, geared to the existing market size; some made component parts to be exported to the parent companies, as in the case of electronics. Almost all of these import-substituting industries were bound by export restriction clauses, thus preventing expansion of production except to take a greater share of the local market. There was no machinery for deciding on the number and size of plants for each industry, to ensure viability and growth and to generate the necessary linkage effects. The motor assembly industry is an interesting case in point (see note 1).

During the period 1971–1980, manufacturing output expanded at an average annual rate of 12.5 percent, and its contribution to the gross domestic product also increased steadily. In 1980, manufacturing constituted 20.5 percent of the gross domestic product, compared with 13.4 percent in 1970. The manufacturing sector also made a significant contribution to employment growth and export expansion. Exports of manufactured goods rose from M$522 million in 1970 to M$5,935 million in 1980. About half of these exports, however, were from the electronics industry, which is owned and controlled almost entirely by foreigners. The second-ranked export industry, textiles, is well behind electronics.

In the early stages of industrial development, these industries were welcomed because they created employment. Many of them took great advantage of the incentives given by the government (especially electronics); they may also have benefited through transfer pricing. Yet, they made no attempt to move up-market. The electronics industries merely assembled imported chips into semiconductor devices, which were then exported. With no forward or backward linkages to increase local value added and with rising labor costs, this industry will lose its competitive edge, especially at a time when the world demand for semiconductors is weak. Anticipating such developments, the authorities waived the import duty on new machinery to help such industries modernize their plants. The electronics industries could, if it wished, move in the direction of integrated production, thereby retaining its competitiveness.

All indications are that Malaysia's industrial investment strategy in the 1980s will be geared toward expansion and diversification of the manufacturing base. High priority will be given to the establishment of labor-intensive, export-oriented, and technology-intensive industries, and to the promotion of intermediate and capital goods industries. In addition, resource-based industries will be further encouraged to generate higher value added and foreign exchange earnings. Policies for other dispersal of industries will promote balanced industrial growth among regions.

The vigor with which the authorities are now pursuing equity ownership goals set in Malaysia's New Economic Policy (NEP) may make some foreign companies reassess their future investment strategies and current ownership structures. Some foreign investors have expressed the fear that while their investments in Malaysia may initially be approved with equity conditions they find acceptable, the government could later decide to alter equity ownership requirements in favor of Malaysians. But a recent Business International study ("Corporate Strategies for Malaysia: An In-Depth Guide for Responding to the NEP") shows that international firms operating in the country with well-constructed strategies can effectively match long-term corporate objectives with the economic goals of the NEP.

To provide broad guidelines on equity participation that will be applied to new projects, the government has specified that:

1. For industrial projects substantially dependent on the domestic market, the government will require majority Malaysian equity.
2. For projects involving the extraction and primary processing of nonrenewable domestic resources, at least 70 percent Malaysian equity, including 30 percent native Malay or Bumiputra ownership would be required.
3. For projects manufacturing substantially for the export market, foreign majority ownership is permitted. Where it is justified, 100 percent foreign equity can be considered.

These guidelines will also apply to that portion of increased investment brought about by any substantial expansion or diversification of existing projects whose equity structure does not comply with the ownership targets of the NEP.

The guidelines will be implemented flexibly. The extent of Malaysian and foreign equity in a particular project will be determined on the basis of the merits of the individual case. Factors to be considered include:

the amount of investment;
the process and level of technology involved;
the location;
the extent of export;
the extent of integration with existing industries;
the promotional effects;
the industry's stage of development; and
benefits accruing to the country through spin-off effects.

Companies are not required to attain the stipulated equity ratio immediately. Companies may begin operations with an equity ratio more favorable to them, with the understanding that the stipulated equity ratio will be reached by a given date.

Though the need for foreign capital and technology remains high, preference will be given only to investments that would help establish resource-based export-oriented industries. As noted earlier, the electronics and textile industries contribute more than 60 percent of

Malaysia's manufactured export earnings. Almost all electronics companies and the more successful of the textile companies are foreign owned, and all of them have gained by the provision of various incentives, as have some of the other packaging industries, such as the milk industries. But none has any significant linkages with local ancillary industries. However, the pattern of industrial growth appears to be changing. Industry is now becoming more autonomous in nature, with a substantial percentage of the equity owned by local nationals. This augurs well, as the products of these investments cater mainly to the local market.

A New Departure in Industrial Policy

During the period 1981–1990 the manufacturing sector is projected, by the Growth Plan for 1981–1985, to expand at a lower rate of about 11 percent. Nonetheless, manufacturing is expected to play a key role in this decade, replacing agriculture, forestry, and fishing as the single most important sector in the Malaysian economy after 1982. The manufacturing sector is projected to generate about 566,000 jobs, or 30 percent of the new employment opportunities during the period 1981–1990, compared with 417,000 or 24.5 percent in 1971–1980. The number of approvals given in the first ten months of 1981 to establish new industries suggests that these employment projections are attainable.[3]

Manufacturing is also expected to promote balanced growth among the regions and spearhead the nation's export drive during the 1980s. Industrialization is seen as a means of improving the conditions of work and living standards of the people in the rural areas. Policy makers have realized that world trade will not be growing as fast as it did during the last two decades. This development will have an impact on commodity prices, and to offset any adverse effects, industries more responsive to the factor endowments of Malaysia have to be identified and developed. It is also widely understood that the process of industrialization cannot be sustained indefinitely if based on the local market alone. Though there is still scope for import-substituting industries, Malaysia has to look to foreign markets for sustained industrialization. With growing unemployment and protectionism[4] in the industrialized nations, Malaysia will have difficulty meeting its export goals unless the quality of the goods and the productivity of Malaysian industries are improved and a more coordinated approach is adopted in the marketing of manufactured products.

Malaysia's manufacturing industries, with the possible exception of electronics, did not suffer sustained recession in recent years, in contrast to some other countries. The primary problem is the absence of a broad techno-economic base on which to build an efficient superstructure of industries in which Malaysia has comparative advantage. Therefore, while continuing to provide all possible assistance to import-substituting industries, Malaysia's new strategy will be to emphasize resource-based and capital goods industries.

HICOM was thus formed "to plan, initiate, implement and manage projects in the field of heavy industries."[5] The new strategy is designed to strengthen the industrial base and to diffuse industrial activity throughout the country with a view to fulfilling the objectives of the New Economic Policy.[6] The key element in the new strategy is to establish heavy "nucleus" industries in the various regions which will help create secondary and tertiary industries. The first of these projects would be a sponge iron/billet plant; the products of this industry would feed its own steel mills and others that presently import from abroad.[7]

The present indications are that HICOM will concentrate in the establishment of upstream manufacturing activities such as basic ferrous and nonferrous metal industries, machinery and equipment manufacture, general engineering industries, transport equipment, building materials, paper and paper products, and petrochemicals.

It is hoped that the establishment of an industrial base will spur industrial growth, with the private sector taking advantage of the variety of downstream industries, ranging from "automotive parts to heavy equipment components, machine tools to agricultural implements, and possibly from military hardware to energy exploration equipment."[8] These "nucleus" plants, which would be publicly owned, may have to coordinate the activities of smaller companies established to supply parts or perform assembly activities. (For example, there are about 2,000 such "feeder" industries supplying component parts to Daimler Benz. HICOM announced recently that it would be adopting the same strategy for its motorcycle project.) Quality control and marketing operations may have to be the responsibility of the nucleus industry, and these functions may be taken over later by the proposed general trading corporations.

The creation of HICOM, with its purpose and direction clearly defined, will make a significant contribution to the building of a broad industrial base. It must, however, be noted that while the establishment of these plants will help Malaysia break free from its total dependence on imports of such items, ways must be found to ensure that such products are produced competitively, without compromising on quality. Failure to ensure competitiveness would set in motion a series of high-cost supporting industries. In the past few decades, the rapid growth of international trade made it relatively easy to use Malaysia's export surpluses to pay for mistakes on the domestic front. The immediate future, however, is less bright. While no one doubts Malaysia's long-term prospects, especially with the revival of the industrial economies and with the vast natural gas deposits coming on stream, the country cannot afford to make many mistakes in the future. Thus, issues such as choice of project, choice of technology, development of management and other skills, the role of multinational corporations and the like will require careful planning and implementation.[9]

Another significant departure in industrial policy is the new administration's "Look East" policy. Much of the fresh promotional effort and diplomatic activities will henceforth be directed toward Japan and the Republic of Korea, though there are no indications of any reduction in efforts to woo investments from other traditional sources.

Japan has recently been Malaysia's number one trading partner and has superseded Singapore as the number one foreign investor.[10] Japan is now on the threshold of a new era in its relations with Malaysia and other members of ASEAN. With the growth of the Japanese economy quickening, the yen strengthening, and anxieties growing about trade tension with most developed and developing countries, the indications are that Japan will soon pursue an outgoing investment policy. Sensing Japan's present motivation to invest in offshore production capacity rather than rely on direct exports alone, Malaysia has launched a strategy of securing a greater Japanese involvement in the economy of the country. Japan imports large quantities of industrial raw materials from Malaysia, and the natural affinity that exists between the two countries might also encourage an inflow of Japanese investments. Moreover, as Japan moves in the more sophisticated industries in the eighties and the nineties, it may wish to relocate some of its traditional industries abroad. Another possible argument is that Japan's circumstance may require it to be more accommodating than the United States or Europe. After all, Southeast Asia is a major supplier of raw materials and an important market for Japanese manufactures.

Means of Policy Implementation

While the Ministry of Trade and Industry and the Ministry of Finance are responsible for Malaysia's policy formulation, the success of efforts to attract foreign investments depends very much on the policy-implementing agencies, especially the Malaysian Industrial Development Authority (MIDA). This organization, which has earned a reputation for a businesslike approach, is strongly represented in variuos international capitals.

MIDA is the statutory body responsible for the promotion and coordination of industrial development in Malaysia. It also functions as an adviser to the Ministry of Trade and Industry on the formulation of industrial policies. For these purposes, it undertakes economic feasibility studies of industrial possibilities and promotional work, and facilitates exchange of information and coordination among institutions involved in industrial development.[11] Issues such as site development, evaluation of applications for pioneer status, and the like are also dealt with by this agency. It is difficult to comment as to whether its advice on the best strategy to industrialize the country is always taken. But MIDA's record reflects sound perceptions and understanding when it comes to advising investors.

Without rich industrial experience, it is difficult for most local industries, especially the medium-sized ones, to see the new competitive realities. Many of them flounder, though there is nothing basically wrong with the projects. An important function to which MIDA has given little attention is active involvement in the improvement of industrial competitiveness. Small and medium-sized industries, in particular, must be made aware of such issues as the fundamental factors determining the nature of competitors, and other aspects of competitive strategies. MIDA has the necessary capabilities for such an activity. The agency is best suited to provide such services for fragmented industries (like automobiles) and declining industries, and to provide guidance for making strategic decisions on such issues as vertical integration, major capacity expansion, disinvestment, and the launching of new enterprises. In an industrializing country, it is not enough to identify and help establish viable industries. Financial assistance and such help as described above must also be offered to those who need them, in order to steer them through difficult waters. This would avoid proliferation of lame-duck industries.

The counterpart of MIDA at the Ministry of Finance is Bank Negara Malaysia, which plays a key role in formulating broad policy objectives and steering the financial system toward implementing the country's industrialization program. The promotion of savings, the development of sound financial institutions, and the direction of lending are all important for the rapid growth of manufacturing industries. But it is indeed a pity that Malaysia has no specific institution to make loans on concessional terms, to basically sound industries that could contribute to the industrial base; such loans might enable them either to consolidate their positions during difficult times or to finance additional investments to make their projects commercially profitable. The Malaysian Industrial Development Finance Corporation Berhad has not done enough. While the recent duty exemption for machinery imported to rationalize production will help somewhat, the general consensus is that there is a case for a specialized agency, or for a special unit in MIDA to assist ailing industries. Projects that need such assistance have to be identified carefully to avoid wasting money on lame-duck industries.

Coordination with Regional and International Bodies

A new policy governing coordination with regional and international bodies had gradually emerged as a consequence of disenchantment with the rich industrial nations. A tough but pragmatic strategy is evolving, taking advantage of every opportunity to emphasize the significance of interdependence.

Another offshoot of the new policy approach will be to make ASEAN speak with one voice and build up its collective bargaining power. ASEAN has worked well in dealings with countries outside the region. Issues such as commodity price fluctuations and protectionism will therefore be taken up more through ASEAN, rather than the disjointed U.N. Group of 77. It is hoped that greater use of the ASEAN forum and the expansion of South-South ties will broaden Malaysia's options. The award of the multi-million Penang bridge contract to Hyundai Corporation of the Republic of Korea was motivated by this objective.

Within the region, however, the road toward implementation of ASEAN industrial projects has been bumpy. Under ASEAN's "package" approach, each member country was allocated a specific project and granted regional status.[12] Unfortunately, although the projects met the stipulated conditions as to availability of resources, profitability, and the like, progress has been stifled. Only two of the five projects identified are progressing satisfactorily; Malaysia's urea project is one of these.[13]

Nevertheless, it may be worth exploring the possibility of formulating ASEAN-wide industrial policies involving private and, if necessary, public sectors as well. This strategy—i.e., a partial customs union cum investment plan—is suggested because economic and political factors would make it hard to realize economic integration at present. A project cooperation scheme is a useful substitute, and such a scheme need not await the sanction of all five members of ASEAN. Two or more countries could launch on such a program and agree on the reciprocal abolition of tariffs or other trade impediments for specific products. While some progress has been made at the governmental level, it may be helpful to encourage the private sector as well to identify viable regional industries and obtain the approval of any two or more governments to qualify for free access. The recently proposed ASEAN Industrial Joint Venture (AIJV) helps to meet these needs. The ASEAN Finance Corporation, which was formed recently by the ASEAN Banking Council, could play the catalytic role.

It would also be very helpful if the ASEAN governments agreed to allow a certain number of commercial banks from the member countries to open branches in the various ASEAN capitals. Availability of such facilities could supplement and complement the ASEAN Finance Corporation's efforts to generate cross-frontier investments, ASEAN joint ventures, and the like. Many industries, such as car components, electronics, and equipment for the oil industries, could be developed economically to serve the home and regional markets.[14]

TRENDS IN GOVERNMENT POLICIES

Public Sector Involvement

Since the May 1969 racial disturbances, the initiative for Malaysia's industrial development has not been left entirely in the hands of the private sector. This incident underlined the urgent need to restructure Malaysian society so as to eliminate inequities in income distribution and employment opportunities among the major racial groups. The urge to assert national goals motivated the government to create and operate a number of enterprises. A characteristic feature has been the absence of a conscious ideological motivation.

Society has traditionally assigned costly and economically unrewarding tasks to the government. In the areas where priorities are set by the community rather than the marketplace, the job is given to the government, but the job and the magnitude of finance involved will in turn affect the marketplace. In most industrial activities identified by HICOM, the question of where to draw the line between public and private enterprises does not arise, since these projects are generally either too big for the private sector to handle or take a long time to gestate. Though the criteria by which the community measures the performance of public enterprises are often multiple, interlinked, and complex, profit is the single most important standard in the case of manufacturing.

Circumstances rather than ideological motivation prompted the Malaysian government to a more active involvement in manufacturing activity. The question of state intervention in the manufacturing sector thus became a matter of degree, rather than of principle. The Malaysian government will be using selected manufacturing activities as a spearhead in pursuing strategic objectives such as the development of depressed areas, applications of advanced technology, industrial rationalization, and defense against foreign intrusion in sensitive sectors. Successful completion of these projects should help the nation achieve its socioeconomic objectives, establish an industrial base, and build indigenous technological and management expertise.

Public-Private Sector Rapport

The usual criticism of the public sector is its inflexibility and failure to respond to the needs of the private sector. In Malaysia, however, there is a relatively high level of interaction between the government and the private sector. The government, intent on achieving high economic growth through industrialization, has tried to be responsive to the needs of the private sector–particularly since, during the Fourth Malaysia Plan period, the private sector is expected to complement the efforts of the government by expanding production to meet demand, improving efficiency, conserving energy, and training and upgrading skills.[15]

The high level of rapport is especially prominent in industry. MIDA has assisted private investors in identifying viable industries. It has also organized investment seminars and investment missions abroad, in which both the public and the private sectors have participated actively. In addition, it acts as an intermediary for local private investors and foreign investors.

Another illustration of the government's responsiveness is the amendments made to the Industrial Coordination Act (ICA) of 1975. The Act required licenses for all manufacturing activities with shareholders' funds of at least $250,000 and with at least 25 full-time paid employees. It also gave the Ministry of Trade and Industry a free hand in attaching conditions to the licenses. Because of substantial opposition to some of the Act's provisions, from both local and foreign businesses, it was amended in April 1977. The authority to impose conditions for licensing was transferred from the minister of trade and industry to the secretary-general of the ministry. In June 1979, the ICA was further amended in response to criticism from the private sector. Those amendments provide for an Industrial Advisory Council, with both government and private sector representation, to advise the minster on matters pertaining to the act.

The government has repeatedly emphasized the importance of cooperation between the public and the private sectors, and its willingness to look into the deficiencies and needs of any particular industry. Before the establishment of the Advisory Councils, consultations with the private sector had been confined to resolving issues and problems faced by the private sector in implementing government policies. With the increasing emphasis on annual budget dialogue sessions and the joint public-private sector committees set up by various ministries, these joint committees will serve as important forums for resolution of issues, thereby strengthening the interdependence of the public and the private sectors.[16]

Technology Transfer

Technology transfer can be horizontal or vertical; developing countries experience primarily the former.[17] Malaysia was swept forward under the lash of changing technology. The unrestricted flow of external capital facilitated the importation of managerial skills and technology. The continued growth and capitalization of the rubber and tin industries contributed significantly to Malaysia's preeminence in plantation and mining technology. Foreign investors brought along the best available plantation technology (and cheap indentured labor from abroad) to produce these goods in the most efficient manner to meet the factory requirements in their respective home countries. The skills and resources of foreign companies therefore not only developed Malaysia's natural resources but also helped spread new management and technological ideas within the country. Some organizations (including banks and trading houses) functioned almost as business schools. Several senior Malaysian industrial executives learned their trades with these foreign companies. But while the best available technology was brought to exploit Malaysia's natural resources, no attempt was made to bring the technology to process these products locally.

Before independence and in the early post-independence era, foreign investors were free to move into any manufacturing industry they wished. As most of these industries were import-substituting in nature, and as new projects and processes were not comprehensively examined before being given pioneer status, foreign investors were free to bring whatever technology they wanted. Despite all the advantages of an open economy, the transnational corporations made litte attempt to transfer technologies suitable to improve, increase, and diversify manufacturing output with a view to selling in the markets of developed countries. A tremendous boost would have been given to the process of transferring advanced technology had the transnational corporations tried to take advantage of the linkage effects and availability of cheap raw materials. The removal of the restrictive trade practices, particularly by the industrialized countries, and accelerated economic cooperation among the ASEAN countries would have assisted the process.

HICOM's planned projects will open doors for the introduction of advanced technology. Some of these projects may be launched with the aid of transnational corporations. In such cases, it will be important to scrutinize issues such as the real cost of the technology acquired, the conditions imposed, the appropriateness of the technology transferred, research and development capacity, and the impact of the transfer on Malaysia's technological and industrial capability. Malaysia's success in extracting the best terms will depend very much on its negotiating capabilities.

Manpower

The realization is growing that industrial development will not benefit from technology unless the talents and skills of the nation's manpower are fully developed, and unless the art and science of management is developed and practised with care and prudence in every sphere of national economic activity. For the successful implementation of the HICOM projects, for example, technological capabilities must be developed in advance to reduce dependence on the foreign joint-venture partners. Formulating an industrial policy alone is not enough. It should be in harmony with the national development policy, which includes development of manpower resources, installation of efficient infrastructure facilities, and all other related paraphernalia to ensure autonomous technological effort. To introduce disproportionate doses of advanced technology and modern techniques without considering the prevailing level of technical competence and management capabilities will impose great costs on the economy. Some sense of timing must be introduced into the transfer process.

Industrialization therefore is not a simple question of transferring technological contrivances. It requires trained personnel, materials, and money. In addition to trained (and retrained) workers, scientists, technologists, and managers are also needed. For example, Malaysia's present engineer/population ratio is about 1:1,500. In developed countries, the ratio is 1:400. In the drive to overcome this problem, it is important to attend to the quality and character of the educational system. The universities should examine syllabuses to ensure that the training given is in keeping with the needs of the economy. Engineers, for example, are no longer asked to design a product for a certain purpose, but to provide a solution to a problem. The changing needs of the professions have to be appreciated, and adequate adjustments have to be made in the teaching institutions. We need a plan for skilled people as well.

CONCLUSION

Malaysia's industrial policies must be viewed in the context of broad social and economic policy objectives. The growing emphasis on self-reliant strategies (including internal structural changes and redistribution policies) is reflected in the present industrial policy.

Industrial strategy is more readily designed than implemented. Bureaucratic procedures, some of which conflict with objectives stated by ministers and parliamentarians, impose significant costs on industry and the country. Industrial entrepreneurship and management are scarce commodities. To maximize the output of these resources, every attempt must be made to streamline the administration and to avoid conflicting policies (governing labor, taxation, credit, and the like) and conflicting interpretations by petty functionaries. Government of course must probe, inspect, influence, regulate, and if necessary punish those who do not comply with the law. But enforcement must be in total conformity with the true spirit of the law, and administered with finesse. In some developing countries powerful vested interests have evolved, both within the administration and the private sector, that make policy reform and policy implementation difficult. Fortunately, Malaysia does not have the sort of regulatory deadlock experienced by many countries (including the United States, which is the most regulated economy outside the Soviet Union). The most debated regulation—the Industrial Coordination Act—has been sorted out through the cooperative efforts between business and government.[18] This is a tribute to the pragmatism of both parties. Occasionally, however, minor regulatory procedures may cause conflict between a government agency and the manufacturing community. With proper briefing of those who are new to implementing policies, such conflicts can be minimized and a successful partnership in accommodating divergent views can be formed as in Japan.

Industrial policy, therefore, cannot be implemented in isolation. Those in charge of implementing the various policies of the government must work in close harmony with each other. Issues such as the exchange rate of the ringgit, credit policies for manufacturing industries, manpower policies, and the like have to be carefully studied and the right policy prescriptions made. In fact, the integration of industrial policy and national development policy is the best means of promoting the efficiency and productivity of Malaysian industries. Such an integrated approach will encourage movement of resources into the expanding industrial sectors, thereby helping the country attain stable economic growth.

Total integration of policies means the inclusion of monetary policy as well. Policy in this area has been reasonably sophisticated, and the financial system is, to a considerable extent, geared to support the industrialization process. It has been argued, however, that the financial community lacks the sort of body of specialists conversant with the process and problems of industrialization that could reduce conflicts, say, between the Treasury and the Ministry of Trade and Industry. If the government and the banks had a corpus of industry specialists, it would be easier to solve such problems as underutilized labor and capital resources, failures to invest or support companies capable of earning real profits, or an inability to innovate out of low-productivity areas. The Fourth Malaysia Plan, 1981-1985, assigns a major role to the private sector, and most of new investments ($74.1 billion) projected for this sector are expected to go into manufacturing. Financial policy makers have an important role to play in helping formulate policies that will address Malaysia's real industrial problems. It is not clear that such a thing as "free trade" still exists. While true protection is counterproductive and weakens the resolve of management and labor to improve efficiency, pragmatic policies are needed in times of economic adversity and early stages of industrial development – of course without fostering lame-duck industries.

Similar pragmatic policies have to be adopted in the case of manpower development. Technological capabilities have to be quickly developed, preferably in advance of the new phase of industrial development. This means more than stepping up the production of engineers and scientists only. An encouraging development is that preparations are being made to send young men for on-the-job training in factory establishments in Japan and the Republic of Korea. Such an investment will have the added benefit of exposing Malaysians to the work ethics of the labor force in those countries. Malaysia needs people who are firm believers in the "theology of productivity."

The 1980s will test the ingenuity of government leaders and the industrial community in implementing the new industrial policy. Malaysia can successfully meet this test if it recognizes the imperatives of careful planning and systematic implementation, and adopts an enlightened framework within which the industrial policies can be carried out.

NOTES

1. There are at present seventeen assembly plants, two of which have not yet commenced operations. In addition to assembling trucks and motorcycles, these plants are associated with about nineteen makes of cars; they assemble about 117 models for a market consuming about 100,000 vehicles a year.
2. In industrialized countries manufacturing represents more than 60 percent of the value added in commodity production. In the case of semi-industrialized countries manufacturing's share is 40-60 percent and in industrializing countries it is 20-40 percent. See Helen Hughes, "Industrialization and Development: A Stocktaking", *Industry and Development*, No. 2 (New York: United Nations), pp. 1–27.
3. The Malaysian Industrial Development Authority (MIDA) approved 522 projects during this period, or 34 percent more than in the same period of 1980, or almost as much

as the whole of 1974, the best year so far. Proposed capital investment in these projects is $4.42 billion (*Business Times,* December 28, 1981).
4. Let us take textiles and garments as an example. The original aims of the Multifibre Agreement (MFA) were to expand trade, reduce barriers, and allow the textile industries in developing countries to grow rapidly. In its application, however, the MFA has generally failed to satisfy the needs of developing countries. See *Economic and Social Survey of Asia and the Pacific, 1980: Recent Economic Developments, 1979-1980,* (Bangkok: ESCAP, pp. 67–68).
5. Apparently the private sector will not be involved in the establishment and operation of heavy industries. "[Heavy] industries are generally large scale by their very nature and require large investment outlays, have long gestation periods and give rates of return on investment which are not considered attractive by normal commercial standards by the private investors in the country. Of course, such projects may still be attractive to and could be undertaken by foreign investors. But because of their importance from the viewpoint of national interest, it is desirable to have the ownership, control and management of these projects in the hands of Malaysian nationals. In view of the lack of interest by the Malaysian private sector in heavy industries, the government has considered it necessary to set up HICOM to specifically initiate, plan, implement and manage such projects and has provided an initial allocation of $125 million to HICOM under the Fourth Malaysia Plan." (Tan Sri Jamil Jan, "The Role of Heavy Industries Corporation of Malaysia in the Fourth Malaysia Plan," a paper presented at a conference organized by the Federation of Malaysian Manufacturers, May 1981. Also see V. Kanapathy, "Industrialisation of Malaysia," UMBC Economic Review, vol. I, no. 2 (1965), p. 8.)
6. The New Economic Policy evolved as a consequence of the May 1969 racial riots and is now being implemented. Its overriding objectives are to achieve national unity by eradicating poverty and restructuring society so as to reduce, and eventually eliminate, identification of race with economic functions. These objectives are to be realized through rapid growth of the economy with equal emphasis placed on the achievement of social objectives; economic growth per se does not satisfy the aspirations of the New Economic Policy.
7. A sponge iron/billet plant, based on the abundant supply of natural gas in the country and imported pellets/iron ore, is planned to be set up in the State of Trengganu on the East Coast of Peninsular Malaysia. This plant, which is supposed to start up in mid-1984, is expected to produce 600,000 tonnes of sponge iron per annum, of which 520,000 tonnes will be for its own billet production and the remaining 80,000 tonnes will be supplied to the local steel mills. Bid proposals for the project have been received and are being evaluated.
     HICOM has also agreed in principle to participate in the equity of another sponge iron project to be set up by the Sabah State Government in Labuan Island, Sabah.
8. From "The Private Sector and Heavy Industries," by Y. B. Datuk Eric Chia, Group Managing Director, United Motor Works (Malaysia) Holdings Berhad, Malaysia. "The tempo of industrial activity has to be stepped up and there seems to be little alternative to the government taking the lead. In all countries, and not the least the United States, much of the initial thrust towards industrial development came from the state. The Malaysian Government has now accepted in principle state participation and intervention in industrial development. Such a measure would not only help to accelerate the pace of industrial development but it would also help to bring about a better balance in ownership and control in the manufacturing sector. . . . Such investments will act as a multiplier and generate considerable secondary and tertiary activities." (V. Kanapathy, "Foreign Investment in Malaysia: Experience and Pro-

spects," Occasional Paper No. 6, Institute of Business Studies, College of Graduate Studies, Nanyang University, Singapore (1971), pp. 18–19.)

9. "Any industry that has an uncertain supply of raw materials or unstable end markets should be kept out of the public sector" (*Financial Times,* December 11, 1981).

10. Foreign equity in the 522 projects approved in the first ten months of 1981 "amounted to M$457 million as against M$209 million in the same period last year. Leading foreign investors in descending order of importance were Japan (M$62.5 million), Australia (M$49.3 million), U.S. (M$45.8 million), Singapore (M$36.0 million), U.K. (M$5.8 million), West Germany (M$23.5 million), Arab investments (M$12 million), and India (M$11 million)" (*Business Times,* December 28, 1981). The capital outlays were mainly in the areas of nonmetallic products, basic metal industry, food manufacturing, chemicals, and chemical products.

11. The Ministry of Trade and Industry planned to participate in eight trade promotion missions and ten international trade fairs in 1982.

12. For information pertaining to the package approach, see Arie Kuyenhoven and L. B. M. Mennes, "Projects for Regional Cooperation: Identification, Selection, Evaluation and Location," *Industry and Development,* No. 1 (New York: United Nations, 1978), pp. 3–37.

13. The other project certain to succeed is the urea project in Indonesia. The soda ash project in Thailand, diesel engine project in Singapore, and phosphatic fertilizer project in Philippines have not taken off for either political or economic reasons.

14. The prime minister of Malaysia called for a grouping together of the ASEAN oil industry, to compete with international concerns that have a monopoly of this region. He said that individually they are too small to compete with the transnational corporations, let alone break the monopoly. (Reported in the *New Sunday Times,* January 3, 1982.)

15. The private sector is expected to play an important role in fulfilling the growth target envisaged under the Fourth Malaysia Plan. "About 72.2 per cent of the total investment targetted for the Plan is expected to come from the private sector. This calls for a more intensified effort on its part, to mobilize resources for investment and to acquire skills, technical knowhow and management expertise. On the other hand, the government will continue to maintain an investment climate conducive to the growth of the private sector and provide the necessary support in terms of infrastructure and other facilities" (*Fourth Malaysia Plan* 1981–1985, p. 251).

16. The Ministry of Finance holds annual prebudget dialogue sessions with associations representing various groups of the private sector, such as the Federation of Malaysian Manufacturers, the Master Builders Association, and the Malaysian Trade Union Congress. Under the auspices of the Ministry of Trade and Industry, public and private sectors are represented on the following committees: Price Review Subcommittee, Joint Public-Private Sector Committees, Committee on the Selection of Participants to Trade Exhibitions. For the financial industry, the Council of the Association of Banks in Malaysia meets the governor of the central bank once a month, and an annual conference is held between the central bank and all the commercial banks, in which views are exchanged.

17. Vertical transfer of technology essentially means the application of science to technology and the conversion of technology into goods and products. Horizontal transfer means the use of scientific and technological information generated in a research institution, a university, or even a firm, and used vertically by another institution to meet its requirements. Vertical transfer generally takes place within an institution, while horizontal transfer takes place between institutions.

18. See *Fortune,* December 28, 1981, pp. 24–32.

Chapter 8

Mexico's Industrialization

*Ernesto Herzberg**

The industrialization of Mexico began with import substitution and a concentration of investment in the highlands. All the benefits of an import-substitution model have now been realized, and thus a continuation of such a policy is no longer recommended. At first import substitution works rather well; it substitutes domestic production for imports of some consumer durables and some intermediate operations such as assembly plants. But because all basic capital goods must at first be imported, rapid industrialization significantly increases the imports of capital equipment, and the import bill goes up rather than down.

The alternative is to design the industrial development process from the bottom up, with the emphasis on basic and heavy industries. The sectors that produce goods and services that go into the making of all other goods and services must be built up and maintained at a world-competitive level. This new stage of industrialization in Mexico has required the establishment of a new industrial policy. A country with 70 million people—a large proportion of whom are between the ages of 15 and 25—needs an industrial system able to create employment and at the same time disperse the population to the coastlands. Moreover, Mexico will require a highly competitive industry in order to increase its exports. A policy of dispersing production to the coastlands has a

*Instituto Tecnologico Y de Estudios Superiores

threefold effect: it creates employment, it provides export competitiveness (by eliminating the need to bring material to the highlands and then return the final product to the ports), and it reverses the demographic process that has concentrated the population in the highlands.

Mexico's population and economic activity have traditionally been concentrated primarily in three urban areas: Mexico City, Guadalajara, and Monterrey. The price mechanism as described by neoclassical economics has been unable to alter industrial location behavior significantly. Instead, the structural approach of unbalanced growth and, to a lesser extent, the radical big-push approach have been used.

Mexico's urbanization trends have been linked to its industrialization process. For example, industrial zone 1 includes Mexico's three largest metropolitan cities, zone 2 includes the next seven largest "secondary" cities, and zone 3 covers the rest of the country, which represents approximately 96 percent of Mexico's area. Industries that locate investments in zones 2 and 3 are eligible for tax reduction of 50-100 percent on import duties, income, sales, capital gain taxes, accelerated depreciation, and lower interest rates, along with a package of technical assistance for smaller firms. However, there seems to be no clear distinction between the incentives offered to zones 2 and 3. Zone 2 includes many cities that are close enough to Mexico City to provide some of its advantages, but far enough to avoid some of its problems of congestion.

Until recently, in spite of these incentives, 80 percent of all new industrial firms established were located in zone 1, many of them in Mexico City. In other words, unless the incentives significantly outweigh the opportunity costs of various locations, they are not likely to attract industry out of the urban areas.

The most recent attempt to decentralize is the national urban development plan. The plan identifies ten specific areas and centers of population priorities, considering the following characteristics: 1) the area's capacity to absorb population; 2) location of natural resources; and 3) the possibility of generating employment. The favored industry sectors are those that can accept location in areas lying outside of Mexico City and the other metropolitan centers.

PLANNING IN MEXICO

The 1980s promises to be the period in which strategic planning, that is long-range formal planning, will become an accepted trend in the top management of the Mexican corporation and within the government. To become increasingly more capable and more competitive in international markets with a diversity of products will require a careful use of resources, which will require acceptance of formal strategic planning. Most Western nations have adopted strategic planning as an important tool for improving the competitiveness of their major industries. In Mexico strategic planning focuses significantly on technology sources, for both the government and companies. Both parties must consider what type of technology developed in other countries can be used with good results in Mexico until the country is able to develop its own through research and development. And each must understand that its strategic planning is highly dependent on that of the other, and must be willing to constantly adjust to the other.

This close interrelationship represents an attempt to incorporate what in France has been known as indicative planning: the government sets the framework of development but does not force the private firms to follow it. Rather, it serves as a guideline and permits private enterprise to anticipate the goals set by the government and thus establish its own strategy. A first example of indicative planning in Mexico is the Alliance for Production, which was designed to combat inflation, raise the economic growth rate, and lower unemployment levels. The Alliance is a pact among the state, the private sector, and labor. The Alliance for Production consists of two parts: a six-year program involving 140 companies in ten major branches of industry, and an initial plan under which the Confederation of Chambers of Industry promised to invest 250 billion pesos (approximately $10 billion) over the period 1977-1978. These goals have been fulfilled. In addition, the Alliance for Production seeks to improve the informational basis on which public, and especially private, decisions are made. Certain assumptions concerning sectoral growth over the next six years were made, giving firms in these areas assurance that their investments were likely to be profitable. The Alliance thus works to reduce the uncertainty that has in the past been a major element in the lower levels of private investment and therefore in growth itself.

Industrial policy in Mexico is developed within the overall structure of the national industrial development plans. The latest of these plans covered the period 1979–1982, with a longer-term plan to guide activities for the rest of the decade. Within this plan industrial output is expected to grow 10–12 percent annually, with the high-growth sectors included in petroleum equipment, petrochemicals, and transport equipment rising to 18 or 20 percent per year. Industry would be expected to provide about 30 percent of the increase in employment, with the service sectors taking up the rest.

PRIORITY SECTORS

Some seventy priority sectors were selected under the following criteria: technology employed, export potential, investment requirements, employment opportunities, income generated, origin of inputs, and estimates of potential market at home and abroad. One of the most important is the origin of inputs, since Mexico puts heavy emphasis on generating demand for local secondary and tertiary industry. Among the sectors given the highest priority is food processing, followed by capital goods, including tractors and farm equipment, and machinery and equipment for petroleum and petrochemical sectors. A lower priority goes to the industries necessary to produce the capital goods: steel mills, cement plants, electrical generating equipment, mining and metallurgic, industrial construction, transport, machine tools, instrumentation, etc. Projected annual growth rates for these third-category industries range from 10 percent to 20 percent. Still lower in the priorities are a group of nondurable consumer goods, including textiles, shoes, containers, household items, school and office supplies, paper, and so on, plus a number of consumer durables and intermediate industrial goods. These are expected to expand at annual rates ranging from 7.5 percent to 20 percent.

Small industry is given a high priority within the plan in order to foster dispersion of industry and because these firms are the tertiary suppliers to the priority sectors.

GOVERNMENTAL INCENTIVES

The major techniques for implementing industrial strategy objectives are federal subsidies, government expenditures and loans, technical assistance, and import protection. The major subsidies are provided through federal tax credits based on investments in fixed assets, increases in employment, or purchases of equipment and machinery made in Mexico. The credit offered is good for five years; its amount depends on the sector and regional priorities established in the plan described above. Small business gets the highest rate of tax credit, amounting to 25 percent of the value of the new investment in fixed assets, while larger companies receive credits of 10-20 percent. The tax credit for additional increases in employment is a uniform 20 percent of the annual payroll cost of the added workers, available for two years, with the requirement that the workers remain at least one year after the company receives the tax subsidy.

The state expects to make a substantial contribution to industrialization through large investments in infrastructure needed in agriculture, transportation, public health, housing, communication, and industry. In addition, the large expenditures in state-owned enterprises will stimulate the secondary and tertiary suppliers. Yet the private sector is expected to supply most of the fixed investment over the planning period: 61 percent is to come from private enterprises, 24 percent from public enterprises, and 15 percent from general government expenditures. By the end of the decade, the private-sector contribution is expected to drop to around 50 percent of gross fixed investment. With the aim of promoting the Mexican-goods industry, state expenditures will be allocated in such a way as to influence the location of industry, output volumes and composition, technical design, production processes, price, and delivery terms. In addition, preferential financing is available for small and medium-sized firms, as are a variety of technical assistance programs—all at subsidized prices and sometimes linked to the investment financing.

Government also assists firms in the process of technology acquisition and transfer from abroad, by analyzing contracts, regulating payments, limiting some of the provisions, and trying to increase the economic benefits realized by Mexico.

The major tool for providing import protection has been the import license, though this is gradually being replaced by duties. (This shift opens the way for Mexico to join the GATT.) On the export side, the foreign trade bank and the foreign trade institute provide information, financing, marketing and promotion services, and fiscal authorities provide rebates of a value-added tax and indirect taxes on goods that are exported. State enterprises are also active in the export field.

THE CHOICE OF INDUSTRIALIZATION PATH

The choice of an industrialization path is an important issue for the future. Two main problems must be solved. The first is to find production processes that can help to alleviate the employment problem but also make Mexican industry internationally competitive. The second is to make the trade-off between imports and domestic production as sources of supply of the domestic market for industrial goods. The industrial plan assumes that the manufacturing industry will absorb 30 percent of the new entrants to the labor force. The problem is that the major investment projects Mexico is now undertaking, especially those in petroleum and capital goods industries (including steel), are by definition highly capital intensive, because they are based on the most modern technology. Nevertheless, the development of large capital-intensive enterprises might encourage the creation of a network of sub-contractors for these industries, consisting mainly of small to medium-sized enterprises using labor-intensive processes. Finally, industrial dispersion patterns must be decided.

DISPERSION OF INDUSTRY

The geographic dispersion of industry has been attempted recently through "border industries" and "in-bond" production for re-export. Both are tied to foreign markets—mostly the United States, but also Japan and Europe—and are therefore composed of industries with special characteristics of separable processes of production, low transport costs, high labor content and so forth.

BORDER INDUSTRIES

The border industry activity consists of firms that turn imported materials, parts, or components into completed consumer goods for export. The process may require imports of machinery, equipment, repair parts, and tools that can remain in Mexico as long as the production continues. According to the program firms are authorized to carry out in-bond operations when either of the following conditions are met:

1. With temporarily imported machinery and any degree of national integration, a firm exports all its products.
2. A firm with an industrial plant already installed or to be installed to supply the internal market carries out temporary imports that will allow the firm to engage in export activities either partially or totally. In this case the products for export should have a minimum of 20 percent of national integration.

During the first eight years of existence the border industry program grew rapidly. In 1966 they were 12 plants; by 1970 the number had grown to 120 and by 1974 it had quadrupled. From 1978 on, the increases continued but at a decreasing rate, reaching 620 firms by 1980.

About 57 percent of the existing plants in 1980 were located in three cities: Tijuana (123), cuidad Juarez (121) and Mexicali (79). Other important locations were Nogales, Sonora (59) and Matamoros/Tamaulipas (50). These five cities accounted for about 70 percent of all border plants in 1980 and 73 percent of the employment. The cities with the largest number of "in-bond" plants located in the interior of Mexico were Guadalajara, Leon and Chihuahua.

The production processes that grew more dynamically were: shoe manufacturing, textiles, electrical appliances and electronics.

In 1978, 9.8 percent of the plants had more than 500 employees, but these accounted for 48 percent of the total employment. At the other end, 53.4 percent of the plants gave employment to fewer than 100 employees, together representing 10.8 percent of the total labor force. In 1980 the revenues of the in-bond industries were $773 million, or 3 percent of the current accounts.

In 1980 total employment was 120,000 people, an increase of 57.3 percent over 1974. Some 85.5 percent of the 1980 total were workers, 9 percent technicians of production, and 6.7 percent administrative. Eighty-nine percent were located along the border cities and 11 percent in the interior. Women represented 77.3 percent of total employment. Their labor is in particular demand for this type of activity, because of the nature of the work, which requires manual and visual activities, especially in areas such as shoe manufacturing, textile, electrical appliances, electronics, and food processing.

Since most of the inputs are imported, the employment effects of in-bond activities are mainly on direct employment, with little development of secondary employment. Moreover the disbursement of income from border industry employment for Mexican products is lower than in other activities because of the high ratio of imported products.

In 1980 the gross value of the in-bond activities was 57,825 million pesos (23 pesos per dollar), minus 40,096 million pesos (69.3 percent of the total value) representing imports of temporary inputs. The remaining 17,729 million pesos corresponds to the value-added by the in-bond industry, including (a) labor, profits, and depreciation of fixed capital; and (b) other costs such as electricity, freight, telephone, telegraph, and custom duties.

MEXICO'S COMPARATIVE ADVANTAGE

Mexico is at least as well situated as Hong Kong, Taiwan, and South Korea to expand its in-bond activities in the future. Some of the most important comparative advantages are the following:

Proximity to the United States. The savings in costs and transport time of raw materials and finished products is considerable. In addition, there is no need to form considerable inventories, as would be the case with more distant countries.

Availability and cost of labor. The minimum salary in the Mexican border is about half the prevailing minimum in the United States (even lower since the February 1982 devaluation of the peso). Other nations in Central America have a still lower minimum salary, but this advantage is offset by transport and other advantages in Mexico.

Productivity. Productivity in Mexico's in-bond activities has been comparable to that in the plants of the United States and other industrialized nations.

Political stability. Stability is of utmost importance in creating an environment favorable to in-bond activities. In addition, legislation guarantees that the plants will operate in accordance with stipulated rules.

Availability of infrastructure and energy sources. More than enough inexpensive petroleum and gas is available to supply the needs of the in-bond industry in Mexico.

STRATEGY TO CONTINUE

Mexico's industrial strategy puts priority on the border industries, as follows:

Continue the expansion of the existing lines of production, with emphasis on areas that have a high proportion of labor costs yet maintain competitiveness over other developing nations with lower labor costs.

Diversify the sources of investment, and attract the establishment of Japanese and European firms that wish to compete in the United States market.

Design a policy that will increase national integration, by developing areas of the economy that are capable of substituting for imported inputs.

Encourage all those products whose volume or weight leads to high costs of transport, insurance, and inventories; in these products Mexico's proximity to the United States represents a competitive advantage.

Identify areas that require rapid reaction. In certain activities, the breakdown of one process can shut down an entire operation. In these cases, proximity to the United States gives Mexico a tremendous advantage, for it is possible to carry out repairs or replace machinery without having to stop plant activities for very long.

Adequate supply of technical skills. Such skills are more readily available in Mexico than in many other developing nations that perform in-bond activities. As a result some manufacturing processes have been developed at the border that are as complex as those in developed nations. Among these activities are automobile parts, nonelectrical motors, office equipment, and several electronic products.

FORECAST FOR THE IN-BOND INDUSTRY IN MEXICO

Even with an aggressive policy, the levels of production and employment in the in-bond industry are largely dependent on the economic activity of the industrialized nations. Thus it is quite difficult to generate accurate forecasts for this industry. Nevertheless, in 1980 an employment of 150,000 to 235,000 was forecast for 1985. This range represented a minimum increase of 25 percent and a maximum of 95.8 percent in five years. Three scenarios were developed.

Low Scenario. A recession in the industrial world could continue until 1983. The economic recovery could bring a new stimulus to the in-bond activity in 1984 and 1985, so that employment would reach 150,000 by 1985.

Intermediate Scenario. If the industrialized countries showed a marked recovery by 1982 and continued to grow at an average rate of 3–4 percent between 1983 and 1985, employment could reach 190,000 by 1985.

High Scenario. If a rapid recovery of the industrialized countries occurred in 1982 and thereafter growth of 5 percent more was maintained through 1985, employment could be estimated at 235,000 people.

Chapter 9

Philippine
Industrialization
Policy

*J. P. Estanislao**

Philippine industrialization policy is difficult to delineate. Not that it has been left undefined. Official policy statements are many and easy to find, but not necessarily consistent with each other. Among those that are in concert, the weight actually given to each is largely unknown and changes over time, sometimes gradually, sometimes suddenly. Thus it is somewhat presumptuous to claim to capture the content of industrial policy—even if reference is made to an official statute, a government document, or a public position paper—because there is no guarantee that what is stated and proclaimed officially is pursued and implemented actually. Dynamic flexibility is, after all, a characteristic of the Philippines. Changes of dramatic proportions can be undertaken rapidly in anticipation of or in reaction to events. Thus, what is enshrined in an official document can be overtaken easily by events.

Interest in industrial policy is conditioned by concern about industrial growth and changes in industrial structure. In fact, Philippine industrial policy is directed less at specific sectors than at overall industrial development. It would be difficult to isolate industrial policy from overall economic policy. Of course, given the interdependence of various sectors in any macroeconomy, a general policy has an influence, often a

*Industrial Economics Institute, Center for Research and Communication, Manila, Philippines.

very significant one, on specific sectors and particularly on those within industry. Thus, credit policy (pursued by blunt monetary instruments, which are often the only ones easily available to the economic managers of a developing country such as the Philippines) often affects industry sectors differently according to their dependence on the organized and monetized segment of the economy. It is difficult then, to delineate where general economic policy ends and specific industrial policy begins; and it would be inappropriate to attempt to trace the Philippines' industrial development and changes in industrial structure apart from general economic policies and a few directed specifically at industrialization.

Accordingly this chapter makes no attempt to identify industrial policy in the Philippines a priori, or to assess the impact of such policy on industrial growth and structural change. Rather, it begins with the facts of growth and structural change within the Philippine industrial sector during the past two decades and infers from these observations the directions actually taken by general economic and specific industrial policies. Recent policy issues and probable future fronts are then explored.

ORIENTATION OF POLICY AFFECTING INDUSTRY

Since growth and structural change are closely related, focusing on the fact of industrial growth may also allow one to observe the structural shifts. For purposes of brevity, this chapter will be limited to a consideration of the more purely quantitative evidence of industrial growth in the Philippines.

In undertaking such a consideration, one must fall back on the traditional framework for analyzing the sources of industrial growth. In particular, one has to look at the market to which industry was being oriented in the hope of determining which demand elements may have contributed significantly to the growth of industrial production. It may also be important to look at the major factors of production that provided as basis for industrial growth and to gauge the relative importance of each supply element in the growth process.

It is within this broad framework of demand and supply factors that the growth of the Philippine industrial sector (i.e., of manufacturing) during the past two decades can be assessed. Over the period studied, the Philippine economy grew at an average annual rate of only 5.7 percent. The corresponding rate of the industrial sector was 6.7 percent. Manufacturing represented a 16.8 percent share of Philippine gross domestic product two decades ago and has since risen to 25.9 percent (Estanislao 1981).

Chenery (1979) suggested ways of breaking down the growth of an economy, a sector, or an industry into four demand elements—final home demand, export market demand, import substitution, and intermediate demand (or interindustry demand)—and of determining the relative importance of each in the growth of production. For the Philippines, roughly half of the industrial growth is attributable to the increase in the final home demand, only about 10 percent to export expansion, about 15 percent to import substitution and 25 percent to intermediate demand (Estanislao et al. 1981).

The findings for the manufacturing sector are consistent with those for the entire economy. Even at the level of specific industries, the same results have been broadly confirmed. At all levels, industrial output growth has depended significantly on final home demand—except for selected basic industries such as sugar, coconut, and wood processing, whose orientation has been more external. In the most recent decade, however, certain industries' dependence on final home demand has fallen, while dependence on export expansion has risen.

Import substitution is no longer significant even in specific industries and, with the exception of textiles and tobacco in the most recent decades (Ranis 1974), has not contributed much at all to industrial output growth. Nor has intermediate demand proven to be a substantial pull factor for the industrial sector. It can not be disregarded in a number of basic industries that process domestically sourced raw materials to which more value is added by other industries. But for most consumer-oriented industries as well as those producing intermediate supplies and capital equipment, intermediate demand has not played a major role in promoting industrial growth.

From the supply side, the growth of labor and capital employed, and more recently also of raw materials used, explains much of the growth of production, with the remainder being explained by productivity increases (Griliches and Jorgenson 1967).

The contribution of labor and capital to an increase in production has always attracted intense interest. More recently, in many developing countries, the concern for appropriate factor proportions in industrial technology has led to calls for a greater use of abundant labor and a lesser use of scarce fixed assets. The importance of domestic and imported raw materials has also been stressed. Indeed, the growth of industries based on an increasing use of domestic raw materials may well represent a structural change considered desirable by many resource-rich developing countries; on the other hand, the growth of industries based on an increasing use of imported raw materials may represent a different set of problems and opportunities for different countries. Finally, even when raw materials are included in the equation, the growth of industry cannot be fully explained by the factors directly used in the production process. Productivity, which ordinarily rises with brisk industrial growth, is said to account for the unexplained residual.

Following this traditional method of breaking down the supply sources of growth, the increase in the use of labor accounts for 12 percent of total output growth in the Philippines, fixed assets for 22 percent, raw materials for 55 percent, and productivity for 11 percent.

The relative contribution of each supply factor to output growth differs somewhat by industry, but the increase in labor input has generally been responsible for 6 percent or less of the increase in industrial output; capital for 35 percent or less; and raw materials for a variable but much higher percentage contribution. The residual for productivity has a variable percentage contribution, tending in most cases toward the low figure. This last result is not surprising, since the growth of factor inputs used has left little room for productivity increases. Labor rose by 3.1 percent per year on average, fixed assets by 4.2 percent, and raw materials, which represent a high share of the value of manufacturing output, by 6.7 percent (Estanislao et al. 1981).

It is now possible to suggest the content of the policies whose impact on industrial growth led to the results described above. First, the Philippines has clearly followed policies that oriented its industries largely to the domestic market. While in the past decade there has been some consciousness of the need to assume a more outward market orientation, industrial growth has been made to depend largely on the growth of final domestic demand, which has been slow.

Second, the pace of change in the structure of Philippine industry has not been rapid enough, and while structural changes through increased import substitution and intermediate demand can account for at least a third of total industrial growth, for most industries there has been no quickening of this pace. It appears that after the initial burst of industrialization, which was motivated by import substitution, Philippine industry lost much of its steam and failed to move on to further stages of import substitution and to strengthen interindustry linkages.

Third, no bias against labor and for capital is evident from a comparison of actual shares paid out and of the implied productivity of each factor. Furthermore, while the use of labor has grown more slowly than the use of fixed assets, labor has contributed less than capital to output growth in specific industries.

Fourth, Philippine policy has banked upon the first phase of the industrial processing of domestically available raw materials as a basis of industrial growth. But instead of moving energetically into the second phase of further processing, the Philippines relied significantly upon imported raw materials. The importation of such raw materials and supplies made industry more dependent upon financing, particularly upon import financing, thereby subjecting it to the vicissitudes of credit policy and foreign exchange availability. It is in this sense that the movements of credit policy and of foreign exchange availability heavily conditioned the ability of Philippine industry to grow.

Fifth, productivity has not been a major concern of Philippine policy toward industry. The strong financial orientation of industry has concentrated concerns on credit access, since this became one of the most important ingredients for successful operations of an industrial enterprise. The more production-based requirements for ever-rising productivity were not even given lip service during the preparation of the current five-year plan.

Thus the Philippines pursued inward-oriented policy for industry; structural adjustments were not paced rapidly, and there was a strong dependence upon imported raw materials, whose availability was contingent upon ever scarce foreign exchange. As a result, industry grew at an annual rate of 6.7 percent during the past two decades. This growth record is far from impressive, especially in comparison with what has been achieved by countries within Southeast Asia. This Philippine policy orientation has remained largely intact through the years. While there have been intense policy debates about certain aspects of how Philippine industry should be developed, and while new official policy pronouncements occasionally set changes in orientation, there has been more continuity than is often recognized.

In the past decade, however, there have been a number of attempts at industrial reform. Changes in actual policy orientation have been proposed; indeed, some such changes have been announced; and a few steps consistent with these changes have been taken. As a consequence, a number of issues have been clearly aired out. They may not refer to industrial policy alone, but to the whole gamut of policies that can influence the direction of industrial growth in the future. It is to these issues that we now turn.

ISSUES OF PHILIPPINE INDUSTRIALIZATION

Industrial issues in the Philippines are debated with varying degrees of heat. But even those that initially seem mere academic debates between economists and policy makers soon attract agitated participants who believe either the national interest or private vested interests will be affected by the final turn taken by industrial policy.

Code words are so often bandied about in these debates that it is sometimes difficult to pin down the basic questions at issue. The tendency is to skirt them: even when they are finally faced, decisions are implemented only gradually, and there is always the possibility of an appeal which can stop or slow down further implementing steps. Thus, the discussion drags on, the debate is kept going over a long period, and there is more than a mere appearance of drift. It is no wonder, then, that the issues of industrialization discussed in the 1970s continue to be points of debate in the early 1980s.

Export Orientation

There is a general consensus that Philippine manufacturing should be much more outward-oriented (Cheetham 1976). This is a code word for promoting nontraditional exports, since certain traditional manufactures have always been undertaken largely for export markets. But many non-traditional export products processed by Philippine industry are not competitive abroad, mainly because the materials and supplies they use are largely imported and pay high tariffs. But high tariffs were established in the first place to protect local industry from external competition. To lower tariffs drastically or to remove them altogether might make some segments of Philippine industry much more competitive in outside markets, but it would also make foreign imports more competitive in the home market. Since different segments of Philippine industry would be affected differently, opinions naturally vary with regard to the tariff-lowering issue. All agree on the general objective of being more aggressive in export markets, but consensus dissolves as soon as this implementation measure is brought into consideration.

Over the past few years, there has been some movement in the direction of simplifying the tariff structure and lowering the tariff rates. But the steps are halting, and the cuts are far from radical. A strong lobby has already materialized to slow the tariff reduction program. It has been suggested that high tariffs are meaningless in any case, because they increase the incentives for smuggling and for graft at Customs; nevertheless, the uneconomic industries understandably attempt to stall the program because their survival is at stake. Since a number of these industries have grown over the years because of their access to and links with those controlling the political levers of the country, the issue transcends mere economic and trade liberalization. The more basic question is that of government and political power working hand in hand with existing industries and those with economic power. Indeed, the politicization of different industrial and business groups has been one of the perennial issues in Philippine society.

Import Substitution

Unlike export promotion, which is almost universally accepted, import substitution divides discussants almost immediately into two camps: those who see it as a necessary first step in postwar Philippine industrialization and those who trace to it much of the weakness of Philippine industry.

Both views have some validity. Outside the traditional industries, which processed locally available raw materials for export markets, the natural first areas for industrialization were consumer products, for which domestic demand was already large to warrant the setting up of local industry to substitute for competing imports. These areas were quickly covered during the first industrial boom after the reconstruction period. But these first import-substituting industries had to be fed with imported materials and supplies, and while they substituted for finished imports, they did not lessen the country's requirements for imports of semiprocessed materials and supplies. In the dynamics of growth, such import requirements became so huge that they could not be met readily, and the scarcity of foreign exchange became an effective drag on economic and industrial growth.

Clearly, a second stage of import substitution is needed, to establish industries that can process the materials and supplies that local industry consumes in bulk. Unfortunately, such industries require large scale and huge capital investments. The eleven major industrial projects proposed and being implemented by the Philippine government are intended to move the country into this second stage of import substitution. From the long-term standpoint, there is little doubt about the eventual desirability of such large-scale, capital-intensive industries.

However, there is an active debate going on in the Philippines about industrial priorities (Villegas 1980). The second-stage import substitution effort will use up a large proportion of foreign exchange resources available to the country, and some have asked whether such resources might not be better used for promoting small and medium-scale industries, especially those that are also labor-intensive. Put this way, the question revolves around priorities. But perhaps a more basic question stems from the size of the eleven major industrial projects. The scale is so massive that the government inevitably has to play a major role, and there is a broad segment of Philippine industry that is wary of government when it not only sets the priorities but also actively implements and runs industrial projects.

Factor Proportions

This wariness is reflected in the third code word used in discussing Philippine industrial policy. Economists and policy makers have long been concerned with the question of what "factor proportions" are appropriate to the resource endowment of the country. In the past, despite protestations to the contrary, the government actively promoted industrialization through an incentives program that favored mainly big business and industrial groups. These businesses were naturally concentrated in metropolitan Manila, whose port was the most convenient for the importation of machinery, equipment, and processed materials and supplies. Many are convinced that the government should continue to pour incentives into new and necessary industrial areas as well as into high-priority sectors. The list of suggestions from Philippine industry on what the government must do to help is endless; the harsh economic facts, however, are that the resources of the government are limited and the incentives it can give out are numbered.

A few economists have recommended the liberalization of factor prices as a means of getting away from the distortions caused by government incentives to industry. The argument has been to let market forces decide the foreign exchange rates, interest rates, and wages. The expectation is that the exchange rates would rise, making exports more attractive; that interest rates would rise also, discouraging the use of scarce working and long-term capital; and that wages would be restrained, encouraging the use of abundant labor. The appeal of the market formula is that it does away with or at least minimizes government arbitration and arbitrariness, and all economic sectors will be subject to the same economic discipline. Such an environment, it has been argued, would be at least somewhat more favorable to small and medium-scale industries, which have been effectively discriminated against by past official dispensation of industrial incentives (World Bank 1979).

It may seem a surprising argument that reliance upon purely market forces would benefit small and medium-scale industries, whose record of employment creation in the Philippines has been better than that of the larger, more capital-intensive ones. It is a measure of the wariness over the distorting effects of government-administered industrial assistance programs that such an argument is put forward. Much of the cynicism about the recently announced official program for government incentives at the grassroots level for small and medium-scale industries stems from such wariness, and indeed the posture of government in actively interfering with market forces for industrial development is at issue.

Base for Industrialization

A fourth code word is the notion of appropriate base for the country's industrialization. Export markets can be one such base, since the foreign exchange earnings from such markets would enable Philippine industry to obtain whatever is necessary to grow energetically with the demands of the large internal market. Thus, the diversification of export products and export markets has been launched with this rationale.

But there is also a long-standing desire in the Philippines to exploit the country's natural resources and use these as basis for further industrialization. On such natural resources, it is hoped, a bigger industrial superstructure can be built up by adding more value through further processing. Thus, a copper smelter is to be set up, an alco-gas program has been framed, and a cocodiesel mixture has been proposed. It has been said that while only a few frontier areas remain unexploited, there is still a long way to go in extracting industrial value from the country's natural resources.

More recently, manpower has been seen as a potential basis for further industrialization. The export of manpower services has given rise to thoughts about a more beneficial use of human resources, in which more investments will be required but from which much greater economic returns can be exacted. Once the quality of the country's human resources is upgraded, it is argued, they can be a more significant source of economic strength, and more specifically of foreign earnings with which to finance further industrialization.

All these bases for industrialization have been examined in discussions concerning Philippine industrial policy. But the relative importance of each remains to be specified. Indeed, Philippine industrialization policy has not considered the various options available and has tended to take them as altogether different strands. As a result, there has been no commitment to pursue an interrelated set of targets for furthering industrialization. The total basis for industrialization remains an issue because it has not been addressed forthrightly.

Productivity

Productivity is an area of more than academic concern, but thus far it has been of interest mainly to academics. While there is wide agreement that productivity is important, little attention has been given to the issue in operational terms.

It is generally recognized, however, that basic services are critical for industrial productivity. The uninterrupted supply of energy and the provision of infrastructure facilities for fast, safe, efficient transport and communication are self-evident imperatives. But brown-outs and temporary interruptions in electricity supply continue; telephone services are inadequate even in metropolitan Manila; the postal system has just been revived; the road network still needs to be properly connected with a system of ports and harbors; even small industries cannot locate in most parts of the country because of the lack of basic industrial services. Much effort will be needed to remove these obstacles to higher industrial productivity; but until they are removed, Philippine industry will continue to find itself bogged down by poor productivity.

In agriculture, the high-yielding varieties of rice with which the green revolution was launched demonstrated the immense possibilities for productivity enhancement. Indeed, in some major crops, most critically in sugar and coconut, productivity has long been deteriorating. While R&D efforts have yielded breakthroughs that promise to arrest the decline, the translation from laboratories and experimental farms is proving to be slow and agonizing. The desire for faster and wider extension work exists, but it has not been operationalized with appropriate urgency.

Because of the limited employment opportunities elsewhere, there is still too much make-work in services. Thus costs rise, and the industrial sector is saddled with higher-than-market fees for services.

The potentials for raising productivity in all sectors of the Philippine economy, including industry, are high. But to convert these potentials into operational realities would require a much greater consciousness of the imperative for higher levels of productivity all around, and a broad, effective assault against the most important stumbling blocks.

It is not easy to resolve all the issues that Philippine industrialization policy has to grapple with. Indeed, these issues have been confronting the Philippines for more than a decade now. It may well be a weakness of Philippine policy making that basic issues are not immediately put in black and white and are consequently not met with forthrightness. While the policies actually carried out show a great deal of continuity, and while there appears to be a commendable realism in combining sociopolitical facts with economic demands, the resulting growth and structural change in industry leave much to be desired. Indeed, few are satisfied with the Philippine industrial record, and frustration with the country's performance is rising, especially since industrial growth has generally been much faster in the ASEAN nations and the whole East Asian region.

In the next few years, the Philippines may face up to some of the basic issues that have been waiting for more clear-cut resolution. Depending on how they are resolved, Philippine industry may continue to grow at below-potential rates or may at last begin to pick up the momentum it lost a few decades ago. It may therefore be worthwhile to speculate on the probable turn of industrial policy in the Philippines in this decade.

TENDENCIES IN PHILIPPINE INDUSTRIAL POLICY

The statements made here are necessarily speculative and probabilistic. They are based on current policy thinking, which has taken shape largely in reaction to perceived problems and thus is likely to persist even if there are changes in the official personalities that influence industrial policy, barring radical changes elsewhere in society.

Trade Liberalization

Trade barriers such as tariffs may be lowered further, and the Philippines may be more willing to go a further distance with respect to intra-ASEAN trade. The Philippines is not likely to lower its tariff rates to the level of Singapore or even Malaysia, however, for the country already has a relatively large industrial base. Moreover, many existing industries will insist on continuing to use the government and its political prerogatives for the protection of their self-interest, which will be equated with the national interest. Indeed, the question is not whether the government will work actively hand in hand with private industry, but whether government leadership will emphasize economically meaningful achievements or pursue more politically motivated goals.

Private industry in the Philippines is highly politicized. Over time, a musical-chairs effect can change the relative closeness of particular business groups to those holding government leadership positions. But the system of close collaboration between economic and political power is likely to continue. Hence, the trade liberalization issue will be resolved in favor of more openness, because of the force of economic need, but the resolution will be diluted by the force of realistic political calculus. The extent of the dilution will be determined by the motivation of the political leadership. If it is oriented more to economic achievements, the economy may be opened much further and Philippine industry may be forced to become more competitive; possibly industrial growth will be higher. But if the leadership is oriented primarily toward holding political power, it may be more timid in disturbing the existing industrial order. The latter alternative is more likely.

Second-Stage Import Substitution

For the past three years, the Philippine government has been supporting eleven major industrial projects as the linchpins of its industrialization program. These projects are: a copper smelter, a fertilizer plant, diesel engines, coco-chemicals, alcogas, six one-million-ton cement plants, an aluminum smelter, petrochemicals, an integrated steel mill, heavy engineering industry, and a pulp and paper plant.

The government has insisted that these projects be oriented towards export. Several would substitute further domestic processing of locally available materials for imports of processed supplies. All would provide a further base for industrialization because of the stimulus they would give to domestic, particularly smaller-scale industries. A few are clearly designed to improve the competitiveness of Philippine industry by raising its productivity. Since these projects are being promoted as the economic environment is gradually being liberalized, the government has been claiming that they meet all the desirable criteria that are most appropriate for the Philippines at this time.

Despite the apparent deep commitment of the Philippine government to all these projects, the road to implementation has been rather rocky. Such rough going had been predicted by the many critics of the program. (In the Philippines, almost any program meets with a great many critics, and this one has not been an exception.)

One problem is that the large size of the projects necessarily makes their viability dependent upon the international economic situation. The export markets that are assumed on paper during the feasibility study stage may shrink dramatically during a period of lower than expected growth. The regional and even the international utilization of competitors' existing capacity in other countries may fall much lower than the project studies assumed. The costs of bringing in equipment and machinery and of putting in place other fixed capital balloon as interest rates rise. Such large projects entail large risks, which are aggravated by the fluctuations in the international market place.

Changes have thus become inevitable. The scale of some projects, such as iron and steel and the aluminum smelter, had to be reduced. The implementation of others had to be delayed, as in the case of the diesel engine, because the project sponsor has doubts about its feasibility. In the case of alcogas, despite government subsidy, the weakness in fuel prices has made it less attractive to go full steam ahead. Because less oil has been tapped and fewer reserves discovered than expected, it is now doubtful that the petrochemicals complex can ever take off. The original plan to put up a full complex where industrial plants could be fabricated has been dropped; instead a smaller project is now being studied for the manufacture of various component parts, so as to increase the local content of industrial plants. Furthermore, because of ecological problems and some doubt about feasibility, the launching of the pulp and paper plant has been long delayed.

Nonetheless, the government has not retreated from its commitment to all eleven major industrial projects. It has been willing to make changes forced upon it, but continues to insist that it wants to pursue all eleven projects as expeditiously as possible.

The determination of the Philippine government should suffice to see many of these projects put in place. Moreover, it is widely held that the Philippines will have to put up most of these industrial projects in any case, since the current industrial structure badly needs them. Much of the argumentation then centers on timing — whether it makes sense to pursue all eleven projects at this time.

Thus far, the government can be complimented for its courage in sticking to the list and its willingness to make changes when necessary. Even if the facts of the marketplace have so far proven the critics right, and even if the business prudence and financial realism of the multinational corporations and lending institutions involved are retarding the government's implementation schedule, most of the projects will go through in the end. They may be smaller than planned. They may not be built on schedule. But many of them will be there.

These large-scale projects will use up a considerable percentage of financial resources available to the country. For cosmetic balance, small and medium-scale industries will be promoted through funding channeled through local politicians to guarantee that the funds will get down to the grassroots.

Much of private industry is cynical about both the major projects and the small industry program. The big industrial projects are carried out mainly under Philippine government auspices. Major responsibility has been assigned to a ministry that has shown little awareness of the dangers of state enterprises. While the major projects have not been planned as a pure state enterprise, for operational purposes they are coming out with strong state control. On the other hand, the record of local politicians in disposing of pork-barrel funds with economic effectiveness does not bode well for the success of the village industry program.

The cynicism of the private sector has been translated into a loss of initiative in undertaking investments of its own and a general loss of drive crucial for the entrepreneurial function. This is a negative factor that must be taken into account in assessing the industrial prospects of the Philippines in the next few years.

Economic Liberalization

A little recognized positive trend in policy that can have a beneficial impact on industry is the progressive liberalization of the Philippine economy. Most price controls have been lifted, and while the price control mechanism has not been discarded, it has been largely deactivated under the policy that price ceilings must be temporary and brief. The new sense is that the most effective medium- and long-term price control is production promotion. Furthermore, there is much greater leeway for wage bargaining, interest rate ceilings have been lifted, and there is much less dirt in the float of the exchange rate.

It should now be possible to test whether a more liberalized economic environment encourages the rapid growth and development of small and medium-scale industries. Meanwhile, major readjustments are being imposed on the financial system and by extension on the ownership and control of components of various industries. Government financial institutions are ending up with more control over some business enterprises, and the bigger universal banks will probably become an alternative rallying point or umbrella for the others.

In the next few years, if small and medium-scale industries can prosper under a more liberal economic policy, they can strengthen the industrial base of the whole economy, because they provide an alternative to the bigger industrial enterprises, which government financial institutions and particularly the universal banks are used to dealing with. To the extent that this happens, despite the seeming difficulties of the larger-scale industries, the economic liberalization program will be a positive factor for industrial development.

Export Basis for Industrialization

The Philippines can rely to some extent on its natural and human resources as a basis for further industrialization. In the next few years, however, despite this cushion, there will be a great reliance upon export markets, to which industrially processed nontraditional export products must be sold.

Traditional exports are useful as a crutch and can provide sufficient resources for the existing industries to run up to a limited level of their capacity. Manpower exports provide not only an employment alternative but also a meaningful contribution to the country's foreign exchange earnings. But it is the growth of nontraditional exports that will determine the extent to which Philippine industry can grow and continue.

But banking upon nontraditional exports means going into partnership with foreign businesses, some of which are multinational corporations, whose investments must therefore be attracted to the Philippines. The country may be unable to control the rhetoric against multinational corporations that issues from selected circles of academe, but it has managed to attract their investment money and open opportunities to use their marketing network abroad.

The lack of attractive and realistic alternatives may force the Philippines to work actively and effectively towards attracting foreign investments with the purpose of significantly raising the country's earnings from nontraditional exports of manufactured products.

Productivity

The Philippines is already committed to spending resources on tapping domestically available energy resources and on improving infrastructure facilities. Today it appears that energy dependence on outside sources can not be reduced as dramatically as planners originally hoped.

But the systematic implementation of infrastructure programs is possible.

The country has learned that, despite protestations and official press claims to the contrary, money is not brought in by butterflies, and only so much can be done properly at any given time. It has a choice, therefore, between (a) scaling down the grandiose plans of trying to industrialize all regions to the same extent at the same time and (b) haphazardly providing infrastructure facilities with little functional use.

Under the first alternative, only selected population centers can be chosen to become major industrial sites, where infrastructure facilities must be concentrated. This alternative will not industrialize the whole country within this decade, but it does offer a good chance that a few regional capitals will become attractive industrial sites in lieu of metropolitan Manila. They will become so only if the needed support services—electricity, water, port, telephone, air services, road network—are in place to serve industries.

Under the second alternative, infrastructure facilities would be put in place with no serious regard for their functional and effective support to an industrial center. Since the claims for infrastructure projects are nationwide, while the capability to undertake and complete them is limited, there is the danger that the projects actually completed would not be functionally related to an operating industrial center. As a result, the concentration of industries in metropolitan Manila would continue, and without industrial centers elsewhere, the promotion of small and medium-scale enterprises would be curtailed.

The likely outcome in the next few years is a combination of the two alternatives. A few industrial centers will be pushed through the coordinated provision of infrastructure facilities, but a good proportion of infrastructure projects will still be undertaken according to a grand design of putting industries across the archipelago.

While the prospects for a regional dispersal of Philippine industry are thus not encouraging, the industries in metropolitan Manila, which constitute the bulk of Philippine industry, can at least benefit from the infrastructure projects destined to serve the country's industrial heartland. As a consequence, there should be a positive influence on their productivity within this decade.

In sum, the outlook for policy affecting industry in the Philippines is slightly more favorable than it has been in the past decade. While the full potential for growth and structural change in the industrial sector is not likely to be tapped, policy is likely to encourage a quicker pace for industrial development. Critical factors will be a more liberal trading regime, greater international economic cooperation, more effective regional cooperation both in the Pacific Basin and more particularly in ASEAN, and greater appreciation for the industrial development needs of all countries on the part of private sector organizations.

REFERENCES

Balassa, B. (1980). "The Process of Industrial Development and Alternative Development Strategies." *World Bank Staff Working Paper* No. 438 (October). The John Hopkins University and the World Bank.

Cheetham, R. (1976). *The Philippines: Priorities and Prospects for Development.* Washington, D.C.: International Bank for Reconstruction and Development.

Chenery, H. B. (1979). *Structural Change and Development Policy.* New York: Oxford University Press.

———and M. Syrquin (1977). "A Comparative Analysis of Industrial Growth." Mimeographed. Paper presented at the Fifth World Congress of the International Economic Association on Economic Growth and Resources, Tokyo, August-September.

Estanislao, J. P. (1981). *Economic Growth and Structural Change in the Philippines.* Manila: Center for Research and Communication.

———et al. (1981). "Sources of Industrial Growth in the Philippines, 1956–1978." Manila: Center for Research and Communication.

Griliches, Z., and D. Jorgenson (1967). "The Explanation of Productivity Changes." *Review of Economic Studies* (July): 34–99.

Kim, K. S., and M. Roemer (1979). *Growth and Structural Transformation.* Cambridge, Mass.: Harvard University Press.

Kubo, Y. (1978). "Sources of Growth Decomposition Equations." Mimeographed. World Bank.

———and S. Robinson (1979). "Sources of Industrial Growth and Structural Change: A Comparative Analysis of Eight Countries." Mimeographed. World Bank.

Nadiri, M. (1972). "International Studies of Factor Input and Total Factor Productivity: A Brief Summary," *Review of Income and Wealth:* 129–55.

——— (1974). "Some Approaches to the Theory of Measurement of Total Factor Productivity: A Survey," *Journal of Economic Literature* 8 (December): 1137–71.

Ranis, G. (1974). *Sharing and Development: A Programme of Employment, Equity and Growth for the Philippines.* Geneva: International Labor Office.

Villegas, B. M. (1980). "Philippine Industrial Strategy in the 80's." Economics and Society Series A (February). Manila: Center for Research and Communication.

World Bank (1979). *Industrial Development Strategy and Policies in the Philippines.* Washington, D.C.

Chapter 10

Industrial Policy and Strategies In the Republic of China

Tai-Ying Liu* and Yie-Lang Chan**

THE BACKGROUND OF INDUSTRIAL POLICY

The Republic of China (ROC) in Taiwan currently has one of the most modern and most highly diversified industrial bases in Southeast Asia. This position has been achieved partly as a result of the Chinese natural business instinct, industrial skill, and determination to attain high production standards as soon as possible—supported by early massive technical and financial aid from the United States. Further contributing factors have been the commitment of overseas Chinese, generally skillful planning, and a stimulating mixture of private and state interests. Finally, growth was accelerated by aiming industrial and consumer products primarily at the sophisticated markets in the Western industrialized countries, rather than at the small home market; consequently, standards have been high and cost has been kept competitive.[1]

Until 1965, ROC growth depended very much on generous economic aid from the United States. As that aid ceased, a new era began, with the ROC still prospering. Its economy has gone through a period of rapid, sustained growth, bringing its per capita gross national product (GNP) from $216 in 1965 to $2,378 in 1981. At the same time the structure of the economy has been gradually transformed. In 1952, agriculture

*Taiwan Institute of Economic Research
**National Chung-Hsing University

accounted for as much as 36 percent of net domestic product (NDP), while industry's share was a mere 18 percent. By 1980, agriculture's share had dropped to 9 percent, whereas industry's had risen to 46 percent.[2] A study prepared by the Organization for Economic Cooperation and Development (OECD) includes the ROC among the ten "newly industrializing countries" (NICs) of the world. Moreover, rapid growth has been accompanied by equitable distribution of income.

The Government and the ROC's Economic Planning

Economic planning has a long history in Taiwan. It started in the Japanese colonial period and developed into a sophisticated, effective system under the ROC government. The ROC's economic development over the past three decades has often been described as a miracle. Among the many factors that contributed to this achievement, successful implementation of economic plans is certainly one of the most important.[3]

On the basis of overall four-year goals set by government leaders, the Council for Economic Planning and Development (CEPD) directs the planning process. Various government agencies, often assisted by private academic and business advisers, submit their plans, which are modified and coordinated by the CEPD, and finally reviewed by the Executive Yuan. In addition to plan formulation and promotion, CEPD is also charged with responsibility for coordination, follow-up, and evaluation to achieve effective plan implementation. Thus, it was designed as the equivalent of a general-staff office for economic development to ensure the fulfillment of the functions of economic planning.[4]

These development plans are designed to guide and sustain economic growth, industrial development, trade, investment, and price stability. Included are progress reports, capital requirement and expenditure plans, and forecasts of macro- and microeconomic growth. In essence, the plans set objectives and provide tax incentives, concessionary loans, or other means of encouraging the private sector to implement the government's policy. However, the ROC's economic planning is not compulsory for the various sectors. Rather, it is "indicative planning" within the overall framework of a liberal economic system, so that the independent decisions taken in the large private sector involve a considerable element of uncertainty.

ROC Strategy for Economic Development

Development strategy and supporting measures in the ROC's economic planning for various periods are listed in Table 10-1. During the first two development plans (1953–1956 and 1957–60), the emphasis was

Table 10.1. Development Strategy Goals and Supporting Measures in the ROC's Economic Planning

1953–1960

1. Develop a planned, free economy and promote private enterprise.
2. Implement a "land-to-the tiller" program, promoting industry from a solid base of agriculture.
3. Utilize U.S. aid effectively and develop labor-intensive, import-substituting industries.

1961–1972

1. Set up export processing zones, implement Statute for Encouragement of Investment, and improve investment climate.
2. Reduce protectionist measures and carry out Foreign Exchange Reform.
3. Establish export-oriented industries to create new job opportunities.
4. Implement Program for Accelerating Economic Development.

1973–1982

1. Increase infrastructure investment and eliminate transport bottlenecks (ten and twelve projects).
2. Promote capital- and technology-intensive industries and backward integration by establishing intermediate goods industries.
3. Establish a Science-based Industrial Park and develop basic and heavy industries to improve industrial structure.
4. Promote agricultural mechanization and institutional reform, accelerating rural development and raising farm income.

on creating a domestic industry to produce daily necessities and reduce heavy reliance on imports for such commodities. A series of labor-intensive, import-substituting industries were established in this period. The third, fourth, and fifth four-year plans (1961–1972) stressed production for export; export processing zones and export oriented industries were established. The sixth plan and a six-year economic plan (1973–1975 and 1976–1981) emphasized infrastructure investment and launched the move toward technology-intensive industry with higher value added.

Economic Development in the 1980s

For the 1980s economic and industrial progress is likely to continue and even accelerate, and the ROC can be expected to become a fully industrialized country.

To accomplish this task, the ROC must face a number of adversities, including diplomatic setbacks and continued diplomatic isolation, prolonged worldwide recessions, stiffer competition in overseas markets from developing countries, spiraling energy costs, the vulnerability due to dependence on Middle East oil, adjustments to economic restructuring, rising labor costs, and the possibilities of raw material shortage.[5] To solve these problems, the ROC's Ten-Year Plan (1980–1989) and its

Four-Year Economic Development Plan (1982–1985) propose a series of programs and objectives.

The Ten-Year Plan (1980–1989). Published in early 1980, the Ten-Year Plan has two basic goals: the maintenance of economic stability and the most equitable distribution of national income. Despite the need to adjust to new constraints–rising energy costs, a tight labor market, and a slowdown in international trade–the average rate of real growth during the 1980s is projected at 7.9 percent per year, with the annual rate of inflation at an average of 6 percent. Per capita income is to be raised from $2,282 to approximately $6,000 by 1989. According to government predictions, Taiwan's economy in 1989 will be 2.14 times its 1980 size in real terms.

The solution envisaged by the Ten-Year Plan is a greater emphasis than in the past on energy-saving, high-value-added, capital-intensive ventures–i.e., a policy to reduce demand for scarce resources, like oil and manpower, and to diversify into more sophisticated exports that are less vulnerable to protectionist sentiments. Industry will remain the engine of economic growth; its annual rate of real growth is set at 10 percent for the entire period. The technology-intensive industries are to grow especially fast. According to the plan, their share of total industrial production is to rise from 24 percent initially to 35 percent by the end of the period.

The various sectors' contribution to gross domestic product will change accordingly. The share of manufacturing will rise from 42.8 percent to 47.7 percent, but that of construction from 5.9 percent to only 6 percent. In foreign trade, the annual rate of growth of imports (12.5 percent) will be negligibly higher than that of exports (12.4 percent), but the trade balance for 1989 is still expected to be slightly positive. Special emphasis is placed on greater independence from oil imports, which in 1989 will still amount to about 20 percent of total imports. By the end of the 1980s, 29 percent of energy demand is to be met by nuclear energy.

Growing government participation in the economy, evident in recent years, will continue through the decade. Government consumption is to grow annually by a real 8.8 percent, while private spending will expand by only 7.3 percent a year. Consequently the share of government consumption in GNP will rise from 14.8 percent in 1980 to 17.6 percent in 1989.

The Four-Year Economic Plan (1982–1985). Within the Ten-Year Plan, the CEPD drafted and the Cabinet approved a shorter-term economic plan, which set the average annual real economic growth rate in the ROC at 8 percent for the next four years. Based on the resolution approved at the 12th National Congress of the Kuomintang in March 1981, the plan will give much importance to the civic role in promoting national economic development during the period. The main projections of the plan include the following:

1. Inflation, as measured by the wholesale price index, is set at 7.5 percent annually.
2. GNP will amount to 2,310 billion yuan, with average per capita income reaching about 163,500 yuan ($4,300) in 1985.
3. Export growth will average 10.9 percent annually in real terms, while imports will increase 11.3 percent.
4. Foreign trade is expected to expand gradually, reaching $72.19 billion by 1985, with exports hitting $36.32 billion.
5. Industrial goods should represent 93 percent of all exports.
6. Supply and demand for labor will rise about 2.7 percent, while unemployment will be maintained at 1.3 percent.
7. Industrial construction will be readjusted by setting an 8.5 percent growth rate for the industrial sector and 2.4 percent for agriculture. The service industry will be up 8.3 percent.

In this new four-year economic plan, the CEPD lists highlights of the nation's future economic development as follows:

1. Continue to keep the small favorable balance in two-way trade.
2. Raise the proportion of exports in key industries and maintain appropriate export growth in other industries.
3. Encourage industries to make more investments in capital goods, accelerate equipment renewal and upgrade products, and lower import proportion of agricultural and industrial raw materials in order to bring greater self-sufficiency.
4. Achieve greater elasticity in economic planning and wider, more diverse markets for ROC-made goods.
5. Establish a healthy foreign exchange market and flexible regulations on foreign exchange acquisition.
6. Continue to encourage long-term foreign capital investment so as to develop critical industries and improve the industrial structure.

POLICIES IN INDUSTRIAL DEVELOPMENT

Over the past thirty years, government economic planners and a skilled group of private sector entrepreneurs have developed and effectively implemented a flexible and highly successful industrial strategy. Between 1952 and 1980, industrial output multiplied more than forty times, while industry's share of net domestic product rose from around 18 percent in 1952 to more than 40 percent in 1972 and 45.7 percent in 1980. Manufacturing's share of NDP during the same period went from 10.9 percent to 34.3 percent. Emphasis shifted from primary import substitution in the early 1950s to export promotion in the 1960s, and thereafter toward secondary import substitution.

In the 1960s, growth in manufactured exports, together with rising domestic demand, accelerated the pace of industrialization. The industrial sector's growth rate rose from 10 percent in the 1950s to 20 percent in the 1960s. Textiles, chemicals, electrical machinery, petroleum products, and coal performed strongly. By the mid-1960s, the cotton textile sector, with its unskilled labor orientation, was overtaken by synthetic fibers. The electronics sector, which used imported intermediate items and was strongly export oriented, grew at least 40 percent in real terms annually between 1964 and 1973. The machinery industry became increasingly capital and skill intensive, aiming at the domestic as well as at foreign markets. By the end of the 1960s, growth emphasis had begun to shift again toward skilled labor, technology and capital inflows.[6]

The ROC was hit hard by the oil crisis of 1973, which drove up prices for petroleum, other key commodities, and shipping, and led to raw material and fuel shortages. Wholesale prices increased 23 percent in 1973, pushed by domestic expansion of the money supply. In early 1974, the government reacted quickly to the general downturn in the economy by introducing an economic stabilization program that included restricted credit, a single but substantial price increase for government-controlled goods and services (oil products, power, transportation, alcohol, and tobacco), and fewer import controls.[7]

The ROC was able to adjust quickly to changing political relations with the United States, Western Europe, and Japan. In many cases, the ROC strengthened economic relations with its main trading partners despite political problems.

In the late 1970s, the second oil crisis exposed the ROC's extreme vulnerability to any reduction or cutoff of energy, raw material supplies, and vital markets, but the concentration on exports helped the island weather the storm. From 1976 to 1979, industrial production increased 53.4 percent, and the share of industrial products in total export rose from 87.6 percent to 90.4 percent. In 1979, foreign investment approvals scored a record high of $328.8 million, an increase of 54 percent over the 1978 level.

In the 1980s ROC industry will undergo major rationalization. Industry will grow by an average of 8.5 percent per year in real terms during the new Four-Year Plan for 1982–1985. The CEPD has selected machinery, electrical machinery, transportation equipment (including automobiles), electronics, and information processing as "strategic" industries, earmarked for special support. These sectors are slated to grow at an average annual rate of 14.4 percent, compared with just over 6 percent for nonstrategic industries. The output of the strategic sectors is expected to rise from 26.6 percent of total industrial production in 1981 to 32.8 percent by 1985.

One major aim of industrial policy during the 1980s will be to reduce the economy's vulnerability to external changes, such as rising oil prices, recession in developed countries, dwindling demand for certain products, and protectionism. ROC textile, footwear, and consumer electronics producers, hurt by protectionism in the United States and Europe, will come under government pressure to streamline and modernize operations.

State Role in Industry

Although the state still plays an important role in industrial planning, its share of industrial production has steadily diminished in recent years. The state is now investing substantially in infrastructure and heavy chemical industries, but the overall share of state ownership in industry has declined over the past two decades because of the rapid growth of private enterprise. Public companies' share in industrial production dropped from 56 percent in 1953 to 20.5 percent in 1971, and then further to 18.5 percent in 1979 and 18.2 percent in 1980.

Trade Policy

From 1955 to 1981, ROC exports grew in value from $0.1 billion to $22.54 billion, imports from $0.2 billion to $21.96 billion. According to the CEPD's estimate, the nation's two-way trade will increase from $44.5 billion in 1981 to $72.19 billion in 1985. The annual export growth rate of ROC products and services will be maintained at 10.9 percent a year. Imported products and services will continue to grow at 11.3 percent a year during the 1982–1985 period. The trade surplus will be reduced from $580 million in 1981 to $450 million in 1985 (compared with a $3 billion deficit in 1980). A firm advocate of free trade, the ROC is currently doing business with 158 countries in the world. With 1.2 percent of world trade, it is the twentieth largest trading nation in the world. It ranks eighth among all countries trading with the United States, which is its largest trading partner.[8]

To achieve its ambitious goal of an average annual export growth of 10.9 percent in real terms from 1981–1985, the ROC will have to overcome problems that include: its weakening competitiveness in major export items such as textiles, electronics, and footwear; the international economic stagnation and slack overseas demand for ROC exports; the prevailing trade protectionism, especially the possibility of restrictions by the United States and Europe on imports from the ROC; the effect of a huge trade imbalance ($3 billion in 1980); the ROC's competitive disadvantage vis-a-vis Japan; continued diplomatic isolation, and the changing approaches by the People's Republic of China.

The ROC's continuing commitment to liberalization of its trade policy, its sensitivity to world trends and opinion, and its growing economic maturity are evidenced by the recent reduction of customs duties on 1,719 items. On September 1, 1980, a new two-tier tariff system effectively granted most-favored-nation status to 113 countries and regions that maintain diplomatic or trade ties with the ROC. The change lowered the average overall tariff rate from 39 percent to 30 percent for fiscal 1981.

Despite the reductions, the new average tariff rates of 30 percent still are higher than those of the ROC's major competitors in the region; Japan's tariffs average 3 percent, South Korea's 25 percent. But government plans include a lowering of the average rate to 10 percent by 1983 as well as the elimination of the surcharge added to CIF prices on imports.

The government's policy aims mainly at strengthening the country's bargaining power when seeking favorable reciprocal trade treatment with other countries. The ROC is not party to the General Agreement on Tariffs and Trade (GATT); with growing protectionist sentiment abroad threatening the island's continued economic progress, the government has been forced to take unilateral action, based on GATT models.

Foreign Investment Policy

Foreign investment and aid have been essential elements in directing and sustaining the ROC's economic development. To encourage foreign investment in ROC industrial sectors is one of the policy objectives in the economic development plan. Between 1952 (when the Statute for the Encouragement of Investment was introduced) and the end of June 1981, new foreign investment averaged almost $100 million annually, totaling $2.86 billion in 2,785 projects. This investment supplemented, and then supplanted, the $1.5 billion in project and program assistance received from the United States until 1965.

Investment by foreign nationals and overseas Chinese in the ROC amounted to $396 million in 1981. The 20 percent decline in foreign investment that year was mainly attributable to sluggish investment on the part of overseas Chinese. However, investment by foreign nationals still registered a remarkable 43 percent growth in 1981. Foreign aid and investment provided technology, management, and marketing skills and stimulated industrial expansion, vocational training, and financial reforms.

An industrial district or export processing zone (EPZ) offers good telecommunications, transport, power, and sanitation facilities plus duty-free privileges for imported raw materials. Taiwan's first export processing zone opened at Kaosiung in 1965, followed by Nantze and Taichung in 1969. With a total area of 180 hectares and initial government investment of 470 million yuan, the three EPZs have attracted 298 factories with an accumulated investment of $346 million as of October 1981. Of the total, foreign entrepreneurs invested $259.4 million (75 percent); overseas Chinese invested $34.3 million (9.9 percent); and the remaining $52.3 million (15.1 percent) came from local investors.[9]

The new Science-based Hsinchu Industrial Park set up near Taipei has so far attracted thirty high-technology firms. Seventeen are already in operation. The park offers investors a convenient location, availability of well-trained manpower, tax incentives, and screening procedures. The park is slated to attract fifteen firms annually, reaching its planned capacity of 150–200 companies by the end of the 1980s. During this period, the park will expand from its present 210 hectares to 2,000 hectares.[10]

With rapidly increasing wages in the United States, Europe, and Japan, the ROC's relatively cheap, well-trained, and cooperative labor force, low utility prices, and infrastructure became even more appealing. The sectors that benefited most from foreign investment were electronics and electric appliances (30.8 percent), chemicals/petrochemicals (11.7 percent), nonmetallic minerals (11.6 percent), services (9.3 percent), metals (7 percent), and machinery (6.9 percent).

Investment has mainly come from overseas Chinese (who have contributed almost 35 percent of the total investment from abroad), the United States (29 percent), and Japan (16.9 percent). Most overseas Chinese investment has been concentrated in services, nonmetallic minerals, construction, and textiles. U.S. investors have tended to prefer electronics, chemicals, banking, and insurance. Japanese firms have emphasized electronics, chemicals, and metal processing. There are more than twice as many Japanese projects as U.S. investments, but the U.S. ventures tend to be larger and wholly owned.

During the late 1970s, foreign investors began to shift from labor-intensive, export-oriented industries toward capital- and technology-intensive sectors and manufacturing products for the island's rapidly growing domestic market.

In summary, for political as well as economic reasons, the ROC will become even more receptive to foreign investors. Improved incentives for favored industries can be expected, but industries not on the priority list will find an increasingly cool reception.

Sectors cited by the government for growth potential, and slated for particular emphasis, include (a) steel and its alloys; (b) nonferrous metals, which include aluminum, copper, zinc, lead, and their alloys; (c) chemicals, including petrochemicals, paper and pulp, cement, ceramics, agricultural chemicals, and pharmaceuticals; (d) heavy plant equipment, such as utility boilers, turbine generators, diesel engines, and processing industry equipment; (e) heavy-duty trucks and lightweight automobiles and passenger cars; (f) sophisticated electronic products and instrument and control systems, including telecommunications equipment, semiconductors, and computers; and (g) machine tools, including measuring instruments and precision engineering products.

Technology Transfer

In recent years, Taiwan has stressed the importance of bringing in foreign capital and technologies to help achieve technical breakthroughs in domestic industry. In 1982 the government planned to increase the funds for the development of science and technology to 1.2 percent of GNP.[11]

Taiwan will strive to gain advanced technology, with an emphasis on achieving greater technical independence for local firms, through foreign investments, licensing, outside consultants, government-supported R&D, and training programs. Technology in areas like information, automation, certain capital-intensive industries, and defense-oriented production will be particularly welcome.

The emphasis on international technical exchange and scientific cooperation with other countries is seen in the fact that in just the first few months of 1982, the Republic of China signed technical cooperation accords with Japan, Singapore, and Saudi Arabia.[12] These agreements are aimed at increasing contacts and cooperation with scientists, engineers, technologists, and institutions of research, development, and engineering in these countries, and giving them frequent opportunities to exchange information, experience, ideas, skills, and techniques with their ROC counterparts, so as to attack problems of common interest and make use of special facilities available in both countries. In addition, during the past few years, substantive relations between the ROC and Indonesia have been promoted through industrial, agricultural, and trade cooperation.[13]

As demand for imported technology becomes increasingly sophisticated, the policies of the past face important challenges. Companies have pointed to the need for more clarity and consistency in regulations. Also required are reforms in patent protection, licensing approval procedures, royalty levels, duration of licenses, and approaches in encouraging foreign firms to bring in new technology.

The government has recently drafted a revision of the Trademark Law under which trademark identification will be based on mark design and the wording of trademarks on export products need not be Chinese.

Moves to revise the ROC's patent and trademark laws and to strengthen penalties and enforcement should benefit foreign firms, particularly those in high-technology, chemical, and pharmaceutical sectors. A revised copyright law was implemented in August 1981, while a new patent statute should be made final by 1984. Generally speaking, the government can be expected to make a real effort to clarify and standardize the criteria for technology transfer. Companies may expect policy changes that will be more attractive to suppliers of advanced technology and more appropriate to the ROC's development goals in the 1980s.[14]

Manpower Policy

The increase in the ROC labor force has not kept pace with industrial growth; the past five years have seen sharp declines in the already low unemployment figures.

According to the government's manpower development program for the 1980s, total employment will increase at 2.5 percent a year, but the employment of skilled, technical, and related workers will increase at the much higher rate of 4.5 percent a year.

The annual increase in employment plus the need for replacements will average about one-third of a million. More than 16 percent of these newly employed will have at least a junior-college education, reflecting the growing demand for higher education, particularly in science and engineering. (Only 9.7 percent of the current labor force has attained that educational level.)

Future skilled labor shortages may pose potential problems for companies operating in the ROC. Deficiencies will be most acute in the technology-intensive industries that are targeted for rapid growth during the next decade. According to surveys sponsored by the CEPD, the current shortage of engineers and skilled technicians will grow steadily during the next ten years to an estimated 16,680 persons in 1984 and more than 22,000 by 1989. Almost 23 percent of the demand for these skilled workers will come from the general machinery sector, followed by electrical machinery with 17 percent. Similar shortages are forecast for electronics, civil engineering, and chemicals.

To meet such rising demands, the manpower development program calls for a strengthening of industrial vocational schools and junior colleges of engineering. Existing facilities, curricula, course content, teachers' competence, and cooperative programs are to be improved to permit a more effective response to the needs of industry. The emphasis will be on quality rather than on quantity.

In the meantime, vocational training will be reinforced to provide for the needs of skilled workers. The manpower development program calls for these efforts. Existing training organizations will be expanded and new ones established so that the target of training 15,000 persons a year by the end of the decade can be reached.

Two familiar concerns cloud the labor outlook for foreign firms in the ROC: wage hikes and high turnover rates. Multinationals are mere spectators to escalating manufacturing wages, which increased 15.3 percent in 1978, 20.4 percent in 1979, and 25 percent in 1980. The impetus behind the hikes is Taiwan's tight labor market. The government shows no signs of instituting wage control policy. In fact, a draft Labor Standard Law for protecting workers has been submitted for approval.[15]

The option of tolerating a highly transient labor force to minimize wage increases is viable for only the minority of firms with a limited, predominantly unskilled labor force, however. Training costs, the tight labor market, and diminishing productivity make it impossible for the majority of companies (which need semiskilled, not unskilled workers) to ignore turnover rates. Wage increases above the market average have successfully brought about abrupt reversals in turnover trends.[16]

The ROC and the Region

Among the countries of the Asia/Pacific region, only South Korea maintains official diplomatic relations with the Republic of China. Yet the ROC is playing an increasingly active and visible role in the area. Currently, the government and ROC enterprises are increasingly turning their attention toward Southeast Asia and Australia.

Traditionally, Japan has been the ROC's primary supplier and its second largest trading partner after the United States. Despite occasional disputes over trade imbalances and some political issues, the ROC will continue to rely heavily on Japan for trade, investment, and know-how.

Economic relations between the ROC and the member states of the Association of South East Asian Nations (ASEAN)—Indonesia, Malaysia, the Philippines, Singapore, and Thailand—have expanded. In 1980, two-way trade between ASEAN and the ROC totaled more than $2 billion, with oil-rich Indonesia accounting for about half. In the future, the ROC will try to expand cooperation with ASEAN, not only in increased trade, but also in such fields as natural resource development, technological expertise, and efficient employment of capital.

The ROC already participates in joint projects with Japan, Korea, and ASEAN nations to develop forest and energy resources, and similar arrangements with Australia have been proposed. Looking forward, relations with other Asian countries should strengthen as the newly industrialized countries of Asia—the ROC, Hong Kong, Korea, and Singapore—transfer to developing nations advanced equipment and technology from the United States, Japan, and Europe, modified and adapted in the NICs, in exchange for raw materials and low-technology, labor-intensive goods.[17]

REFERENCES

1. Anton Gälli, "Taiwan: Economic Facts and Trends," Ifo: Institut für Wirtchaftsforschung, 1980.
2. Kwoh-ting Li and Wan-an Yeh, "Economic Planning in the Republic of China," The Institute of Economics, *Academica Sinica*, 11, December 1981.
3. Ibid.
4. Ibid.
5. "Taiwan to 1987," A Business International Multiclient Study, *Business International* Asia/Pacific Ltd, December 1981.
6. Kwoh-ting Li, "Policies and Strategies for Economic Development," *Economic Review* No. 200, ICBC, March-April 1981.
7. T. L. Yu, "Retrospect and Prospect of Industrial Development in Taiwan in 1980's," *Economic Review*, ICBC, July-August 1980.
8. Kwang-shih Chang, "Outlook For the Industrial and Trade Development in the Republic of China," *Economic Review*, ICBC, November-December 1981.
9. "Export Processing Zones in Taiwan, Republic of China," *Economic Review*, no. 98, ICBC, November 1981.
10. "Taiwan's Hsinchu Park: Tempting Invitation to High-Tech Firms," *Business Asia*, June 19, 1981.
11. "Premier Sun Requests Business to Foster Technology," *China Post*, February 12, 1982.
12. Ibid.; "ROC, Saudi Arabia Sign Accord on Scientific, Technological Cooperation," *China Post*, January 12, 1982; "ROC, Japan Sign Technological Cooperation Accord," *China Post*, January 22, 1982.
13. "Sino-Indonesian Economic Ties Growing," *China Post*, January 16, 1982.
14. "Taiwan to 1987."
15. "Draft Labor Standard Law Approved," *China Post*, January 18, 1982.
16. "How Companies Cope with Rising Turnover in Taiwan's Labor Market," *Business Asia*, October 24, 1980.
17. "Taiwan to 1987."

Chapter 11

Industrial Policy and Economic Restructuring In Singapore

*Pang Eng Fong**

INTRODUCTION

Industrial policy, defined broadly as a set of state measures to influence the development of manufacturing firms and their adjustment to changing national and international economic conditions, has a history of only two decades in Singapore. Before self-government in 1959, Singapore functioned essentially as a regional entrepôt. Its industrial sector was small, and colonial efforts to promote industrial development were hampered by a shortage of funds. In 1959, the newly elected government under the People's Action Party (PAP) embarked on a deliberate program of industrialization to expand and diversify the island's economy. It introduced investment incentives, provided protection for import-substituting firms, and initiated development of infrastructure to attract industry.

In the early 1960s, government planning was predicated on access to the market in Peninsular Malaysia, the island's traditional hinterland. In August 1963, after protracted negotiations over the terms of its merger, Singapore gained access to an enlarged domestic market by becoming a constituent state of Malaysia. But Singapore's experiment at integration failed, and it separated from Malaysia to become a sovereign city-state in 1965.[1] After 1965, the government reoriented its development strategy to emphasize export manufacturing led by foreign

*Economic Research Centre, National University of Singapore

firms. This strategy proved remarkably successful, thanks to the boom in world trade in the late 1960s and early 1970s. The oil crisis of 1973 and the world recession that followed broke the republic's growth path. Since the late 1970s, however, the Singapore economy has returned to high growth. In the first two years of the 1980s, despite sluggish growth in most industrial countries, Singapore's growth averaged nearly 10 percent a year, in line with the government's growth target range of 8–10 percent a year set for the 1980s.

INDUSTRIAL POLICY, 1959–1965[2]

Singapore's industrial development since self-government can be divided into three periods. From 1959 to 1965, the emphasis was on the domestic market and import protection. The second period, from 1966 to 1978, was marked by rapid growth in labor-intensive manufacturing exports and economic diversification. The third period began in 1979, when the government announced new measures and incentives to restructure Singapore into a modern industrial economy by 1990.

After the PAP government came to power in 1959, it asked the United Nations to recommend an industrialization program. The UN Mission, led by Dr. Albert Winsemius (who remains a trusted advisor of the government), recommended a strategy of selective import protection to secure the domestic market, antidumping legislation, five-year tax holidays for approved enterprises, liberalization of immigration permits for foreign managers and technicians, expansion of technical and vocational training, machinery to settle industrial disputes, and the establishment of a quasi-government body, the Economic Development Board, to spearhead the promotion of manufacturing investment. The Mission identified the shipbuilding and repairing, metal engineering, electrical equipment, and chemical industries as ones that would make good use of the skills of Singapore workers, had good prospects for expansion, and could capitalize on the island's strategic location in Southeast Asia.

The Mission's program outlined a long-term strategy for industrial development, in which the state was to play a major role in developing infrastructure and ensuring a healthy investment climate. At about the same time that it received the Mission's recommendations, the Singapore government drew up a State Development Plan covering the period 1961–1964, and indicating the type and level of government spending needed to speed up economic growth. The Plan, however, was only moderately successful because of labor unrest and political uncertainty in the early 1960s arising from factionalism in the ruling party and the strained relationship between Singapore and Malaysia, which deterred foreign investment. Consequently, the industrial base expanded less than had been planned. Some diversification of the industrial structure occurred because of international developments. Textile and clothing firms from Hong Kong and Taiwan relocated themselves on the island to gain increased access to developed-country markets, and the long-established oil refining industry expanded because international petroleum firms were seeking out new production centers. Apart from modest product diversification, the first half of the 1960s also saw the creation of efficient state organizations to carry out industrial and social policies.

INDUSTRIAL DEVELOPMENT AND POLICIES, 1966–1978

After its separation from Malaysia, the Singapore government reoriented its strategy to promote export-oriented manufacturing activities. Because its experience with import-substituting industrial development was short and no strong interest groups had developed, it was able to reduce protective tariffs and quota restrictions quickly to promote export-oriented manufacturing. Before its new development strategy could produce results, Singapore was shocked to learn in 1967 that Britain would complete its military pullout from the island by 1971. Thus to the problems of building a viable nation and economy was added the need to step up defense spending and create an additional 40,000 new jobs for people laid off by the pullout.

Fortunately, world economic conditions and state policies welcoming foreign capital and emphasizing competition combined to produce an unprecedented period of double-digit growth from 1966 to 1973. The 1974–1975 world recession knocked Singapore off its high growth path. Since 1976, however, growth has again picked up, despite a slowdown in the world economy, the second oil crisis in 1979, and rising protectionism in developed countries.

Economic growth since independence has derived mainly from the export of goods and services. Exports of goods, dominated in the 1960s and early 1970s by labor-intensive manufactures such as clothing, textiles, footwear, and electronics, are increasingly concentrated in such industries as petroleum refining machinery, shipbuilding and oil rig construction, precision engineering, and chemicals. At the same time, the export of services has expanded with the growth of the transport and communications sector and the financial and business services sector, especially after 1974.

Structural change has accompanied rapid growth. In the 1960s, there was a diversification from import substitution into trade in labor-intensive manufacturing, and in the 1970s a further diversification into trade in services, namely tourism, transport and communications, and financial and business services.

Rapid growth since 1965 has greatly transformed the labor market. Unemployment, which stood at over 10 percent in the early 1960s, fell steadily during the late 1960s and early 1970s, when full employment was reached. The 1974–1975 recession raised the unemployment rate marginally. Since 1976, the labor market has tightened with the inflow of new labor-intensive manufacturing firms from industrial countries, especially Japan. By 1979, the labor market was overheated, leading to rapidly rising wages and widespread labor shortages.

Since independence, with the exception of the 1974–1975 recession period and its aftermath, manufacturing has been the fastest-growing sector of the economy, with annual growth rates in output of between 20–25 percent. Manufacturing now employs more people than any other sector, contributes the most of all sectors to gross domestic product (GDP), and exports two-thirds of its output. The industrial composition of its output has changed with growth. In the early 1960s, output was mainly sold locally, and food and printing were the largest industries. In the 1970s, petroleum, transport equipment, and electrical and electronic products were the dominant industries, together accounting for half of manufacturing value added. As a result of the growing export orientation of its manufacturing sector, Singapore is increasingly integrated into the world economy. Its economic fortunes are strongly influenced by investment and technology decisions taken in industrial countries, which are its main export markets and sources of investments.

The experience of the electronics industry is a good example of the impact of industrial decisions taken in developed economies on a stable, low-wage and outward-looking country. In the 1960s, technological and market changes in electronics led to worldwide sourcing and the multinationalization of the industry. Electronics manufacturers developed an international division of labor, locating the manufacture of labor-intensive products and processes in low-wage developing countries while retaining research and development and the manufacture of high-value products in developed countries. Because of its stability, its large pool of low-wage labor, and its openness to foreign investment, Singapore became in the late 1960s a favored offshore location for electronic multinational companies headquartered in North America, Western Europe, and Japan. American semiconductor multinational companies led the way, followed by European and Japanese component manufacturers. Since the late 1960s, Singapore has developed into a major regional and world manufacturing center for the international electronics industry.

Over the years, the electronics industry in Singapore has been upgrading its activities into higher-value and more skill- and technology-intensive products and processes. Since the late 1970s, both local and foreign electronics manufacturers have begun transferring labor-intensive assembly activities out of Singapore to Malaysia and other neighboring countries. Processes remaining in Singapore have been increasingly automated and mechanized. At the same time, multinational firms have been moving new, higher-value product lines from their headquarters to Singapore in response to world product competition and favorable domestic conditions.

Favorable external conditions contributed to Singapore's rapid industrial expansion. But the country would not have been able to take advantage of these conditions had the state not introduced policies to influence the structure of the manufacturing sector. After independence, the government consolidated the industrial investment incentives first introduced in 1959 and also introduced new ones. Besides providing five-year tax holidays for designated pioneer enterprises, it introduced a concessionary tax rate of 4 percent on approved export profits and a 20 percent concessionary tax rate on payments to foreigners of royalties, technical assistance fees, and research and development contributions. (The company tax rate is normally 40 percent.) In addition, it exempted from tax the interest earnings on approved foreign loans and allowed manufacturers double tax deductions for export promotion expenses and accelerated depreciation allowances. The objective of these incentives in the 1960s was to attract investment, especially foreign investment, in labor-intensive industries.

The rapid success of export industrialization and mass employment creation led to a change in industrial policy as early as 1970. The original strategy of promoting labor-intensive industries was replaced by one that encouraged investments in more skill- and capital-intensive industries. But this policy was relaxed following the recession of the mid-1970s.

These additional incentives were not the only or even the most important factor attracting investors to Singapore. The government also expanded industrial facilities. In 1968 the Economic Development Board, which had been established in 1960 to provide a wide range of services to investors, was restructured. The Board retained its investment promotion and evaluation functions, but new institutions were created to take over its other functions. The Development Bank of Singapore took charge of industrial financing, the Jurong Town Corporation handled industrial estate development, and the Singapore Institute of Standards and Industrial Research provided industrial consultancy services.

The government also took steps to ensure industrial peace and expand the supply of trained manpower for industry. The Employment Act and the Industrial Relations (Amendment) Act of 1968 set limits on negotiable fringe benefits and defined as nonnegotiable such issues as hiring, promotion, transfer, layoff, and dismissal. Together with Singapore's other attractions—openness to foreign investment, political stability, excellent location and infrastructure, honest government, and so on—these incentives and controls helped to create a healthy investment climate favoring labor-intensive investments.

INDUSTRIAL POLICY AND RESTRUCTURING SINCE 1979

In 1979, the government launched what was termed a "Second Industrial Revolution" to restructure the economy into one based on high-value activities. The rationale for this strategy is detailed in Singapore's indicative development plan for the 1980s, which sets a GDP growth target of 8-10 percent a year and identifies manufacturing, trade, tourism, transport and communication, and "brain" services (including financial, medical and architectural services) as the five pillars of growth.[3] Both internal and external factors prompted the restructuring strategy. Internally, the economy was experiencing widespread labor shortages, which were likely to become more severe because of the diminishing pool of new labor force entrants.

Politically, a strategy of relying on labor-intensive activities could not satisfy workers' rising expectations for better pay, which could only be met by the creation of more skilled jobs. Externally, Singapore was beginning to lose its competitive advantage in producing labor-intensive manufactures to other developing countries, and faced the ever-present threat of protectionism in developed-country markets. Moreover, the industrial countries were likely to continue growing slowly in the 1980s, and Singapore had to develop new markets in developing countries.

To encourage firms to upgrade and mechanize, the government adopted three sets of policies: a wage correction policy designed to raise labor costs to promote efficient use of scarce labor; additional investment incentives for desired industries; and expansion of training and educational facilities for new labor force entrants and workers in industry.

Wage Correction Policy

Before 1972, market forces determined wages in Singapore. To ensure orderly wage changes, the government set up a tripartite National Wages Council in that year. Since then, voluntary wage guidelines have strongly influenced wage increases in both the private and public sectors.

During the world recession of the mid-1970s and in the few years immediately thereafter, the Council recommended modest wage increases to ensure the competitiveness of the labor-intensive export industries. These guidelines, while helping to keep exports competitive, did not encourage firms to use labor efficiently or to upgrade their operations quickly. As a result, labor shortages intensified and manufacturing productivity suffered, growing by an average of only 2–3 percent a year until 1979. In that year the Council began a three-year wage correction policy; that is, it recommended high wage increases, averaging 20 percent a year, to restore wages to market levels. In 1980, it introduced the idea of a second-tier payment to reward above-average workers. The government has indicated that in the future, wage changes will be closely tied to productivity gains. The Council's guidelines will be more flexible, to reflect more fully than in the past the diversity of productivity gains among firms.

The wage correction policy has apparently met with some success. Employment creation in the economy, especially the manufacturing sector, has slowed. National productivity gains have doubled, averaging over 5 percent a year since 1979. Foreign investment commitments, mostly in desired industries, have risen to record levels, despite the large wage increases. At the same time, there has been a resurgence of local manufacturing investment commitments.

Industrial Investment Incentives

To stimulate investment in desired high-value activities, the government has modified old fiscal incentives and introduced new ones.[4] The basic tax incentive was, and still is, pioneer status, which provides for zero tax on company profits for five to ten years, depending on such factors as the level of investment, its capital and skill intensity, and the extent of its linkages. Pioneer status can be granted to deserving projects even if the investment is less than $1 million. The period of tax exemption can be longer than ten years for projects involving advanced technology and long gestation periods.

A second important incentive, first introduced in 1967 and liberalized since then, encourages exports by taxing approved export profits at 4 percent rather than at the usual rate of 40 percent. The normal incentive period is five years, but it can be as long as fifteen years for projects with fixed capital expenditure of over $150 million, provided Singapore permanent residents own at least 50 percent of the paid-up capital.

Firms that do not qualify for pioneer status or export incentives can obtain an investment allowance under which an approved manufacturing or technical servicing project receives a tax credit of up to 50 percent of new fixed investment in plant, machinery, and factory buildings. The credit can be set off against the profits of the company for the year in which the capital spending takes place.

In addition to the pioneer status, export incentive, and investment allowance schemes, the government has a variety of other incentives to encourage plant expansion, automation, computerization, and R&D spending. Capital equipment can be completely written off in five to ten years; plant and machinery for R&D can be completely depreciated in three years; double deduction of R&D spending is permitted; lump-sum payments for manufacturing licenses can be capitalized and written off in five years; and an investment allowance of up to 50 percent of the capital investment in research and development is available.

A Capital Assistance Scheme was set up in 1975 with a budget of $100 million to provide equity and/or loan capital to industrial investors with specialized projects that will benefit Singapore economically and technologically. About half the budget has so far been disbursed. The Economic Development Board, which is in charge of the Capital Assistance Scheme, also has a Small Industries Finance Scheme to help small firms to upgrade their operations and diversify their product lines. Local firms are also eligible for small development grants under a Product Development Assistance Scheme, another scheme administered by the Board.

By legislation, all the incentives schemes except those aimed specifically at small or local firms are available to both local and foreign enterprises. In practice, however, foreign enterprises, which dominate the manufacturing sector in terms of value added and exports, have benefited more than local firms, because of their larger investments and higher technology levels.

Compared with those of the 1960s and 1970s, investment incentives are now more selectively awarded. Favored projects are those that are technologically sophisticated and also capital and skill intensive. The Economic Development Board has drawn up a list of industries for priority development, which includes those making such products as computers, instrumentation and industrial controls, telecommunication equipment, advanced electronic components, solar cells and optical fibers, precision machine tools, photographic and optical instruments, medical instruments and devices, office equipment, industrial machinery including robotics, oilfield equipment, aircraft components, automotive components, ship machinery, diesel engines, mining equipment, specialty industrial chemicals, pharmaceuticals, and engineering plastics.[5]

Besides planning to attract investment in priority industries to broaden Singapore's industrial base, the government is encouraging local manufacturers who cannot pay market wages to relocate to other countries. The relocation of such firms, it believes, will help neighboring economies and give industries in Singapore ready access to key inputs. It will also encourage, with loans and incentives, the expansion of supporting industries to link up with high-value-added industries. In short, the Singapore government is clear about the industries it wants and the adjustment that both local and foreign firms must make to remain viable in Singapore in the future.

Expansion of Training and Educational Facilities

A third vital component of the restructuring strategy is the accelerated expansion of educational and training opportunities, not only for new labor force entrants but also for workers already in industry. With the emphasis on skill and technology upgrading, postsecondary technical and professional training has become a high priority of government policy. Since 1979, the National University of Singapore has sharply increased enrollments in its professional faculties, particularly engineering. A new Nanyang Technological Institute will open in 1983 to train practically oriented engineers for industry. The Singapore Polytechnic, Ngee Ann Technical College, and the Vocational and Industrial Training Board will significantly increase the numbers of technicians and skilled workers for industry in the 1980s. Government planners project that the various formal postsecondary institutions will need to enroll as many as 35,000 students each year during the 1980s if the growth targets for manufacturing and the economy are to be met. This number exceeds the available pool of qualified Singaporean school-leavers, who are already in short supply relative to the number of available training places. To meet intake targets, the government will admit increasingly large numbers of foreign students, mostly Malaysians, who will be required to work in Singapore for varying periods of time after their graduation.

In addition to the formal postsecondary institutions, the government has developed, in some cases jointly with private industry or with the support of industrial countries, many practically oriented industrial training institutes. The Economic Development Board runs four Joint

Industry Training Centres, three of them established jointly with international companies (Philips, Tata, and Rollei) and the fourth with the Japanese government. Two other training institutes, with the German and French governments respectively, are also being set up. Plans are also under way to develop new training and retraining programs to upgrade the skills of the one million persons already in the labor force.

In the past, manufacturing firms relied mostly on self-financed in-plant training. Skilled workers might be sent overseas for training and work experience, for example, in the parent plants of multinational companies. The Economic Development Board subsidizes some of these training programs through its Overseas Training Scheme, Industrial Development Scholarship, and Industrial Training Grant Scheme.

In 1979, as part of its restructuring strategy, the government set up a Skills Development Fund to upgrade skills and retrain workers who might be made redundant by the restructuring strategy. Firms most contribute to the Fund an amount equal to 4 percent of the wages of their employees earning less than $750 a month, but they can apply for grants to cover as much as 70 percent of approved training costs. Since 1979, the contributions collected by the Fund have accumulated rapidly, partly because the wage correction policy did not cause any massive retrenchments and partly because of bureaucratic delays in processing applications for training grants. The purposes of the Fund have recently been widened to permit grants and loans for mechanization and technological upgrading.

Government training and educational programs are not restricted to Singapore citizens. Because of the declining number of qualified Singaporeans, the government has increased the intake of foreign students into postsecondary and tertiary institutions. At the same time, it is encouraging foreign skilled and professional (but not unskilled) workers to settle in Singapore. Its long-term policy is to expand the locally available supply of skills needed for a modern industrial economy, and not to become dependent on unskilled foreign labor. High dependence on unskilled foreign workers, it believes, not only retards industrial restructuring but also creates problems of integration, especially if the foreign labor is imported from countries that differ from Singapore in their social and cultural characteristics.

ROLE OF STATE

The state plays a highly interventionist role in Singapore's economic development. The ruling party, in power since 1959, wields complete political control through its near exclusive representation in parliament (all but one of the seventy-five members of parliament belong to the ruling party) and its de facto control of the government bureaucracy, the labor movement (through the National Trades Union Congress, whose secretary-general is also a minister without portfolio), and local community organizations. Development policy is decided by the government in limited consultations with groups of workers, employers, and other citizens.

Though it intervenes heavily in the economy and society, the government believes strongly in free enterprise and open competition. It has strived since independence to make the Singapore economy more and more open to foreign participation, especially by multinational companies, which it sees as crucial in helping the island to overcome its handicaps of size, small domestic market, and lack of natural resources. In consequence, there are few government controls on private investment, including foreign investment, which is allowed to enter any industry except telecommunications, utilities, and other infrastructure services provided by state agencies.

Since Singapore is a free port, there are few import duties; those that exist serve mostly to raise revenue and to curb consumption of certain "luxury" items, such as tobacco, alcohol, and motor vehicles. Protective duties apply to only a few items, including clothing, nonessential foodstuffs, and refrigerators. Domestic price controls exist only for a few items such as sugar, steel, and cement. Licenses are required only for the importation of rice, refined sugar, chlorine, and refrigerators, and for imports from a few socialist countries. There are no export duties, and export licensing applies to only a small number of items.

In the manufacturing sector, apart from minor health, safety, and pollution regulations, and regulations on the employment of labor and industrial relations, there are virtually no controls on private enterprise and investment. There are no antimonopoly laws, no approval or licensing process for foreign or local investments, no technology transfer controls or required registration of contracts, no requirements for domestic purchases by foreign firms, and no restrictions on profit or capital repatriation. In short, the Singapore economy is characterized by an absence of restrictions on trade and investment. Government policy is to encourage economic efficiency and quicken the transfer of technology and expertise by helping private industry to adjust to changing international conditions.

Though it subscribes to an economic philosophy of free trade and competition, the government does not behave like the state in a laissez-faire economy. The government actively influences the sectoral allocation of resources and industrial adjustment through its various investment incentive schemes, which grant tax exemptions, write-offs, and other subsidies and allowances to desired investments.

The Singapore government does more than provide infrastructure and incentives to industry. On its own or in partnership with private enterprises or shareholders, it also finances or engages in direct production of goods and services. Government-owned or -managed companies, joint ventures with private companies, and some statutory boards are involved in a wide range of secondary and tertiary activities, including steel manufacturing, oil refining, shipbuilding, shipping, trading, banking, and property development. The government's reasons for participating in direct production are many, but the main one in the early years was to lead the way in large, high-risk projects. The government, however, is not ideologically committed to bailing out unprofitable state enterprises. All its enterprises are market oriented and profit-making, and despite its commitment to private enterprise, it has not divested itself of profitable ventures. State encroachment on traditional private sector areas was strong until the late 1970s. Of late, with the government's emphasis on privatization, it has slowed down and may well be reversed in the future.

Because of its heavy direct and indirect involvement in the economy, the state can exercise considerable leverage on the domestic macroeconomy, beyond the use of conventional public revenue and expenditure instruments. More than half of domestic income passes through government hands in one way or another. The state influences wage changes through the National Wages Council, and construction activity through its own property development activities and controls on the private sector. Through the Monetary Authority of Singapore, a quasi-central bank, it also regulates financial markets and the domestic money supply.

Despite its powers, the government has rarely chosen to manage the economy in the Keynesian countercyclical manner. Since independence, it has consistently had budget surpluses, which have had a deflationary effect on the economy and helped Singapore to maintain a low inflation rate.

Of the three main actors in Singapore's economic system—enterprises, workers, and government—the government is clearly the leader in the development process. It sets development priorities, executes policies, and influences and even directs the decisions and actions of the other two actors. Although foreign enterprises dominate the industrial sector and are strongly represented in other sectors of the economy, they do not have a strong say in economic policy making. Like local enterprises and workers, they respond essentially to government policy initiatives and provide feedback and comments on government policy on an ad hoc basis. Employers' associations—like the Singapore National Employers' Association, Singapore Chinese Chamber of Commerce, Singapore Manufacturers' Association, American Business Council, and employers' groupings of other nationalities—are only indirectly involved in the formulation of economic policy. They are, however, represented on various statutory boards, including the Economic Development Board, Jurong Town Corporation, National Wages Council, and National Productivity Council.

Unlike many countries, Singapore has experienced little conflict between the government and private sector enterprises, mainly because government programs and policies are guided essentially by market forces. The government recognizes the primacy of the private sector in deciding what, how much, how, and for whom to produce, and does not interfere in private sector production and marketing decisions.

There is also little conflict between business and labor, largely because of the government's intermediary role in their relationship. Workers' rights and powers are limited by government legislation and administrative powers, and the government controls and union movement. The government promotes unionization as a means of extending its control over the labor force. Its wage guidelines also remove a potential source of conflict between employers and workers.

The peaceful cooperation of workers with employers and with the government has been achieved by political, economic, and social means. Politically, the ruling party has historically been identified with moderate trade unionism. It influences strongly the appointment of national union leaders. Economically, the workers have gained from rapid development progress, which they see as the result of pragmatic government development policies. The government has thus been able to persuade workers to identify their interests with those of the nation. In particular, it has had no problems selling its restructuring strategy to workers. Those who have been laid off by the strategy's impact on weak, labor-intensive firms have had no difficulty finding alternative employment in Singapore's expanding economy. Socially, workers have benefited from government social subsidies, which have raised real living standards and made it possible for the government to maintain a policy of wage restraint for a long period.

The relationship among the three actors will change somewhat in the future because of the government's new policy to reduce workers' dependence on the state for various social benefits and to decentralize worker-employer relations to the firm level. Workers' dependence on the state may lessen and their dependence on employers increase in the future, but their relationship will still be strongly influenced by the state. As in the past, the government will play the leading role in national economic policy making, including the formulation of industrial policies to quicken Singapore's adjustment to changing international economic conditions.

SINGAPORE AND REGIONAL INDUSTRIAL DEVELOPMENT

In the last few years, as part of its restructuring strategy, Singapore has encouraged low-wage, labor-intensive firms to relocate in neighboring countries where there is still an abundant supply of labor. It views the accelerated development of industries in the region as important to the growth of its own manufacturing and service industries. The more developed its neighbors are, the more Singapore, as the commercial and financial hub of the region, will benefit.

In recent years, many export-manufacturing firms in Singapore have shifted increasingly to service-oriented activities while moving out part of their production facilities to neighboring countries. They now not only manufacture products in Singapore but also serve as regional warehousing, purchasing, servicing, sales, and R&D centers for their plants in the region. The expansion of regionally oriented activities in Singapore by multinational companies indicates that regional integration led by market forces is increasing.

However, regional industrial integration initiated by the Association of Southeast Asian Nations (Indonesia, Malaysia, the Philippines, Singapore, and Thailand) has so far made slow progress. Economic integration has not progressed much beyond the five ASEAN industrial projects, which are joint ASEAN government ventures. Of those five, only the Indonesian area project is on schedule. An agreement on guidelines for industrial complementation has also been signed by the member countries. These guidelines give an expanded role to the private sector in promoting industrial complementation. So far, however, the application of the guidelines has been limited to automotive parts. Regional industrialization through cooperative development of industrial infrastructure, training, and exchange of information and marketing know-how has received little attention.

CONCLUDING REMARKS

Since independence, the objective of Singapore's industrial policies (which may be considered a subset of general development policies) has been to quicken the industrialization process. In the 1960s, the strategy was to attract investors, particularly foreign investors, into labor-intensive export-manufacturing industries. In the 1970s, the emphasis shifted to the promotion of higher-value industries, but this emphasis was played down in the mid- and late 1970s because of the world recession. Since 1979, the government has introduced new industrial policies and expanded investment incentives to upgrade the economy through the establishment and expansion of high-value activities, particularly manufacturing activities. So far the restructuring strategy is working well. Whether Singapore can continue to attract the industries it has identified for priority development remains to be seen. Domestic conditions favoring foreign enterprise and investment are likely to remain unchanged. But there is much uncertainty about regional and international trends that might influence firms in desired industries to relocate themselves in Singapore rather than elsewhere. For this reason, a global perspective on the factors underlying the relocation of industries internationally is useful for the formulation of industrial and economic policies in Singapore.

NOTES

1. For an account of the many conflicts between the government in Singapore and the federal government, see R. S. Milne, "Singapore's Exit from Malaysia: the Consequences of Ambiguity," *Asian Survey* VI:3 (1966), p. 175.
2. This and the next three sections use materials from the following papers: Pang Eng Fong and Linda Lim, "Rapid Growth and Relative Price Stability in a Small Open Economy: The Experience of Singapore," paper read at the Conference on Experience and Lessons of Small Open Economies, Santiago, Chile, November 11-13, 1981; Pang Eng Fong and Linda Lim, "Foreign Labour and Economic Development in Singapore," paper read at Department of Economics and Statistics seminar, National University of Singapore, Singapore, September 17, 1981; Linda Lim and Pang Eng Fong, "Technology Choice and Employment Creation: A Case Study of Three Multinational Enterprises in Singapore," ILO Multinational Enterprises Programme Working Paper No. 16 (1981); and Pang Eng Fong, "Economic Development and the Labour Market in a Newly-Industrializing Country: The Experience of Singapore," *The Developing Economies* XIX:1 (March 1981), pp. 3-16.
3. "Highlights of Singapore's Economic Development Plan for the Eighties," Appendix I of "Towards Higher Achievement," Budget Speech 1981 by Goh Chok Tong, Minister for Trade and Industry (March 1981).
4. For a full list of the various incentives for manufacturing and servicing activities, see Singapore International Chamber of Commerce, *Investor's Guide to the Economic Climate of Singapore* (Singapore: SICC, July 1981), pp. 21-30.
5. The full list of priority industries is given in Appendix A.

APPENDIX A

List of Priority Industries To Be Promoted in the 1980s

Electrical/Electronics

Computers and peripheral equipment and software development
Instrumentation and industrial controls

Telecommunication equipment
Advanced electronic components, including semiconductor wafer fabrication and silicon crystal growing
Power generation and distribution equipment
Electrical motors and switchgear
High-value home appliances
Solar cells and optical fibers

Machinery and Precision Engineering

Conventional, NC/CNC, and other precision machine tools and accessories, metal-cutting and metal-forming machinery, tools and dies
Photographic and optical instruments—e.g., cameras, microscopes, spectographs
Medical instruments and devices—e.g., surgical instruments, dental equipment, diagnostic and patient monitoring apparatus, prosthetic devices
Office equipment—e.g., copiers, typewriters, cash registers, facsimile
Precision measuring tools—e.g., micrometers, comparators—and components—e.g., hydraulic/pneumatic valves, sensors and transducers
Industrial machinery and components—e.g., plastic fabrication machinery, woodworking and textile machinery, robotics

Transport Equipment and Heavy/Basic Metal Engineering

Oilfield equipment and services
Aircraft components—e.g., hydraulic flight control equipment, fuel pumps, avionics
Automotive components—e.g., transmission, clutch, brake assemblies, carburetors, automotive electronics
Industrial process plant fabrication, pumps, compressors, valves
Ship machinery and equipment
Special steels, forging, investment casting, precision sheet metal, and other supporting industries
Diesel engines, turbines, and related components
Mining, construction and agricultural equipment, and related components

Petroleum/Chemicals/Petrochemicals/Plastics

Specialty industrial chemicals
Fine chemicals
Pharmaceuticals
Engineering plastics

Chapter 12

Industrial Policy of South Korea: Past and Future

*Young Yoo**

This chapter describes the industrial policy of South Korea. After a review of past policies and programs, it examines the country's present industrial policy and likely trends within the next five years.

REVIEW OF PAST INDUSTRIAL POLICY

Overview of the South Korean Policy

The economic progress of South Korea during the last two decades or so has been phenomenal. Beginning from a position uncomfortably close to the bottom of the international income scale and without the benefits of significant natural resources, South Korea launched itself on a bold series of economic development plans, which have transformed the nation from a marginally subsistent agricultural economy into one of Asia's major industrial countries. In the twenty-one year period between 1962, when the country's first Five-Year Economic Development Plan started, and 1981, the last year of the Fourth Development Plan, gross national product (GNP) grew from $12.7 billion to $63 billion in 1980 prices, a

* Korea Institute for Industrial Economics and Technology

five-fold increase. GNP per capita at current prices grew from $87 in 1962 to $1,636 in 1981.

Though South Korea's rapid economic growth has clearly been the result of a number of interacting economic, political, and social factors which cannot be easily quantified, certain key factors can be singled out.

Among the tactical factors involved in the nation's remarkable growth, export expansion and an outward-looking strategy played a particularly important role. Indeed, manufactured exports can be called the engine of growth. South Korean exports rose from $55 million in 1962 to $21.3 billion in 1981. Another important factor was the change in the composition of exports. In 1962 primary products accounted for 73 percent of the total value of exports, manufactured products for 27 percent. But by the end of 1981, the share of primary products had declined to 7 percent, while that of manufactured exports rose to 93 percent; heavy and chemical products have been increasingly more important than light manufactured goods.

The rapid economic development of South Korea has been accompanied by a change in the country's industrial structure, transforming it from a largely agricultural society into a semi-industrialized economy in a relatively short time. Highlighting these changes, the share of manufacturing in GNP rose from 14 percent in 1962 to 34.3 percent in 1981, while that of the primary sector declined from 37 percent to 18 percent and that of the social overhead capital, and other services sector rose from 47 percent to 48 percent.

"Industrialization" or "Industrial" Policy

Industrial policy is a rather new policy tool added to the government policy mix, and it is a very broad concept. It can best be understood as government's policy to shape business activity and influence economic growth. It may work through a wide range of policy areas (fiscal, monetary, credit, R & D, and so on) and is geared to a long-term perspective. The concept of industrial policy is usually associated with the long-term economic management of industrialized countries. In other words, for advanced countries, it involves the protection and upgrading of existing industries and the introduction of new ones in the face of domestic and international pressures released by prior stages of industrial development.

But for less developed countries industrial policy has different connotations, because it may entail the classic processes that transform agricultural economies into industrialized economies. These countries must first industrialize their economies before taking measures to upgrade their industrial structure. Thus their industrialization policy is part of grand development strategy and is more general in scope and more historical in time span.

South Korea and other newly industrialized countries are in a peculiar position as far as government policy toward industries is concerned. Having transformed a rural economy into a relatively more industrialized economy, the South Korean government must now take a new perspective on industrial policy in the face of dramatic changes in the international economic environment and the domestic economic slowdown in recent years. In effect, the government is moving from an "industrialization" policy to "industrial policy," by adopting a new approach characterized by long-term structural considerations, greater emphasis on sectoral policies, and more attention to R&D, management, and marketing.

Review of Past Policies and Programs

Industrial policy in South Korea over the last two decades can be divided into four distinct phases of evolution: (a) 1962–1964, (b) 1965–1973, (c) 1974–1979, and (d) 1980 to the present. We will focus on the third and fourth periods, which mark the threshold of the country's transition from "industrialization" to "industrial" policy.

From 1962 to 1964 South Korea pursued an import-substitution policy. Investments were undertaken to replace foreign imports in such areas as cement, oil refining, and fertilizers. During this period the country attained an annual growth rate of 6.9 percent, but at the cost of incurring a substantial degree of inflation. The growth strategy based on import-substitution soon reached its limits however, because of small domestic markets and large capital requirements, as well as foreign exchange constraints, which became increasingly serious following a decline in U.S. aid in the early 1960s. Therefore, Korea adopted an outward-looking industrialization strategy in the mid-1960s.

The second period, from 1965 to 1973, can best be characterized as export-led economic development. During this period the growth of manufactured exports was encouraged by the government. The three industries that received the greatest government support were textiles, clothing, and electronics. To promote exports, the government provided exporters with tax exemption, and an almost unlimited supply of credit at a preferential interest rate. Besides these various export incentives, the government devalued its currency successively to encourage exports and adopted a relatively liberal import policy.

During the third period, from 1973 through 1979, South Korea concentrated its efforts on developing heavy and chemical industry. The aim was partly to carry out import substitution in capital goods and intermediate industrial inputs. Thus 1973 marked a turning point for industrial policy in South Korea. As the emphasis of industrial policy shifted from export promotion toward promotion of the heavy and chemical industry, a number of important changes occurred in the industrial incentive system. A series of preferential tax and credit systems were devised to induce investment in the heavy and chemical industry. The government established a National Investment Fund (NIF) in 1974 to help the entrepreneurs' long-term investment in the industries. The NIF, composed of funds from government subscriptions, various public funds, and savings from banking institutions, is used to finance procurement of land, fixed and working capital, and long-term export finance requirements. Loans are made at a preferential rate, and the interest rate differences are subsidized by the government.

Besides this indirect financing through NIF the government also made substantial direct investments, in the form of infrastructure construction or subscription to important industries. Various tax incentives were also provided in 1974 for the promotion of heavy and chemical industry. Those who invested in "important industries" were given a complete exemption from corporate and income tax for the first three years and a 50 percent exemption for the following two years. The important industries were petrochemicals, shipbuilding, machinery, electronics, steel, nonferrous metals, fertilizer, defense, electric power plant, aircraft, and mining. Since export industries such as textiles, clothing, and shoes were not included in the "important industries," such government policies discriminated in favor of import substitution and against exports.

As a result of various government support policies, there was a rush of investment into the heavy and chemical industries in the latter part of the 1970s. Investments in heavy and chemical industry doubled in real prices between 1977 and 1979 while investment in light industry increased by only 50 percent. Thus the investment in basic metals, machinery, electronics, and shipbuilding exceeded the targets of the Fourth Five-Year Economic Development Plan by the end of 1979. This excessive investment in heavy and chemical industry created some serious structural problems for the economy, thereby contributing to the high rate of inflation in the late 1970s. This in turn helped to erode the international competitiveness of the country's exports.

Structural Problems of South Korean Industry

One of the most serious problems that resulted from the excessive investment in industry was the inflationary pressure exerted on the economy. As a policy preference, loans were extended to heavy and chemical industry projects at interest rates that were negative in real terms, and an excessive demand for funds developed. With the increase in the money supply, prices rose, and workers demanded higher wages. When workers were granted higher wages, export competitiveness suffered. And when the government devalued the currency to restore export competitiveness, the economy experienced a new round of inflationary pressure stemming from the high cost of imports in local currency.

The second serious problem had to do with unbalanced growth among firms and industries. Since funds were allocated to investment in the heavy and chemical industries on a priority basis, investment in other sectors of the economy suffered. In addition, economic power was concentrated in the few industrial groups that were able to undertake such projects.

The third problem had to do with the weakened competitiveness of South Korean industry. As part of the effort to accelerate the development of heavy and chemical industries they were given excessive protection. Furthermore, the extensive government controls and regulations that accompanied policy preference loans to the heavy and chemical industries allowed little room for private initiative and creativity.

As a consequence of the structural problems associated with past industrial policies, among other things, the Korean economy experienced a negative economic growth rate of 5.7 percent in 1980; this was the first experience of negative growth since the introduction of economic development plans in 1962.

INDUSTRIAL POLICIES OF SOUTH KOREA AND STRUCTURAL CHANGES

Although the negative growth of the South Korean economy in 1980 was due in part to the adverse effects of higher international oil prices, domestic unrest, and unusually bad weather, the government realized that the recent recession of the economy was structural rather than cyclical. This led the government to take a new, longer-term perspective on its industrial policy, as can be seen in the present Five-Year Economic and Social Development Plan.

The single most important change in industrial policy during this period so far has been the reduction of the government's role in promoting so-called strategic industries. Investment choices will be left to the initiative of the private sector, and the government will provide only the general framework in which choices will be made by private entrepreneurs in cooperation with their bankers and financiers. That is, industrial policy will aim at reducing preferential treatment for selected industries and at exposing domestic producers to foreign competition in order to enhance their international competitiveness. In line with this policy, and also to provide long-term guidance to the private sector, the government established the Industrial Policy Council, which consists of various economic ministers. The Council is charged with coordinating industrial policies that emerge from different economic ministries, and is headed by the senior economic minister and vice premier of the Economic Planning Board.

The guiding principles for South Korean industrial policy during this period will be: (a) a more efficient allocation of investment resources; (b) attainment of an advanced industrial structure; (c) development of the agricultural industry; and (d) a more rational energy policy. These guidelines have been adopted to help South Korean industries develop more in line with shifting comparative advantages in the world market.

Overall Investment Policies

The top priority during the Fourth Five-Year Economic and Social Development Plan period will be given to investments in energy conservation, technology, and manpower development. The government will attempt both to induce investments in energy-saving industries and to encourage investments for energy conservation, thus substantially reducing the GNP elasticity of energy demand.

Investments for technology and manpower development will receive equally high priority, to enhance the competitiveness of South Korean products and to provide a still better qualified labor force for industries. Top priority will be given to the development of comparative advantages of South Korean products in skill-intensive industries.

Key technologies that will receive increased government support through reinforced tax and financial incentives will include the electronics, fine chemical, and machinery industries, and industrial safety technology and systems development. Meanwhile, more effort will be devoted to the import and proper assimilation of advanced foreign technologies through such activities as expanded technical information services, more overseas training opportunities, and employment of more foreign technicians and engineers.

Sectoral Plans in Manufacturing Industries

Machinery Industry. The machinery industry will be one of the keystones of the fourth period, in the sense that its development will determine the growth pattern of the South Korean economy. The incentive system will thus be reoriented to develop an industry that can compete more effectively in the world market.

In the first place, to promote domestic demand, the current system of producers' credit will be changed to a buyers' credit system by expanding the Procurement Fund for Locally Produced Machinery and Long-Term Export Credit Financing. At the same time, tax incentives to promote use of domestic machinery will be reinforced through expanded tax exemptions, and special depreciation allowances.

Second, to enhance the competitiveness of the industry, the government will strongly encourage the development of the parts industry through expanded tax and financial incentives, increased technical extension services, and specialization. The government will also make every effort to stabilize domestic prices so that interest rates can be lowered smoothly in the future. However, preferential loans will be kept to a minimum.

Shipbuilding capacity will be expanded to meet the rising domestic and export demand from four million gross tons in 1981 to six million gross tons in 1986. The automobile industry will also be expanded, but with the emphasis predominantly on economies of scale through specialization and the subsequent enhancement of capacity utilization.

Electronics Industry. The major task of the electronics industry during the period will be to improve its international competitiveness through technological innovation and development of high-quality new products. In particular, the development of industrial electronic machinery such as semiconductors, computers, and communications equipment will be stressed more than that of consumer electronics.

Research institutes will lead the development of key technologies and expand the base for absorbing foreign technologies. To encourage the introduction of fast-changing technologies, such as that for semiconductors, majority ownership will be permitted to foreign firms.

Concurrently, through enlargement of the domestic telecommunications system and computerization of government administration and business management, sources of domestic demand will be reinforced. Some overseas investments will also be undertaken to exploit the experiences South Korea has accumulated through exports of consumer electronics during the past decade.

Raw Material Industries. The expansion of the steel industry will be geared to the provision of a stable supply to replace imports in the future. The Second Pohang Steel Mill, which will break ground in 1985, will increase annual production by three million metric tons.

The nonferrous metal industry will be more cautiously promoted, taking into consideration the availability of the ores and competitiveness in the world market. Unreasonably high self-sufficiency for nonferrous metals will not be sought in the future.

The completion of the Second Petrochemical Complex at the time of severe recession and the oil price shock in 1979-1980 created serious structural problems for the industry last year. Thus, future development of the industry will be more gradual and perhaps more fragmentary than in the past.

Light Manufacturing Industries. During this period, light manufacturing will continue to be a major export industry, even though its share in total exports is expected to decline. To improve the quality of simple labor-intensive products, the government will encourage replacement of obsolete facilities in the textile industry and development of dyeing technology. Likewise, new products will be developed to meet the ever-changing tastes of foreign consumers, while small-lot production of high quality and high-value-added products will be expanded. To help promote such developments, the government will reinforce information systems about markets and technologies.

Small and Medium-sized Industries. The development of small and medium-sized industries will be one of the most important tasks of industrial policy during the period. To improve the efficiency of these firms, the government plans to enlarge the technical and management extension services, through such organizations as the Small and Medium Industry Promotion Corporation and the Korean Production Technology Service Corporation. In addition, overseas training opportunities will be increased for managers of small and medium-sized firms, and financial support for modernization of their facilities will be expanded.

To promote a balanced development of both large and small firms, specialization of products will be sought for small and medium-sized firms, and efficient vertical integration will be implemented through their cooperation and fair trade practices. A venture capital system will be introduced by such organizations as the Small and Medium Industry Bank, the Long-Term Credit Bank, and the Technology Development Corporation to finance activities of technology-intensive small and medium-sized firms. The financing will mainly take the form of equity investments or convertible bonds, and will be extended to such diverse activities as market surveys, feasibility studies, trial production, and full production of new products.

Changed Industrial Structure and Prospects for Foreign Participation.

Changes in the emphasis of industrial policies are likely to transform the South Korean industrial structure during this period. Thus, the share of manufacturing in GNP will increase from 29.4 percent in 1980 to 34.0 percent in 1986. Within the manufacturing sector, the share of heavy and chemical industry will increase from 54 percent in 1980 to 57 percent in 1986.

The restructuring of South Korean industry will also lead to a change in the composition of exports. The share of light industrial goods in total exports will decrease from 46.2 percent in 1982 to 39.5 percent in 1986. The share of heavy and chemical industrial products in total exports will increase from 44.7 percent to 55.0 percent during the same period. Particular attention will be paid to the growth of exports in machinery, whose share will increase from 23.9 percent to 36.0 percent in 1986. In the meantime, the export growth target is projected to reach $53 billion by 1986 (up from $21 billion in 1981), rising at an annual rate of 20.3 percent during the period 1982 to 1986.

To sustain long-term growth of exports and the economy as a whole, import liberalization is essential, but must be implemented gradually to avoid serious domestic industrial and market disruptions.

For all changes in tariff and other forms of protection, due advance notice will be given; and for products that are not produced locally, the government will reduce tariff rates and at the same time phase out import quotas. To control importation of products that are competitive with domestic products, the government will first replace the present nontariff barriers with high tariffs and then gradually reduce tariff rates.

Imports of technology will also be further liberalized. One way to accelerate the inflow of advanced technology is to promote foreign direct investment, including joint ventures. Accordingly, the government will actively seek the inflow of foreign direct investment through such measures as the establishment of foreign investment promotion offices abroad and further simplification of administrative processes for foreign investors. (In April 1982, the Korea Economic Institute was established in Washington, D.C., to provide information on South Korea's economy and government policies to foreign businessmen.) At the same time the government will make serious efforts to diversify sources of foreign direct investment, since most such investment in the past has come from the United States and Japan. Thus, foreign direct investments from European and Middle Eastern countries, other things being equal, will receive more favorable treatment in terms of tax exemption and ownership.

As the government has placed a priority on restructuring the industrial base of the country, it will actively seek the inflow of foreign direct investment in accordance with its industrial policy priorities. Some industries will be encouraged more than others. The government's criteria and incentive systems will favor:

Large-scale complex projects including metal, machinery, and electronics, which are difficult for a domestic company to undertake alone.

Projects with high inter-industry linkage effects.
Projects with large employment effects.
Technology-intensive small and medium industry products.
Projects necessary to the further development of domestic industry.
Projects with large balance-of-payments effects.
Projects that contribute to the diversification of sources of foreign direct
  investment.

Industries fitting these criteria are classified as "encouraged industries" while others are termed "general industries." The encouraged industries will be given more favorable tax treatment and will be allowed to establish wholly owned subsidiaries.

The encouraged industries that meet these criteria are as follows:

Machinery, metals, electrics, electronics, and chemical industries.
Energy-related projects.
Food processing industry.
Pharmaceutical industry.
Distribution and service industry.
Other industries that the Minister of the Economic Planning Board
  deems necessary to the further development of the domestic
  economy.

For actively promoting the inflow of foreign direct investment, the government will eventually switch from a negative to a positive screen system, in which all foreign investment applications will be automatically approved except in a few restricted cases. To this end, the government will gradually expand the range of industries open to foreign direct investment in the positive system. The general industries will be the first to be liberalized in the transition to the positive system; all foreign investments, including the encouraged industries, will be liberalized by the end of the late 1980s. The adoption of the positive system is part of the government's overall plan to liberalize the inflow of foreign capital and to make the economy more competitive in the world market.

Chapter 13

Swedish Industrial Policy

*Bengt Belfrage and Bengt Molleryd**

Governmental activities related to industrial policy have grown in number in Sweden during the last decade. The measures taken have varied in character depending on the specific sectoral or regional objectives, the levels of technology and the innovation processes, and so forth. The consequences have not always been as anticipated, and the coherence of all the measures is practically impossible to verify.

Given its ad hoc nature, differing in virtually each instance of application, Swedish industrial policy presents a complex picture with intricate connections among the various activities. It is therefore difficult to generalize about governmental support and interventions and their impact on industrial and business practices, especially in their international dimensions.

It has become increasingly apparent since the mid-1970s that Swedish industry is in a period of crisis. This crisis is structural and thus can be expected to be drawn out over time. This was a main conclusion of a study of the competitive potential of Swedish industry conducted by the Royal Swedish Academy of Engineering Sciences (IVA). The study report, entitled "Technical Capability and Industrial Competence," revealed that both domestic and international factors underlie Swedish industry's acute problems. Many of these problems are related to inadequate adjustment to a changing international environment. The dynamics of this environment have created greater demands to adjust while at the same time industry's ability to change has lessened.

* Royal Swedish Academy of Engineering Sciences.

Other recent studies have concluded that substantial structural problems exist in a few industrial sectors in which international competition has grown more intense during last decades. These sectors include mining, iron and steel, shipyards, and textiles. The analysis indicates, however, that conditions are comparatively healthier in the engineering industry, which constitutes 40 percent of total value added in mining and manufacture and over 40 percent of exports. But here also we have problems or problems-to-be. The engineering sector is too small, although it is expected to grow.

Each of these sectors has an important international dimension. But it can hardly be said that Swedish industrial policy pays due regard to its international aspects. Rather industrial policy is developed largely on an ad hoc basis. But because Sweden is an open society and a small economy, closely related to what is happening outside, it is extremely important that it follows national and international economic and technological developments.

These sectors show the strain of internal restructuring as a result of international market changes. Steel's growth has declined over the past ten years; shipyards have declined absolutely; textiles' growth has decreased sharply, as has the wood, paper, and pulp sector; the energy sector has expanded significantly, as has food; the large engineering sector has continued to grow but at a declining rate. These and other circumstances together have produced continued governmental interventions.

The Royal Swedish Academy of Engineering Sciences (IVA) has sponsored several studies related to industrial policies. In 1979 it finished a report on Swedish technical and industrial capability and competitiveness, which included a comprehensive analysis of the industrially oriented R&D system in Sweden. It is now engaged in two internationally oriented studies concerning energy-related engineering and the building construction sector. A third study examined Swedish international and industrial marketing in technology-intensive products, and a fourth reviewed national security and industrial policy. These studies have been the background for a more extensive public discussion of industrial policies, in which IVA has participated. The positions it has reached are outlined below.

PREREQUISITES FOR INDUSTRIAL EXPANSION AND RENEWAL

Strengthening of the Swedish industrial base and structure must come about primarily through efforts of industry itself. With their knowledge of techniques, markets, and business conditions, businesses themselves are best equipped to evaluate and choose areas for renewal and expansion. The nation's policies, administrative apparatus, and so forth must be designed so as to support the capacity of business to expand and renew itself.

THE RANGE OF GOVERNMENT INVOLVEMENT

Through its agencies and other channels, the government influences both directly and indirectly many of the factors that are important for industrial activity and development. The government's domain of responsibility includes the establishment of the framework and conditions for industrial activity and development. Individual firms are then free to make their own decisions within this setting.

The element of time is an important aspect of the process of industrial change and development and, as such, is a key factor in considering the effects of government involvement. For example, measures affecting elementary education will usually take considerable time to exert an effect on industrial development, whereas the impact of financial market policy can be immediate. Both types of effects are important. What is essential to note is that policies differ significantly in the timespan between measure and effect.

DIMENSIONS IN INDUSTRIAL RESTRUCTURING

Industrial research and development has the utmost importance as means to renewal and expansion in industry. Absolute levels of R&D expenditures are low in comparison with other European countries, but Swedish industries are quite R&D intensive. Consequently, Swedish technical knowledge of products and production processes in areas where firms are currently active is on a comparatively high level.

Nevertheless, several factors restrict or impede R&D efforts. The most important is a relatively high cost level compared with international competitors. More efficient production techniques can only partially and temporarily compensate for this disadvantage. Inflexible planning and organization within the firm, as well as isolation from markets, have also often been cited by firms as constituting impediments.

In one of the IVA studies mentioned earlier, marketing was found to constitute a considerable limitation to international expansion. The

Swedish domestic market provides a comparatively small base for firms. Any increase in the international and global orientation of Swedish business will necessarily place greater demands on international contacts and sales channels. These demands are extraordinarily difficult to meet in the short run.

It is important to emphasize the long-term aspects of marketing. To a significant extent, the development of international marketing channels must be viewed as a long-term investment. For example, it took time for Swedish building consultants and building firms to establish themselves in the Middle East and North Africa.

As the international dimension of Swedish business is being developed, the production network must adapt itself to accommodate this change. The network concept and its implications for marketing in technology-intensive products has been developed further in the marketing technology study mentioned earlier.

POTENTIAL FOR EXPANSION AND RENEWAL

After examining the possibilities for developing Sweden's industrial structure, IVA has concluded that competitive production must be expanded within the current industrial structure in the short and medium term. This will require a broadening of existing industrial activities that will complement the present structures. Wholly new business and technological ventures can gain weight in Sweden's production and export structure only in the long run, however.

To any assessment of this type must be attached a strong reservation. The development of new business activities and technology takes time. Efforts of this type cannot guarantee quick results but are nevertheless vital for the economic health of Sweden in the long run. The competence for industry's technical development in the 1990s has to grow from seeds sowed today!

UNIFIED POLICY FOR BUSINESS DEVELOPMENT

A unified policy emphasizing the development of industry and business has not really been pursued in Sweden. Yet such coordination of governmental policy as it affects industry, both directly and indirectly, is important for industrial development. At times isolated measures have been implemented in different areas without taking into consideration the total effect on the general development of industry. In some instances, new political goals and restrictions have been established without concurrently instituting the operative means or methods for establishing priorities among conflicting goals. A large number of examples can be cited from energy, environmental, regional, and labor-market policies. An important partial goal of industrial policy is to represent industry's demands on resource development and use. The government's influence on industrial activity has only to a limited extent been guided by an intention to promote technical development and renewal. In some cases environmental restrictions have been imposed on firms without regard to economic consequences. The consequences for the competitiveness of firms have been considerable.

There has been an increasing tendency for government to introduce regulations affecting the details of production, for example in regard to various types of technical specifications. It is important that necessary regulations be constructed so that technical quality and competitiveness are promoted. For example, it is often preferable to formulate requirements in functional terms. It would then be up to industry to generate and propose technical solutions.

In the longer run, government policy to promote industrial development ought to be directed toward improving the functioning of the market. General policy should be aimed at bringing about a more efficient use of production resources. In the absence of well-functioning markets and reasonable economic balance, short-run measures of an acute nature will be perpetually necessary and will take over.

In areas without functioning markets, policy must be designed so that the development and use of resources reflects society's long-run desires. Education, research, and developmental activities are examples of areas in which the goal of policy must be to see that sufficient scope and quality are achieved.

GENERAL OR SELECTIVE MEASURES?

There are already a large number of instruments available to promote industrial innovation in various ways. General measures are frequently more important than selective ones. These must be complemented, however, by measures of a more selective character to remove specific obstacles obstructing the path toward industrial change and renewal. Yet Swedish experience with selective measures shows that there is often a risk of negative side-effects not apparent at the outset.

To minimize these problems, measures must be evaluated and re-examined on a continual basis.

Support of technical research and development is one of the most important instruments of long-term industrial policy. In larger, established firms research and development are integrated into the firm's total activities. Investments in research and development thus compete with alternative investments in the formation of the firm's long-term strategy. R&D investments of Swedish firms have maintained a high international standard. The rate of increase has slowed down, however, and if allowed to continue, this deceleration will result in stagnation during the early years of the 1980s. Stagnation in the R&D investments of Swedish firms would have serious repercussions for long-run competitiveness.

For several reasons, it is desirable that the government offer comprehensive support of technical R&D with more long-run ramifications, complementing the firm's short-run application-oriented R&D.

A primary goal of R&D is to strengthen the firm's competence within already established technical areas and to prepare the ground for growth in new areas. Swedish investments in long-run-oriented R&D have been insufficient in comparison with those of other countries. For this reason it is of the utmost urgency that support aimed at developing long-run-oriented industrial technical knowledge and competence be both comprehensive and goal oriented. Public support should be directed toward building up fundamental competence. It is important to make sure that the level of basic competence covers an acceptably broad range. Research on the frontiers can be pursued only within a limited number of areas, however. Our goal here has to be fairly broad and thus the main direction should not be markedly commercial; the purpose cannot be to solve our acute industrial problems. Instead, our aim must be to strengthen our capacity to accommodate and generate long-term change.

It is particularly important that the universities, in their planning and in pursuing their activities, strengthen their organizational flexibility and readiness to assimilate and promote the formation of knowledge in new areas of technology. Educational institutions should be prepared to accommodate justifiable demands for increased internationalization. Among other things, the conditions for bringing in foreign instructors and researchers must be radically improved. Possibilities for study abroad should also be improved. In addition, efforts should be made to create a more innovation-oriented atmosphere in education.

At present R&D planning is fragmented at the highest political level, falling within the domain of responsibility of the Ministries of Industry and Education, as well as other ministries. The need for a unified effort has recently intensified and requires close attention by the government.

GOVERNMENT PROCUREMENT AS INDUSTRIAL POLICY

One specific technique for promoting an industry sector is government procurement. The organizational prerequisites for this sort of policy continually shift. Generally, the procurement policy of the national government has had a favorable impact on industrial development. This successful experience cannot be projected directly into local government procurement, however. The organizational forms for procurement by this level of government must thus be examined carefully. Through experimentation more efficient forms for procurement at this level can undoubtedly be developed.

NEWLY ESTABLISHED TECHNOLOGY-BASED FIRMS

Among the more general industrial policy measures, some of the most important are those that improve the climate for innovation and creativity. Support to smaller technology-based firms for financing and dealing with technical administrative functions during the development phase of a project can be of considerable importance.

Small technology-based firms differ from other small firms in a number of ways. There are important differences in their growth and consolidation patterns and need for market contacts. Support forms must thus be differentiated. It is particularly important that supportive measures cover the whole innovation cycle up to the point of market entry and initiation of regular production. "Technology development companies," similar to Small Business Investment Corporations (SBIC) in the United States, should be established by the government, with banks and private business joining in the sensitive development phase and assisting with market entry, organizational problems, and so forth.

DEVELOPMENT SUPPORT FOR SPECIFIC SECTORS

Industrial policy can be most effective by directing support to areas in which Sweden is capable of maintaining a comparative advantage in the future. The defense supply industries have the sort of technical competence that can gain market competitiveness. Increased defense material procurement, even within the framework of given defense budgets, can be useful as a means of promoting future-oriented growth of technical competence within supplier industries.

Another area in which government policy can be directly decisive is energy. Today's energy policy is characterized by extraordinary uncertainty because of changes in the global system, fluctuations in power structures, shifting judgments of the course of technological developments, and so forth. It is important that the government have a clear short- and long-run energy policy. In the absence of a national strategy for the provision of energy, many large energy users, such as municipal power companies, are reluctant to initiate projects involving new technology. Also, it should be stressed that a governmental energy research program is not sufficient by itself to create the conditions necessary to reduce Sweden's oil dependence.

Building construction is a third sector in which social involvement operates through many channels. At present, the building sector is beset with extremely grave economic problems. For both general and economic reasons, a strong increase in building following traditional lines cannot provide a motor for growth within the foreseeable future. If some fundamental problems can be solved, there are substantial possibilities to stimulate growth in the construction industry by consciously directing policy toward the promotion of specialized construction, concentrating on the technical aspects of renovation, energy use, the lifespan of structures, and general installation problems. Investments in structures within the areas of energy and transportation should be initiated as soon as possible by the public sector.

Given the uncertainty of international developments, the framework for long-run industrial policy in Sweden cannot be firmly fixed at any given time.

An important task of industrial policy must be to scan the frontiers of industrial development and contribute to the foresight needed to improve industry's ability to respond to the requirements of various alternatives. Cultural and industrial ties to other countries should be tightened, especially in the fields of R&D and industrial marketing. Some of these international contacts will come through Sweden's foreign representatives and businessmen working abroad. The flow of information and personal contacts between scientists in different countries is also important. Virtually all (99 percent) of our total R&D is carried on outside Sweden: thus it is very important to get information on it, increase our capacity to exchange ideas, technology, and goods.

LABOR'S ROLE

A very important dimension of Swedish industrial development concerns the functioning of labor markets and the relations between business and labor. Sweden has long had good relations between government, labor, and employer organizations. Labor in Sweden is relatively highly organized, and by tradition is highly involved in decision-making processes at several economic levels (firm, industry, national). Although a non-labor government is currently in office in Sweden, the involvement of labor in the business life of the country persists, although, for obvious reasons, it is somewhat weakened. To some extent these relations are institutionalized. To some extent interests and perspectives of the Labor Party and big business also have coincided.

This type of relation is particularly important in a time of industrial restructuring and adaptation, when the demands on labor to relocate and adjust are high. Generally speaking, blue collar unions have taken a more positive attitude toward technical change than have some white collar groups. Blue collar groups have long been exposed to international competition and technical change. Now white collar groups are increasingly influenced by technical changes. Development is in a sense now more dependent on the white collar groups, whose values are a bit different, often more resistant to adjustment.

Chapter 14

National Industrial Strategies
and
International Industrial Mobility:
The Case of Switzerland

Otto Hieronymi,* André Gabus,* and Heik Afheldt**

INDUSTRIAL POLICY

Swiss governments, at both the federal and at the cantonal level, have traditionally pursued policies favorable to economic development. The main objective of these policies has been to provide an environment that allows the harmonious development of industry, services, and agriculture. Swiss economic policies have been highly successful, as witnessed by the level of output (the highest gross domestic product (GDP) per capita among the industrialized countries), domestic price stability (on average the lowest rate of inflation among the countries of the Organization for Economic Cooperation and Development (OECD) in the last ten years), and the low level of unemployment (also the lowest rate among the OECD countries).

In contrast to most of the other OECD countries in Western Europe, Switzerland has had very little or no industrial policy to speak of. Two broad factors have limited the proactive role of Swiss governments in industrial affairs: (a) the liberal economic and political tradition of the country, which spurns direct government intervention in the decision-making process of the private sector, and (b) the vitality and success of the private sector, within Switzerland and abroad, and the healthy state of the Swiss economy in general. The lively federalist political

*Battelle Centres de Recherche, Geneva
**Prognos AG, European Center for Applied Economic Research

tradition of Switzerland has also acted as a brake on the encroachment of government, and especially of the federal government, in industrial decision making.

It would be wrong, however, to assume that the federal and cantonal governments are passive in the economy or that Swiss economic policy is based entirely on the laissez-faire precepts of the nineteenth century. The Swiss authorities at all levels follow economic developments at home and abroad at least as closely as other OECD countries do. Nor is the liberal economic tradition incompatible with an active social and labor market policy. The economic role of the central government, in particular with respect to stabilization policy, is described in amendments to the federal Constitution.

The principal features of Swiss economic policy are the following:

1. The final responsibility for the success or failure of companies rests with the management; government should not get involved in business decisions.
2. Economic policy tends to have an overall rather than sectoral scope (in line with the principle of equality of treatment). The principal areas of government influence are monetary policy, labor market policy, exchange rate policy, foreign trade policy and fiscal policy.
3. Swiss economic policy also includes certain measures in favor of specific regions or sectors, but these are exceptional.
4. The Swiss political system has two distinctive features that are also very important in economic policy making. First, all important policy decisions, and in particular the introduction of new laws, are preceded by a very close and systematic consultation with all organizations, companies, and associations that could be affected by the contemplated measures; this search for a consensus on specific topics increases considerably the effectiveness of economic policy. Second, virtually all important decisions and laws at the federal, cantonal, and municipal levels may be subjected to a referendum or a popular vote; in fact, new laws may be proposed and subjected to popular vote outside the elected legislative bodies.

The crisis of the international economy in the 1970s brought about changes in the objectives and the instruments of Swiss economic policy. In addition to global measures like exchange rate policy, selective measures have been introduced to assist specific areas and industries. Their overall impact has remained rather limited, however, so far.

On the whole Swiss economic policy in recent years has aimed less at providing special assistance to selected industries or companies, and more at securing or maintaining favorable competitive conditions for Swiss firms. These policies have included exchange rate policy, anti-inflationary policy, and agreements and measures aimed at reducing or eliminating trade and payment restrictions or discrimination on Swiss goods and services. A major example is the trade agreement with the European Economic Community, which effectively eliminates trade discrimination against most Swiss products entering the Common Market. Another example is on agreement with the EEC on international insurance.

INDUSTRY STRATEGY

Even among small countries, Switzerland has one of the highest degrees of integration with the world economy. Exports and imports of goods and services account for 30 percent of GDP, and the Swiss economy is also very closely linked to the Western European economies and the rest of the world through the flow of capital and the movement of labor. Numerous foreign industrial and service companies are established in Switzerland, and there is an even stronger Swiss presence abroad through direct investments in manufacturing, distribution, banking and insurance, and other services such as transportation.

A number of large Swiss companies are among the leading multinationals in their respective sectors (food, pharmaceuticals, heavy electric equipment, international banking, insurance, transportation). Switzerland also has many so-called mini-multinationals—relatively small companies that have manufacturing in one or several locations abroad. Such companies, which may have fewer than 1,000 employees overall, have acquired or set up foreign subsidiaries for reasons similar to those of their much larger counterparts; they are trying to reduce production (particularly labor) and distribution costs, to be closer to foreign markets, as well as to acquire new technologies. Mini-multinationals are found in various sectors, including machine tools, other nonelectric and electric equipment, and textiles and clothing.

On average, the twenty-five largest manufacturing companies in Switzerland generate about 68 percent of their total sales abroad, whereas about 73 percent of their staff is employed at foreign locations. The importance of foreign activity decreases with the size of the company; for the 100 largest industrial companies taken together, sales generated abroad amount to almost 60 percent of total sales, while their staff abroad represents 64 percent of the total. The number of staff in foreign subsidiaries of Swiss companies represents about 45 percent of the industrial employment in Switzerland.

These percentages are averages, which, of course, do not fully show the differences among the individual companies or the weight of a company like Nestlé, for example. However, the data also show that manufacturing abroad represents a significant portion of the activity of not only the largest but also the medium-sized Swiss companies. Moreover, a company-by-company comparison also shows that although foreign manufacturing activity is particularly important in some sectors, there is some production abroad in virtually all industrial sectors.

Direct investment abroad is a long-standing feature of the Swiss economy, and the establishment or acquisition of manufacturing facilities abroad has been part of the business strategy of Swiss companies since well before World War II. The internationalization of the production of Swiss companies, however, gained considerable momentum in the 1960s and has continued during the period of slower growth and increased uncertainty since the early 1970s. In geographic terms, the Swiss industrial presence is predominantly in Western Europe and the other OECD countries, especially the United States, but there is also a large Swiss manufacturing activity in the newly industrializing countries.

Several factors have contributed to the internationalization of Swiss industrial production. The growth of the economy in the 1950s and 1960s led to a chronic labor shortage, which could be alleviated only through a huge inflow of foreign labor. Since the mid-1960s increasingly severe restrictions have been placed on the inflow of foreign labor; still, in 1980, foreigners represented about one-third of total Swiss industrial employment. In fact, the tight labor market has probably been the single most important factor encouraging Swiss direct investments abroad in the last fifteen years, and discouraging or limiting foreign direct investments in Switzerland. A related factor has been the relatively high cost of labor. Many companies have tried to transfer at least part of their most labor-intensive production to lower-wage areas.

For many companies an important, and often decisive, reason for manufacturing abroad has been the desire to be closer to specific markets and/or to overcome high tariffs or other obstacles to exports from Switzerland. Geographic distance or transportation costs have been often less important than trade restrictions or the political, social, or even market pressures to have a production facility in order to be able to sell in a given market.

Finally, one should also mention the role of technology transfers in the internationalization of Swiss companies. Production in foreign locations may be a means of acquiring know-how or new technologies, or conversely, of opening up new markets for Swiss technologies.

Notwithstanding frequent complaints about the high costs of production, the lack of suitable land, or the impact of zoning laws, Switzerland remains an attractive location for manufacturing industry on the whole. The unemployment rate in industry is very low. While some foreign multinationals (e.g., General Motors, Goodyear) have closed manufacturing or assembly operations, such decisions were usually part of worldwide rationalization measures, rather than a corporate vote against Switzerland.

Because of the general labor shortage in Switzerland, the control of foreign work permits has become a powerful instrument, particularly for the cantonal governments, in influencing the sectoral pattern of investments and production. Although overall restrictions limit cantonal authorities' flexibility in granting new work permits for promising new investments, virtually all major investment decisions – expansion of existing plants or the creation of new production units – are coordinated with cantonal authorities. This is true for both foreign and Swiss companies investments in Switzerland.

INDUSTRIAL POLICY PROBLEMS AND PERSPECTIVES FOR THE 1980s

The concept of "industrial policy" is still less frequently involved in Switzerland than in other OECD countries. In recent years some have called for a more active economic role on the part of government, even at the sectoral level, but this remains a minority view. The liberal, noninterventionist policy framework is likely to enjoy a broad popular support into the 1980s. Limited changes in the economic order have been suggested in the proposed revision of the Swiss Constitution, but have met with widespread criticism. Thus, short of a major cataclysm, direct government economic intervention will remain fairly limited in Switzerland in the future. To the extent that Switzerland pursues any industrial policy, it will be affected by the considerations outlined below.

First, there is widely shared concern in Switzerland, both in government and in business circles, about the spreading of government intervention in industrial decisions abroad, both in countries that are markets for Swiss products and in countries that are major competitors (OECD countries and newly industrializing countries as well). This preoccupation with the "industrial policies" of other countries is motivated by practical rather than ideological concerns; it is felt that government intervention under various forms of industrial policy results in protection of domestic firms or subsidies to national industries. Experience has shown that these policies are only imperfectly dealt with under the Articles of GATT and other international agreements. The relatively small size of the Swiss economy and the country's generally liberal economic policies make it more difficult for Switzerland to counteract the effects of these policies through negotiations.

Second, efforts to maintain the competitiveness of Swiss industry by checking the rise of costs and prices will remain the central concern of the Swiss authorities with respect to their own economic policies. There are likely to be recurring tensions between exchange rate policy and domestic monetary policy, with the emphasis shifting back and forth between the objective of avoiding an excessive rise in the external value of the currency and the objective of moderating the increase in domestic prices.

Third, the growth of productivity and the adaptation of Swiss industry to changes in demand and competition on world markets are areas that have been largely outside the competence of government in Switzerland. The bulk of R&D spending, for example, is financed by the private sector in Switzerland, and the Swiss government does not have a significant science and technology policy, although in recent years there have been specific measures in favor of selected technologies, such as electronics. Government spending for fundamental and applied research is likely to increase, however, in the 1980s, and new policies (research programs, new institutes) in favor of specific technologies may be introduced in the years to come.

Fourth, because of the country's federalist structure and tradition (and because of low overall unemployment), Swiss economic policy has tended to aim at preventing excessive regional economic differences. The measures that have been adopted in favor of the watch industry have more of a regional than a truly sectoral objective. In the 1980s too, regional policies (including attempts to attract new industries to certain areas of Switzerland) will probably predominate over industrial policies in the narrow sense of the word.

Fifth, because of the size of the country and the interdependence with the rest of the world, foreign economic policy has been and is likely to remain one of the principal Swiss instruments for defending and promoting the interests of the nation's industry. As in the past, Swiss policy will remain liberal and pragmatic in international negotiations.

STRATEGIES IN SELECTED SECTORS

The strategies of Swiss companies in the 1980s will be essentially determined by two broad sets of factors: (a) the search for profits and growth and efforts to reduce costs, and (b) security and attempts to minimize the impact of uncertainty and instability in the world economy on the company's operations.

The specific strategies that are likely to be adopted in line with these considerations will vary from sector to sector, and there may be considerable differences among individual companies within a sector. A common feature of Swiss industry across various sectors is the relatively large share of high-quality and specialized goods in the product range. A major question for the 1980s is whether, under the impact of new competition and new technologies, this characteristic will change or become even more pronounced. Another major issue that is attracting increasing attention in Switzerland is the geographic diversification of Swiss industry: will it continue in the future, partly under the impact of other countries' industrial policies, thus possibly leading to an effective loss of jobs in Switzerland?

The Mechanical Industry and Electronics

The mechanical industry, in the broad sense of the word, has been a highly diversified, very strong sector of the Swiss economy. Part of its dynamism results from its linkages to both the consumer goods industries and electronics. The importance of this relationship is evident in the example of either machine tools or watches.

Investment Goods. Swiss capital goods (machine tools, textile machinery, turbines, and so on) are characterized by a high degree of specialization and high quality. As a result the volume of production is relatively low, whereas the life of the products is usually long. This characteristic has to some extent slowed down the introduction of digital technology to replace electromechanical commands and mechanical controls.

An important question for the future is whether the industry will migrate toward the major centers of digital technology, i.e., California and Japan. And in terms of general strategy, will Swiss companies be able to remain competitive as suppliers of small-series or even of custom-made products? A possible alternative could be an increased emphasis on turnkey projects.

Switzerland is the sixth largest producer of machine tools in the world outside the communist countries. The machine tool industry is very strongly export oriented, and Switzerland's net export of machine tools is the third largest in the world, after the Federal Republic of Germany and Japan. The machine tool industry is very heterogeneous in structure, with many highly specialized small and medium-sized companies. The pace at which electronics have been introduced in this sector has been rather uneven, although it has accelerated in recent years. There is also an awareness that Switzerland will have to play a role in robotics as well if the machine tool industry is to maintain its current strong position.

Consumer Goods. The principal Swiss consumer goods industries are watches and, to a lesser extent, electrical appliances. The watch industry was the first sector in Switzerland to experience the impact of microelectronics. While it has succeeded in resolving the challenge of integrated circuits (by setting its specifications and manufacturing in Switzerland, using American technology), it has not yet been able to solve the problem of assembly. The Swiss watch industry has thus remained a producer of quality watches in the medium- and high-price classes, and has also become a supplier of components to low-wage watch makers in the Far East.

Major questions will confront the watch industry in the future. Can it regain a strong position for cheap watches by introducing automated assembly? Can it find new solutions that will enable it to remain competitive for components? And can automated assembly be introduced for medium-priced watches?

The answers to these questions will determine whether the Swiss watch industry continues to move its production toward lower-cost countries, and whether it can strengthen its position as a supplier of components. In general, the mobility and the overall strategy of the watch industry will depend on its ability to master new technologies and to control its distribution channels.

Chemical Industry. The major branches of the Swiss chemical industry are pharmaceuticals, agrochemicals, dyes, and aromas. Overall, the industry accounts for about 6 percent of Swiss industrial employment, and for almost 9 percent of the value added of industry. While exports account for about 60 percent of production in Switzerland, they represent an even greater share of production by chemical companies.

The Swiss chemical companies have been responsible for over 50 percent of industrial R&D expenditures in Switzerland, a much higher proportion than in other industrialized countries. (R&D spending is over 10 percent of total sales). The R&D activities of the major Basel chemical companies outside Switzerland have also increased in recent years.

The environmental laws in Switzerland are still in the formative stage, but already act as a brake on the possible expansion of chemical production in Switzerland.

It should be noted that Switzerland grants nonreciprocal tariff preferences to developing countries for chemical raw materials.

Textiles and Clothing. For a highly industrialized, high-wage country, Switzerland has a surprisingly important textile and clothing industry. This sector accounts for about 5 percent of total industrial value added, but about 8 percent of industrial employment. Foreign workers account for 50 percent of employment in the textile industry and almost 65 percent in the clothing sector.

Exports, mainly to Europe, represent about one-third of total output, there is also some production by Swiss companies abroad, particularly in other European countries that have lower wages.

The Swiss textile and clothing industry are specialized in high-quality, higher-priced products: in the last five years export prices for clothing were about 50 percent higher than import prices.

In recent years drastic structural changes and a radical modernization have improved the industry's competitive position and business outlook. While employment has been shrinking, the industry still resents the limitations imposed by the existing restrictions on the hiring of foreign workers.

Recently, the government has offered only limited assistance to this sector, such as subsidies for participation in commercial fairs abroad and the partial delaying of Tokyo-round tariff cuts (20 percent instead of 50 percent). There are no quantitative restrictions on imports.

Insurance. Insurance is a worldwide activity, insured risk requiring the widest geographical coverage. Traditionally, Swiss insurers have maintained or developed their business in national protected markets by reinsuring domestic companies. Hence the predominant role of reinsurance for the Swiss insurance industry.

Present trends in developing countries reproduce European history in that each country tends to develop its own national insurance system. To reinsure risks of domestic newly founded companies in those parts of the world is the goal of all leading reinsurance companies in the world. How Swiss reinsurance companies will remain competitive in a very difficult market is one of the major issues facing the Swiss insurance industry.

In contrast to developing countries, Europe has moved toward a common insurance market (by conceding freedom of establishment and freedom of services). Swiss companies, outside the EEC, must adjust to this changing environment, which will eventually concern reinsurance as well.

Finally, financial and monetary factors may affect the still strong position of the Swiss insurance industry. Investment opportunities may well prove to be a limiting factor, at least more so than in the past. Low yields could be detrimental to the currently high solvency margin of the Swiss companies in the long run.

Chapter 15

Industrial Policy in
The United Kingdom

*Stephen Young and Neil Hood**

THE BACKGROUND OF INDUSTRIAL POLICY

British economic performance has been markedly poorer than that of most other industrialized countries over a long period of time. The fundamental problem has been the relatively low level and slow rate of increase in output per capita of the working population. It is not just labor productivity that is low, but total factor productivity as well. This has been an important and continuing influence on price, employment, balance of payments, and investment problems in Britain and on the low rate of growth of living standards of the population. These trends, furthermore, have been accompanied by a 34 percent decline in industrial employment—roughly four million jobs—between 1966 and mid-1981. The scale of that loss has no comparison anywhere else in the world.[1]

In such an environment, economic policy has been in the forefront of debate. But there has been very wide divergence of opinion on the extent to which, and the means by which, government should intervene on both macro- and microeconomic issues. Some argue that the principal need is for a solution to the problems of the macroeconomy and stable macroeconomic policies. Industrial policy, in such circumstances, should attempt merely to remove unnecessary distortions to market forces and to strengthen incentives to enterprise. The other view is that monetary, fiscal, and exchange-rate policies have a role only in managing the level of demand and the balance of payments and have not been

* University of Strathclyde

directed towards innovation and productivity improvements. Industrial policy, by this view, should be more active and interventionist, with the aim of stimulating productivity growth and thereby stemming deindustrialization.

The present Conservative government has perhaps gone further than any other in pursuing the former approach to economic policy, which may be summarized as:

Economic strategy giving the highest priority to reducing inflation.

Supply-side and other policies designed to improve the efficiency of markets and to create a climate in which private enterprise can flourish [e.g., abolition of pay, price, dividend and exchange controls; introduction of measures to encourage the growth of small firms; measures to promote competition in the private sector and nationalized industries; industrial relations measures].

Expansion of the market-oriented sector of the economy by a vigorous programme of privatisation [i.e., handing whole industries or parts of industries back to private sector control].[2]

Specific constructive support for industry in limited areas.

Current Labour Party policy, by comparison, calls for:[3]

Substantial reflation, through, for example, special emphasis on major public investment projects.

National planning, and the introduction of planning machinery to coordinate government intervention.

Planning agreements with major firms in each sector, including multinationals, backed up by sanctions.

Industrial democracy.

Establishment of a publicly owned stake in each important sector of industry and take-back into public control of those sections of industry that have been privatized. Increased public sector role in high technology fields.

Establishment of a Foreign Investment Unit to scrutinize and monitor the effects on the economy of inward and outward investment.

Establishment of import penetration ceilings on an industry-by-industry basis across a broad range of sectors.

In both cases the actual reality of policy may be rather different from the versions quoted above. Experience suggests that politicians often enunciate principles of economic policy, but under the pressure of events act in a diametrically opposed fashion. There remains, nevertheless, a wide gulf between the general economic policy and industrial policy objectives of the two political parties that have governed Britain for the past sixty years; and this lack of consensus extends further to cover, for example, the widely differing approaches favored by industrialists as compared with the trade union movement.

Most objective observers have been highly critical of attempts to formulate and implement industrial policy. They argue, first, that policy has often tended to be "slogan-oriented," revolving around some vague concept such as nationalization, planning, restructuring, or industrial democracy; second, that policy has been changed too frequently, varying according to the party in power and the state of the national economy; and third, that policies have been adopted on an ad hoc basis as governments responded to some short-term or local problem. A related point is that policies have discriminated by sector, with measures focusing on industries in long-term decline (e.g., shipbuilding) or those with well-publicized problems (e.g., machine tools, automobiles), those that are glamorous and related to defense (e.g., electronics), or indeed those that are effective at lobbying. It should also be added that policies have discriminated by firm within sector. In this context Rolls Royce, ICL (Interntional Computers (Holdings) Ltd.), Chrysler UK, and, most spectacularly, British Leyland come immediately to mind.

INDUSTRIAL POLICY IN THE UNITED KINGDOM FROM THE 1960s

Main Policy Areas

Although politicians and others in Britain use the term "industrial policy" very loosely, so that it could encompass virtually all aspects of economic strategy, the term is here applied more conventionally to refer to industrial support and regulatory measures and programs to influence industrial structure and performance. Most observers within Britain would include regional (i.e.,within Britain) measures as an important component of industry policy—including controls over development in particular areas, various financial incentives, provision of advanced factories, and infrastructure investment—but these are not considered here.

Many of the instruments of policy employed in Britain are similar to those used elsewhere in the world. These include monopolies and restrictive practices policies; the use of tax allowances and investment grants to influence capital investment in industry; manpower policy measures relating to labor mobility, industrial training, and market clearing; and policies on industrial innovation. Since much of British industrial policy has tended to be defensive in nature (aimed at job preservation), it is worth noting that by far the largest proportion of government aid for industrial innovation has been allocated to the space and aircraft industries or nuclear power.

Where Britain differs from some other countries is in the importance of public ownership of industry and in the policies pursued toward these industries. Until recently these nationalized industries could be categorized into three main industrial sectors: fuel and power, transport and steel, and a miscellaneous sector (including the Bank of England and the Post Office). Most of these were brought into public ownership immediately after World War II by the labor government. These traditional nationalized industries are of major importance to the performance of the economy as a whole, simply because of their size, level of investment, and central position in the economy. In the late 1960s, for example, the nationalized industries' gross investment accounted for about 22 percent of total U.K. investment. Similarly the Post Office, the National Coal Board, British Rail, and the British Steel Corporation are, or were until recently, the four largest employers in the country. It is perhaps not surprising that the nationalized industries have been treated as a political football in the U.K. Political differences have related to the ownership of these concerns; their objectives and the role they should play in the achievement of broader macro-objectives of economic management; the optimal degree of ministerial control, and so on. According to a recent report, government interventions in the affairs of the nationalized industries increased in the 1960s and 1970s, the effect being "to delay decisions, or to back-date them, to disrupt plans previously agreed, to invalidate criteria for planning and assessing performance, to produce financial deficits, and most important of all, to damage the morale of the management and personnel."[4]

Public ownership of industry goes beyond these traditional sectors to include, for example, the British National Oil Corporation. The BNOC was established as a public sector commercial enterprise in 1976, with the aim of acting "as an all purpose instrument for the implementation of North Sea oil development, production and marketing."[5] In addition, public ownership has been extended into a variety of manufacturing enterprises, especially enterprises in crisis situations. On the other hand, the present Conservation administration came into power with a call for privatization, and by late 1981 the government had completed the sale to the private sector of a majority of shares in British Aerospace and had passed legislation to sell shares in British Airways and the National Freight Company.

Within an industrial policy context, it is fair to say that in recent years Britain has given most attention to the role of public money in the private sector. The interest and concern attaches first to the very large sums of money involved and second to the nature of enterprises that have been the recipients of government money: the latter issue extends further into the whole debate concerning the management of industrial crisis, stemming the tide of deindustrialization, support for winners versus support for losers, and so forth.

To follow and understand the policy developments that have taken place, it is necessary to go back at least as far as the Industrial Expansion Act of 1968, which gave the government powers to provide loans, grants, and guarantees; to underwrite losses; or to subscribe share capital to various categories of projects. The Act was applied first in March 1968 to a government-initiated merger in the computer industry, from which emerged ICL. The Government provided £13.5 million in the form of grants in general support of R&D expenditure and subscribed for 3.5 million £1 shares in International Computers (Holdings) at par. Assistance was also given under the Act to a scheme to establish a major aluminum smelter industry in Britain, as an import-saving project. Other controversial projects included the £100 million loan and credit guarantee arrangement for the Concorde aircraft and loans for the construction of the Queen Elizabeth II.

The Conservative government that was elected in 1970 regarded "disengagement" as its industrial strategy priority, allied to a policy of applying much more stringent tests before granting state support than the former administration had. Yet only three months after this "lame ducks policy" had been articulated, the government announced its intention to take over most of the assets of one of the country's most famous companies, Rolls-Royce, after a spectacular collapse. By this single action the whole strategy had been thrown off course, particularly when other interventions were soon required to support firms in the shipbuilding industry. The government thus found itself moving back to the need to formulate a support policy, expressed in the Conservative Industry Act of 1972. On the question of assistance to industry, it was recognized that there was a need to establish firm and objective criteria for the expenditure of money under this 1972 Act. In an attempt to introduce some logic and predictability into government response to the threat of corporate collapse, a document entitled "Criteria for Assistance to Industry" was produced late in 1975. It was pointed out that while the broad thrust of selective assistance would be to invest in success, there were three types of rescue operations in which the government might appropriately become involved:

A limited number of important undertakings where . . . the Government will intervene to ensure that the capability and as much of the employment as is economically possible is retained (although . . . redundancy and streamlining may be necessary).

A number of cases where it is thought that given a reasonable amount of assistance, the company is capable of viability.

In exceptional cases, assistance to a company in receivership, where a modest contribution may make all the difference between a continuing operation and eventual liquidation.[6]

It is at least arguable that the first of these categories provided the justification for the huge and continuing government involvement in the rescue and restructuring of British Leyland (BL) Ltd., Britain's only indigenous car manufacturer. The shock to the economy of a complete liquidation of BL would have been too great for any government to contemplate. The company was thus taken into public ownership and funds committed against a long-term plan for the company, the end result of which, it is hoped, will be a return to profitability by 1984. The cost to the taxpayer has, of course, been staggering: between 1974 and 1980 the company had a cash deficit of £1.762 billion, financed by grants, borrowings guaranteed by government, and share issues subscribed by government. When this is coupled with the cash flow of at least £1.14 billion that the company has projected it will need for the years 1981–1984, the total cash deficit over eleven years will have been on the order of £3 billion. (During this time BL will have lost around 100,000 workers.[7])

Even if this is justifiable, the same could hardly be said of the rescue operation mounted in the same industry around the same time for Chrysler UK Ltd., the British subsidiary of the Chrysler Corporation. Here the government committed itself to the provision of up to £162.5 million between 1976 and 1979 to cover potential losses and to finance specific capital projects. This followed Chrysler's threat to liquidate the U.K. subsidiary as one of a series of options, which included giving the U.K. company to the government or transferring a majority interest to the government. The deal aroused a storm of protest: the cash came virtually without strings and without any government stake in the operation; long-term viability for the British subsidiary was unlikely; Chrysler UK was foreign owned; and there was enormous resentment of what was seen as a multinational blackmail in extracting government aid.[8]

In this and other rescue packages that followed, the criteria for assistance to industry were seen to be set aside. Government reaction has frequently seemed to be motivated by noneconomic criteria. In the Chrysler case, for example, the rise of Scottish nationalism would have been assisted by closure (the company had a plant in the west of Scotland). So every industrial crisis has tended to produce a unique response, a problem that has become particularly embarrassing since the mid-1970s with the increased incidence of industrial crisis. Nor has the present Conservative government been able to follow its desired hands-off approach to corporate collapse—witness the rescue of ICL in March 1981. As one author has commented: "In the last analysis, none of these interventions was a policy. They were reactions to events, sometimes vigorous or innovative, more often reluctant and despairing expedients, rather than policy."[9]

Institutions in the Policy Process

Since the 1960s, in response to the apparent success of institutions in other countries, Britain has set up a number of bodies concerned with national and sectoral planning and the improvement of industrial performance. In 1962, the National Economic Development Council (NEDC) was established, involving high-level representatives of government, management, and labor. At the same time, Economic Development Committees (EDCs) for individual industries were set up with a similar tripartite composition to consider the problems of particular sectors. Although they are currently in something of a trough in terms of their activity and influence, the very survival of the NEDC, the EDCs, and some Sector Working Parties is evidence of the useful work they have undertaken over a good period of time.

More ambitiously, the Industrial Reorganisation Corporation (IRC) was introduced in 1966 and survived, with the Labor government, until 1970 to encourage concentration and rationalization in industry with the aim of promoting increased efficiency and international competitiveness. The feeling was widespread in Europe at this time that increased firm size was necessary to permit effective competition with the American multinationals. With a capital of £150 million, the IRC was given wide powers and considerable freedom from government control to encourage mergers and rationalization. Among the noteworthy mergers promoted by the IRC were BLMC (later BL), the outcome of a merger between British Motor Holdings and Leyland Motors; Rowntree Mackintosh, formed after the U.S. corporation General Foods had put in a bid for Rowntrees; and RHP (Ransome, Hoffmann, Pollard), formed as a result of the IRC aim to create a major British-owned ball-bearing company.[10] The main criticisms of the IRC were that it concentrated mainly on horizontal mergers and that its objective was to create industrial giants by finding the most efficient firm and merging the rest into it, when the increased size could adversely affect the efficiency of both the key company and the entire group. The IRC became, in addition, a further source of government subsidies to private sector companies.

While the life of the IRC was cut short in 1971, the Labor party in opposition was actively contemplating the establishment of something similar—a state holding company, the National Enterprise Board (NEB). When the NEB was finally set up, its form was a good deal less interventionist than that envisaged by its original proposers. Its major functions were specified as the improvement of industrial efficiency; assistance to companies that were short of funds; the take-over of existing government shareholdings to ensure profitable public enterprise; the promotion of industrial democracy; the purchase of shares of private companies in the open market; and the provision of funds to firms in return for an equity stake. To fulfill these roles it was granted external borrowing rights of £700 million, with a possible extension to £1,000 million.

From the beginning the NEB was handicapped by its role as a holding company for a number of publicly owned firms, particularly BL and Rolls Royce. At the end of 1978, these two companies accounted for 89 percent by value of total NEB shareholdings. Similarly £720 million of the £1,000 million external borrowing limit had been committed by the end of September 1978, of which £510 million had gone to the transferee companies. Fears that the NEB would be used as an instrument to take over successful private firms were thus unfounded; between 1975 and 1978, the NEB acquired thirty-eight companies (excluding the transferees) but in only eight cases did the acquisition cost more than £1 million.

When the new Conservative government came into power in 1979, the NEB was not, as might have been expected, wound up. But its overall remit was reduced and now includes high technology projects, regional investments, and loans of up to £50,000 for small businesses. It is required to work with private sector partners wherever possible, to concentrate on ventures that would not otherwise go ahead, and to sell off its investments as soon as they become profitable. On the other hand, the millstones round the neck of the NEB—BL and Rolls Royce—were transferred to the government's Industry Department; in addition, the NEB's assets in various companies have been sold to raise funds for the Treasury, and there have been a number of other voluntary sales as well as several closures.

The NEB's biggest investment is now that in Inmos, a company set up by the board in 1977 to give Britain an indigenous stake in the microchip business. This company has government and NEB backing of £85 million, the latest tranche of which is being used to build a factory in South Wales, which will operate in parallel with another Inmos facility at Colorado Springs, in the United States. The NEB tried to raise private investment for Inmos during 1980, but had to accept that the project then looked unattractive; it now hopes to privatize the company in 1983/84. The NEB also owns another three much smaller advanced electronics companies, but further major state-owned greenfield projects seem unlikely. More likely are joint ventures with the private sector costing around £3–5 million, with the Board (or more strictly its successor, the British Technology Group) hoping to put in not more than £0.25–1 million to act as a catalyst.[11]

As this discussion indicates, the NEB has never operated as a "controller of the commanding heights," the role originally conceived for it. Under the Labour government, its strategy was hampered by the inclusion of British Leyland and Rolls Royce in its portfolio, and most investment was therefore in smaller companies. While the Conservation administration relieved the NEB of its major problems, it much reduced its funding and activities, essentially treating it as a venture capital agency. Even if there is a gap in the provision of such finance, the fact is that the NEB in such a role can only have a marginal impact on industrial structure and performance in the U.K. and even in providing the very necessary stimulus to indigenous high technology ventures. It is arguable that the IRC was a good deal more successful in its rather clearer role of attempting to promote changes in industrial structure, accompanied sometimes by changes in management, as a means of improving efficiency and international competitiveness.

Sectoral Policy

In the United Kingdom, sectoral policy during the 1970s consisted of two related strands of activity. First, U.K. governments have operated a mild form of indicative planning through the National Economic Development Office (NEDO). The NEDO Sector Working Parties (SWPs) and EDCs for particular industries numbered sixty-one at a maximum and covered a very substantial part of U.K. private manufacturing industry. The principal task of these groups has been to look at the development of their respective sectors, identifying problems and priorities for both private and public sector action. In addition, some have acted as effective pressure groups, tackling issues such as dumping (in industrial electrical equipment); pressing the case for uniform standards through Europe for military work (electronic components); and confronting government with the special needs of their sectors (as in clothing, where the case of Industry Act financial schemes was pressed, as was that for a strengthening of the Multifibre Agreement). Perhaps the most serious limitation of these SWPs has been the lack of effective instruments for implementing their recommendations. At the firm level, the industrial investment decisions may or may not be influenced by the sector view, however sound. At the sector level, the effectiveness of the groups would have been enhanced by the existence of a coherent national industrial policy.

The second strand of sectoral policy represents an attempt on the part of the government to exert a more direct influence on investment policies within sectors. The general aim of these sectoral schemes, which have been operating since 1973, was to improve the efficiency and competitiveness of companies by encouraging new product developments and the investment in contemporary technology. All of the schemes were introduced for a limited period of time and with a specified budget, although in some special cases both the time and financial constraints have been exceeded. The size, industrial spread, and duration of these schemes has varied considerably. The criteria by which industries were chosen to be incorporated within the schemes are not readily determined. They include a mixture of overcapacity sectors (textiles, clothing, and machine tools); newer developing technologies (micro-electronics); sectors where performance was influenced by European Economic Community (EEC) regulations (poultry meat); and those suffering severely from import penetration (footwear). Most of the schemes were organized in terms of clearly specified conditions pertaining to location, timing, types of eligible expenditure, project viability, and so on, with fixed levels of support (around 20–25 percent of eligible expenditure) being generally given to companies complying with the established conditions. Where a selective discretionary element existed in a scheme, a series of parameters were established to guide the allocation of government funds.

A number of these schemes have now been phased out. The remaining annual funding level is now much reduced. Although a number of the schemes have been the subject of government reports evaluating their effectiveness and showing improvements in productivity and competitiveness, there are some obvious problems with support of this type. There is, for example, an element of indiscriminate subsidy involved, and, given the size of some of the schemes, the available assistance is often spread too thin. Again, these schemes have largely adopted the principle of additionality; i.e., to receive support it has to be shown that the project would not have gone ahead (or not so soon or on such a scale) without assistance. This can have the effect of encouraging inflated projects and, with the bunching of applications that is associated with the end of time-limited schemes, can bias against companies starting much-needed projects for fear of prejudicing grant claims. Examples of some of these specific sectoral approaches adopted in Britain are presented as brief cases in the following paragraphs.

Machine Tool Industry.[13] U.K. government activity in this sector dates to the 1930s, when the industry was afforded import protection.

During the postwar period it has been the subject of continued scrutiny, concern being frequently expressed over its structure, performance, and level of innovation. The Machine Tool Industry Scheme (MTIS) was introduced in 1975 with the aim of encouraging the develop of new products and processes. Two kinds of support were offered: (a) loans for the manpower and equipment necessary to design, develop, and market a new machine tool, and (b) grants or loans for the modernization of production facilities. In 1976 the scheme was extended to include firms manufacturing one-off tooling and assembly machines, while a third type of assistance was subsequently brought in to aid the undertaking of studies of efficiency in small and medium-sized companies. The budget was £30 million, but in the end it was not fully taken up because of the effects of the recession on investment plans. A second scheme (Product and Process Development) was introduced in 1977 for the promotion of innovation throughout manufacturing industry, and there was some direct machine tool spin-off from this.

The parallel problems of one company within the industry – Alfred Herbert – should be noted as indicative of another strand of policy. The major share of NEB money invested in machine tools after 1975 was devoted to trying to overcome this company's liquidity problems. Finally bought out by the NEB in 1975, the firm was severely rationalized and received an additional £18.5 million of public investment from 1976–1980; nevertheless it was closed in 1980. Substantial funding had also gone into this company for product innovation, but the strategy of leading the sector through its major operation failed miserably.

In spite of these forms of assistance, the U.K. machine tool industry has continued to pose real problems. There has been little sign of any definite rise in innovation; Britain's share of numeric-controlled production has failed to grow at the same rate as in other countries; and U.K. exports are mainly of standard machine tools, while its imports are largely of high-performance, precision tools.

Electronics and Information Technology. From the mid-1970s the main thrust of U.K. government policy in these areas was exerted through the National Enterprise Board. Charged with developing the U.K. economy, the NEB had not had the opportunity to develop a broad strategy before it found itself with investments in ICL and ownership of Ferranti and Data Recording Instruments (DRI). This immediately established NEB with a presence in mainframe and small computers, electronic systems, integrated circuit manufacture, and computer peripherals.[14] Finding an appropriate strategy for the coordinated development of these activities was, however, only part of the NEB problem of determining an appropriate modus operandi for British activity across this sector. In the event a variety of approaches was adopted. For example, in mainframe computers, ICL was already the largest European producer, and the NEB's role was largely to provide financial support. In contrast DRI was still small by the standards of U.S. peripheral companies and it was considered necessary to promote a joint venture with the U.S.-owned Control Data Corporation in order to gain access to new technology and have sufficient volume to be internationally competitive on costs. Again in the office equipment field, while the major U.K. companies such as GEC and Plessey were pursuing independent strategies, the NEB set up Nexos as a completely new company to bring together the products of many of the smaller U.K. companies, thereby creating a comprehensive and integrated product system.

There was much debate as to the appropriate U.K. government strategy in the microelectronics base technology of silicon chips. Among the issues was whether it was wise to rely on the continued availability of microchips on the world market and to develop "custom" chip production within the United Kingdom. Whereas this view had merits in terms of market size, price, and value added, it posed problems of security of supply. Moreover it was argued that many of the significant technological advances would come through the standard chips; that 80–90 percent of the demand would be for standards; and that there were inherent problems in relying on production from multinational sources. Most U.K. companies remained in the "specials" side of the business, although GEC announced a joint venture with the U.S.-owned Fairchild in 1978 to manufacture standards at a plant in Cheshire. Schlumberger took over Fairchild, however, and this proposal did not come to fruition. Out of all of this the NEB decided to support the establishment of Inmos in April 1978.

To complete this brief review, two other types of U.K. initiative should be mentioned. The Microelectronic Industry Support Scheme is in the relatively early stages of its life. It has a total budget allocation of £70 million and is designed to support a variety of product and application developments in this sector. Allied to this is the second scheme, the Microprocessor Application Project (MAP), which promotes a variety of activities including an extensive program of awareness seminars; crash training programs; grants towards consultant's costs for the feasibility study of a new application; and contributions of 25 percent of the development costs of viable new applications.

* * *

While sectoral policy has existed in various forms in the United Kingdom for a number of years, the strength of commitment to it has varied and the net effect is very limited. Moreover, the period since 1979 has witnessed a dismantling of some of the limited forms that existed, the numbers of both sector working parties and funding schemes having been reduced. At present there is, therefore, almost no government commitment to sectoral planning as such, even though the apparatus continues in skeleton form.

FOREIGN DIRECT INVESTMENT AND TRADE POLICIES

Just as there is little coordination between the various components of domestic industrial policy in the United Kingdom, so there are few links between the planning and implementation of domestic and international policy. However, the principle of liberalization as regards international trade and direct investment has been a guiding theme. And despite an apparently wide divergence of attitudes between the two political parties, policy as pursued has been less subject to radical shifts of direction.

Inward Direct Investment Policy[15]

The United Kingdom is both a major home of and a major host to foreign direct investment (FDI). On the inward FDI side, studies until fairly recently have tended to suggest significant net benefits to the economy, which partly explains the liberal attitudes taken by successive governments. The U.K. interest in maintaining a fairly open world system for its own multinationals is also relevant. Policy has thus focused on methods of attracting foreign-owned multinationals into the country, and a wide range of bodies (national, regional, and local) are active in promoting FDI. In the attraction process, the most powerful weapon is the financial incentives that can be offered to the prospective inward investor. The predominant schemes are related to varying regional needs throughout the country and do not in principle discriminate among investors in terms of nationality. But discretionary finance available under the terms of the Industry Act of 1972 has primarily benefited foreign investors. On occasion very large sums of money have been made available, as in the attraction of a Ford engine plant to Wales and the De Lorean sports car project in Northern Ireland. Such aid is subject to EEC constraints upon the financial packages offered by member states.

On the control/regulatory side a variety of policy instruments are available, but these are mainly "potential" in their nature. Large and politically sensitive foreign direct investments may be subject to performance requirements imposed by the government, although the companies will benefit from the substantial financial assistance payable by the government. A current example is Nissan, which is in the process of negotiating terms for the establishment of a vehicle assembly plant in Britain. The need for a unified, consistent approach has increased, since evidence suggests that multinationals in Britain are producing relatively low-value-added goods and are operating in the sectors that have seen the greatest deterioration in trade performance during the 1970s.

Outward Direct Investment Policy[16]

Traditionally, close controls were placed on the method of financing outward direct investment flows, to ensure that the cost would not fall on the foreign exchange reserves until after equivalent benefits had accrued to the balance of payments through the repatriation of earnings. In the autumn of 1979 these exchange control regulations were completely abolished, a move strongly linked to the expansion of oil production in the North Sea and a desire to ease upward pressure on the exchange rate brought about by the improved balance of payments position. For intra-EEC investment this relaxation was required to fulfill Treaty obligations, and it was also argued that it would help to overcome the apparent U.K. problem of a surplus of investment capital and a shortage of attractive investment opportunities.

In line with their attitudes on inward FDI, the trades unions were strongly opposed to the ending of exchange controls. The unions have argued that possibly one-third of British outward FDI could be competitive with domestic investment (with a consequent loss of jobs at home[17]). In fact there have been no comprehensive investigations of the impact of outward FDI for fifteen years, although in the last few years academic observers have pointed out a number of important trends. These include a large increase in outward investment in high technology sectors such as chemicals and engineering and a decline in the ratio of U.K. exports to Western Europe to the U.K. direct capital stake in the region. This latter point in particular has been interpreted as evidence that the U.K. is becoming less attractive as a production base, and certainly persistent low growth in the U.K. economy has led a number of corporations to declare publicly that their policy was to spread their asset base away from the former emphasis on the British market.

Trade Policy

There is reasonable agreement that for twenty-five years after World War II, "trade policy was a relatively uncontroversial aspect of Government economic policy" in Britain.[18] Since that time, as elsewhere in the world, pressures for interventionism and protectionism have increased. In the United Kingdom particular concern relates to the deterioration in the trade balance for manufactured goods. According to those urging general import controls, the rapid increases in import penetration are the international manifestation of deindustrialization and industrial crisis in Britain. The position, it is argued, is exacerbated by North Sea oil, where the substantial improvement in the current balance of payments because of oil must be matched by a deterioration in the nonoil trade deficit and/or by offsetting net capital exports.

Another set of arguments in favor of trade protection focuses on the view that free trade is not an optimum policy, given the severe constraints on trade allegedly imposed by the Communist bloc, Japan, most less developed countries, and some EEC members. By this view, the country that adopts free trade policies allows its industrial structure to be determined by others. Some have gone further to argue that non-Western traditions have rocked the trade boat. And specifically there are fears that British manufacturers may abandon down-market and simple assembly operations to the newly industrializing countries (NICs) only to find they cannot compete in more advanced goods with U.S. and Japanese producers. And "if Britain's industrial performance continues to decline in international terms it will be the first of the major industrial countries to cross paths with the NICs which are on the way up."[19]

Those who see a need to continue Britain's fairly liberal, free-trading traditions tend to highlight the international links of the British economy and the point that over 30 percent of U.K. gross national product is exported. For this reason and because the country has relatively few resources apart from coal and oil, it is highly vulnerable to retaliatory action. The "re-spending effect," applying particularly to developing countries, is also noted. Finally, many would suggest that import controls are more likely to cause "degeneration" than "re-generation."

To date the case for general or wide-ranging import controls has been resisted, although a change of government in 1984 could alter this position. Nevertheless, Britain has played a role in seeking a more restrictive renegotiation of the Multi-Fibre Agreement and has applied voluntary export restraints on a range of goods, including textiles, footwear and leather products, television receivers, automobiles, ball bearings, cutlery, and so forth, particularly from Japan.[20] However, it has been argued that protectionism in Britain happened after earlier policy decisions had actually increased adaptive pressures from imports.

Curiously, U.K. trade policy discussions focus largely on imports and import protectionism rather than on the promotion of exports. The major methods for assisting exports are still Export Credit Guarantees. In the financial year to March 1981, the Export Credits Guarantee Department (ECGD) insured exports worth over £17,000 million and by its guarantees to banks, it made available to exporters credit finance of £3,300 million at preferential rates of interest.[21] Apart from this, all that exists are a range of government schemes for export marketing research, overseas missions and seminars, exchange risk guarantees, and so forth. As one author has observed on the basis of such evidence, "no attempt has ever been made in the U.K. economy to develop a coherent strategy of export-led growth."[22]

CONCLUDING COMMENTS

No attempt has been made in this chapter to consider the European Economic Community dimensions of industrial policy in the United Kingdom. To date, it is fair to say, EEC rules in areas such as competition policy, state aids to industry, regional policy and trade, and foreign direct investment policy have had only a minor impact upon the U.K. industrial scene. And particularly in the area of industrial assistance, the EEC has been more active in a defensive role than in promoting high technology and growth sectors.

From a purely domestic policy perspective, there has been no shortage of industrial policy initiatives and innovations in Britain. As has been noted, however, commentators have been severe and sweeping in their critiques of British industrial policy. Terms such as "incoherent," "inconsistent," and "ad hoc" appear frequently in the literature, and criticisms stress the lack of clarity in basic objectives, the fact that trade-offs between competing objectives have not been estimated in advance, the bewildering revisions and reversals of policy, and so forth.

To a large extent the confused history of industrial policy in Britain merely reflects a sense of frustration, almost despair, in that the country's relative economic decline has seemed irreversible. Deindustrialization is proceeding apace, and the so-called "British disease" (expressed in the low level and rate of growth of productivity) still exists and is certain to continue to tantalize industrial policy makers. The prospects for a policy consensus are not good, as the appallingly high level of unemployment increases internal strains and widens the gulf between political parties and between unions and management. Even for the detached observer, it is genuinely difficult to assess whether a comprehensive, planning-based approach to industrial policy is preferable to a hands-off approach, or indeed whether either can make a difference in the long-term performance of the British economy.

NOTES

1. Some recent contributions on British industrial decline are: F. T. Blackaby (ed.), *De-Industrialization* (London: Heinemann, 1979); R. E. Caves and L. B. Krause, *Britain's Economic Performance* (Washington, D.C.: Brookings Institution, 1980); K. Pavitt (ed.), *Technical Change and British Economic Performance,* (London: Macmillan, 1980); S. J. Prais, *Productivity and Industrial Structure* (Cambridge University Press, 1981); C. Carter (ed.), *Industrial Policy and Innovation* (London: Heinemann, 1981); and A. P. Thirwall, "Deindustrialisation in the United Kingdom," *Lloyds Bank Review,* No. 144, April 1982, pp. 22–37.
2. *British Business,* July 24, 1981.
3. *Labour's Plan for Expansion: The Alternative Economic Strategy,* Labour Party broadsheet.
4. W. A. Robson, "Control of the Nationalised Industries," *National Westminster Bank Quarterly Review,* November 1977, commenting on a report by the National Economic Development Office.
5. R. Bailey, "BNOC's New Phase," *National Westminster Bank Quarterly Review,* November 1979.
6. Eighth Report from the Expenditure Committee, Session 1975–76, *Public Expenditure on Chrysler UK Ltd.,* Vol. 1, HC596 (London: Her Majesty's Stationery Office, July 1976).
7. T. Lee, "What Cash Flow Analysis Says About BL's Finances," *Financial Times,* October 23,1981.
8. N. Hood and S. Young, *Multinationals in Retreat: The Experience of Scotland* (Edinburgh University Press, 1982).
9. S. Golt, "Government Organization and Support for Private Industry: The United Kingdom Experience," in S. J. Warnecke (ed.), *International Trade and Industrial Policies* (London: Macmillan, 1978), p. 79.
10. S. Young and A. V. Lowe, *Intervention in the Mixed Economy* (London: Croom Helm, 1974).
11. The British Technology Group has been formed from a merger of the NEB and the National Research Development Corporation (NRDC). The latter has, since 1948, been the main body administering state aid for R&D. The merger took place in the autumn of 1981 although the two are to remain separate statutory bodies until legislation is passed.
12. Among other specific references noted, see D. Imberg and J. Northcott, *Industrial Policy and Investment Decisions* (London: Policy Studies Institute, 1981).
13. A. Daly, "Government Support for Innovation in the British Machine Tool Industry: A Case Study," in C. Carter (ed.), *Industrial Policy and Innovation.*
14. W. B. Willott, "The NEB Involvement in Electronics and Information Technology," in C. Carter (ed.), *Industrial Policy and Innovation.*
15. N. Hood and S. Young, "British Policy and Inward Direct Investment," *Journal of World Trade Law,* Vol. 15(3), May/June 1981.
16. N. Hood and S. Young, *The Economics of Multinational Enterprise* (London: Longman, 1979), pp. 307–11.
17. Trade Union Congress, *The Trade Union Role in Industrial Policy* (London, 1977), quoting a Department of Industry estimate.
18. C. Milner and D. Greenaway, "Rethinking Trade Policy?", *National Westminster Bank Quarterly Review,* February 1981.
19. V. Cable, "Britain, The 'New Protectionism' and Trade with the Newly Industrialising Countries," *International Affairs,* Vol. 55(1), January 1979.

20. B. Hindley, "Voluntary Export Restraints and Article XIX of the General Agreement on Tariffs and Trade," in J. Black and B. Hindley (eds.), *Current Issues in Commercial Policy and Diplomacy* (London: Macmillan, 1980).
21. *British Business,* December 25, 1981.
22. A. P. Thirwall, "Deindustrialisation in the United Kingdom," p. 36.

Chapter 16

Industrial Strategies in the United States

*Jack N. Behrman**

The United States officially avoids any semblance of an industrial policy. Public discussion tends to avoid even the word "policy," favoring "industrial strategies" or "reindustrialization." This rewording helps to reject any concept of national economic planning and also to reject what is perceived to be the content of industrial policies employed by other countries. However, numerous activities of the government do help to shape the industrial structure of the United States—just as an industrial policy would—though in different directions and with different techniques. The U.S. government is taking tentative steps in the direction of guiding industrial development through its examination of the role of technology in U.S. exports, its concern for international competitiveness of U.S. industry, its examination of potential disadvantages of locating U.S. industrial activity overseas, and its support of individual segments of U.S. industry in the face of strong foreign competition.

Industrial policies, whether explicit or implicit, are a response to the question of *where* industrial activities *should* be located—that is, the determination of the international division of labor. This question would be resolved in one fashion under free-market criteria, in another by the movement of direct investment under decisions by transnational corporations (TNCs), and in still another by governmental decisions, whether

*University of North Carolina.

taken unilaterally or jointly, continuously or ad hoc. Whatever the decision-making process, the shape of industrialization will be affected by changes in four inputs: worldwide *markets,* the strategy orientations of *TNCs,* governmental *policies* and guidance, and developments in *science and technology.* These four factors operate separately and interactively, but their impacts on industrial location will differ according to the extent to which free markets provide the dominate signals in the decision making, TNCs are given major decision responsibility, or governments assume that role.

The U.S. government is still, in principle, wedded to the concept that the decisions should be made by TNCs and other (private) corporations in response only to market signals, with governments merely setting the broad rules of the game. Other countries have shifted more toward government guidance, partly in response to the breakdown of the Bretton Woods system and partly in reflection of a long-standing activist role of government. U.S. policy is readily inferred from the following official statement on the effects of investment performance requirements imposed by other countries. These requirements are officially considered "an economic detriment to the extent that they create economic behavior inconsistent with market-dictated forces." The statement continues:

> In particular, trade-related performance requirements can lead to distortion in trade and investment flows and in the uneconomic use of resources. For example, local content requirements mandate the use of domestic factors of production irrespective of relative costs. Similarly, export requirements force a firm to export a certain amount of its production, irrespective of comparative advantage. Such exports can cause trade diversion through displacement of another country's exports to the third country markets or through increased imports in another country from the firm complying with the export requirements. Possible losses incurred in such exports can be made up by exploiting what are often monopoly-like positions in the host country. These requirements have effects similar to trade protection or subsidies in altering international trade flows and adversely affecting other countries. Trade distortion is most severe when two or more requirements are used in conjunction with each other (e.g., local content and export requirements in the same industry) or when they are used in conjunction with other restrictive practices (e.g., tariffs) or incentives.[1]

However, the United States finds it hard to hold to its principles in the face of low growth rates, continued high unemployment, and shifts in international economic conditions, which in turn are reflected in four major developments: the increased difficulties of moving any further toward liberalized trade through the General Agreement on Tariffs and

Trade (GATT); the inadequacy of the International Monetary Fund (IMF) in maintaining free and stable exchange rates; the growth of and concerns over the roles of TNCs in international industrial integration; and the efforts to handle problems of specific industrial sectors through bilateral or multilateral agreements, as in orderly marketing arrangements. "Orderly marketing arrangements," when translated, means "prevention or dampening of shifts in the location of industry." This interference constitutes an industrial policy (at least for one sector), even though not adopted with the full consideration of the objectives or the best mechanisms for industrial change.

The U.S. government, therefore, is applying strategies that are normal under industrial policies, but that it would not consider as constituting either an industrial strategy or policy. But the government is not necessarily happy with its position. For example, a Bureau of Economics staff report to the Federal Trade Commission in June 1980 argued that orderly marketing agreements, as applied by the United States, have operated significantly to the net detriment of consumer interests and have imposed an (in)efficiency cost on the economy several times any calculable benefits. This loss is incurred largely by passing to the foreigner the scarcity rents from the restriction of imports into the United States. The report recommends the elimination of such barriers, rather than their adjustment, to shift the locus of the scarcity rents to the United States.[2] Although this report is not necessarily reflective of the policy positions of the Trade Commission itself, it does accord with the top government officials' pronouncements of the principles underlying U.S. policies.

Congress is also generally in accord with these principles, but it is frequently pressed to take differential action with reference to specific sectors. It would prefer not to have to make policy on an ad hoc basis, however. In the words of the staff director of the Congressional Subcommittee on International Economic Policy and Trade of the House Foreign Affairs Committee, "Congress has exhausted−and is increasingly exhausted with−ad hoc 'fixes' for industries suffering from foreign competition, and cannot relish the prospect of having to pass judgment individually on what could be a long procession of troubled industries seeking government help." He goes on to argue that a national industrial policy might well become infused with political rather than economic considerations and thus could well "perpetuate diseconomies rather than eliminate them".

Of course, neither the Federal Trade Commission nor the Congress formulates the policy of the U.S. government, but both have significant roles to play. At present, however, U.S. policy makers are not guided by either the market or a comprehensive analysis of economic strengths and weaknesses. Majak and others have argued that if we are going to move to assistance to specific sectors, it must be done in the context of much wider national economic planning. The U.S. is certainly not yet ready for such a move. Therefore, the government has, despite its distaste, provided specific assistance and support to "distressed" sectors including textiles, footwear, autos, steel, citizens' band radios (transreceivers), color television, steel, and a variety of agricultural products, as well as a series of other products that have been given safeguards under the Escape Clause provisions of the GATT.

PRINCIPLES OF U.S. POLICY

The basic principles underlying U.S. policy toward international integration are still those embodied in the Bretton Woods Agreements. Government is to stimulate aggregate investment and employment, without much attention to where either occurs geographically or sectorally. There is, therefore, no policy on a desired mix between agriculture and industry or between industry and service sectors. The shift of employment from agriculture into industry and from industry into services has not been guided in any sense directly by the government, and no preference is shown for one or the other, save in exceptional circumstances (e.g., a distressed area). Nor is there any policy preference shown as to the distribution of activities between rural and urban areas or among particular regions of the country. Although support is sometimes given to specific agricultural activities (wheat, tobacco) and to particular service sectors (shipping), these aberrations are a response to strategic political pressures. Much less is there any guidance as to the degree of concentration of the particular conglomerate structure on industry; its sectoral composition, even as between high-wage and low-wage industries; or the location of specific sectors within the country or abroad.

The conclusion to be drawn is that the U.S. government has not seen itself as an appropriate decision maker on the location or activities of industries, but as a supporter of industrial growth and competitiveness in general. *In principle,* it stands ready to see the United States develop industrially in whatever way the international markets and private companies decide. But this is in principle only; the principle is violated whenever it begins to hurt seriously, and "political harm" is more likely to catalyze interference than "economic harm." In addition, if state governments wish to operate on different principles, they are permitted to do so, so long as they do not violate national law or international treaties to which the United States is a party.

STATE GOVERNMENT INCENTIVES

The authority to grant incorporation is reserved in the United States to the individual states. There is no federal incorporation law, but companies operate across state boundaries under federal laws prohibiting restraint of trade among the fifty states, and they invest nationally under principles of comity. Corporations have been wooed by states just to get them incorporated within their jurisdiction for purposes of taxation, even if the manufacturing headquarters activities are located elsewhere. Other states have sought corporate investment for the purpose of increasing employment opportunities or expanding port activities through foreign trade.

Probably none of the states has developed a coordinated set of tactics that could be called a "strategy" in the sense of determining precisely what sectors it would like to have enter or locate in specific areas of the state. On the contrary, most of the states are simply interested in larger payrolls and higher tax bases. However, a few of them have sought to shift the structure of economic activity away from agriculture into industry and, within industry, to the higher-wage jobs associated with high technology industries. In other states, industrial diversification is sought so as to reduce dependence on a dominant industry or a few sectors, which might be hit hard by economic recession or by obsolescence of product lines. Some also seek a dispersion of job opportunities throughout the state, to prevent concentration in a few urban areas and to reduce the infrastructure costs of such agglomerations. A few states have selected specific industry sectors they would like to promote and have established industrial parks to attract them—such as the Research Triangle Park in North Carolina, where high technology industries are attracted by the limitations on types of manufacturing, the requirements for a high percentage of R&D operations, and the ambiance provided by three nearby universities.

The techniques states use for attracting industry have included low-cost loans and grants, the donation of land, low-cost leases of manufacturing facilities, tax waivers or credits, and the training of the work force or technical personnel needed by the company.

Particular states that have chosen specific industrial segments to sponsor have sometimes been exceptionally successful—Massachusetts with the electronics industry (after the loss of the textile and shoe manufacturing sectors to southern states); California with Silicon Valley; Texas in aerospace—and several states are now interested in promoting biotechnology centers. These efforts do not reflect a search for a high degree of specialization or any concerted or coordinated industrial policy looking to the future structure of industry within the state. Rather, they reflect only a high priority given to *one* sector in the total economic development of the state. In some instances, the efforts of one state have conflicted with the objectives of another, leading to some competitive extension of incentives, which probably did not significantly alter the decisions of the companies as to locations or product lines. Municipalities also have offered tax and loan incentives, with the probable result of simply reducing the tax revenues to both local and state governments.

In the absence of federal government coordination of these activities, or even any prohibition of the use of incentives to attract foreign industry, foreign investors benefit as much as U.S. investors and share in the market distortions that result. These activities of states and cities are an embarrassment to the federal government in its efforts to encourage other countries to eliminate their national incentives and disincentives.

FEDERAL POLICIES

The federal government has rejected any active role in estab-lishing the *pattern* of industrial development in the United States and is supported in this decision by the views of both business and labor. Neither of these groups sees an important role for the government in the stimulation of specific sectors to increase their competitiveness or to alter the market forces determining the location of activities in that sector. The only exceptions to the rule against government guidance (stimulation or preclusion) are in the national security, communication, transportation, utility, and shipbuilding sectors. There a variety of direct and indirect subsidies and constraints are provided, and foreign firms are precluded from some of these. Stimulation is different from protec-tion, however, and both labor and business have urged government to *protect* existing interests when they are threatened (as discussed below).

Federal policies, therefore, tend to be ad hoc and essentially political in purpose rather than economic. This view is illustrated by the man-ner in which assistance has been given to specific sectors; by the ex-tension of safeguards and adjustment assistance for labor, firms, and communities threatened by imports; and by programs of regional develop-ment assistance. None of these has been set within a larger framework of industrial strategy.

Within the past few years, the government has begun to see the desirability of stimulating industry, but has done so under the commonly designated policy of "reindustrialization." It is a policy of nondiscrimi-nating encouragements to industrialization, increased productivity, and improved competitiveness. The stimulation is achieved through ag-gregate tax incentives of accelerated depreciation, investment credits, reduced taxes on capital gains, and provisions that encourage leasing of capital equipment—all to accelerate investment in new facilities, thereby improving productivity and competitive position, it is hoped, as well as increasing employment by increasing sales volume.

In addition, a stimulus to reduce costs and therefore to raise productivity is sought through deregulation of industry, which has been assessed as too costly in terms not only of the regulations themselves but also of the administrative burdens of compliance and constraints on the decisions of industry.

Further, the federal government has recently adopted a policy stance of weakening, or at least not strengthening, the bargaining position of labor unions, in the hopes of reducing wage pressure and thus increasing the cost-effectiveness of manufacturing in major segments of industry. The government has also examined ways in which it might provide a stimulus to R&D activities of companies so as to accelerate innovation and thereby increase sales at home and abroad. These investigations have not led to any specific encouragements; for example, there are no new grants or subsidies to R&D activities, and no sectors have been singled out to be encouraged on a priority basis. The major effort on the part of the federal government has been vocal persuasion to companies to undertake more R&D.

The closest that the U.S. government has come to sectoral priorities is its consideration that the future of U.S. industry rests with the high technology sectors. It is hoped that U.S. industry will find ways to move more extensively into electronics, informatics, biophysics, genetics, and medical specialties—in each case with the purpose of expanding markets at home and abroad. But the government has not sought the entrance of foreign high technology companies into the United States to bolster this development.

Despite its *preference* for the development of certain industrial sectors, the U.S. government has no policy for the stimulation of science and technology for these sectors, though it recognizes that their growth will depend heavily on R&D expenditures. Rather, its attention is drawn to "key" sectors, which are those with enough political power to command governmental support—shipbuilding, national security industries, chemicals, petroleum and petrochemicals, textiles, automobiles, aircraft, and a variety of industries that are seen as injured by the effects of a negotiated redistribution of duties.

Thus many sectors are not seen as either preferential or "key" in the political sense—including pharmaceuticals, rubber products, wood products, paper and pulp, metals and metal products, instruments and instrumentation, electrical and other machinery, agricultural and construction vehicles and equipment, transport equipment, optical and photographic products, and so forth. From its present and historical stances, it would appear that the U.S. government would permit the demise of any one of these sectors, or at least of major producers therein, thereby reducing significantly the U.S. participation in any given sector.

It was assumed, of course, that the reduction of barriers to trade, as accomplished in several GATT negotiations since 1945, would cut into U.S. industry only at the margins, eliminating the inefficient producers and thereby raising the gains from trade. Obviously, like other countries, the United States has availed itself of the Escape Clause provisions of the GATT when imports threatened a given sector more than marginally. The use of such safeguards is merely to "save what exists" rather than to develop any overt industrial strategy.

Apart from the usual safeguard procedures, the U.S. government has provided support or protection of a quite special nature to six different sectors or companies within them: textiles and apparel, footwear, color television, aircraft, steel and automobiles.

Textile Multi-Fiber Agreement

The textile industry has long been protected by a fairly high level of tariffs covering a large portion of the products and imposed against all suppliers. In addition, quantitative restrictions are imposed on most of the leading foreign exporters under a procedure known as "voluntary export restraints." These negotiations produced bilateral agreements that established annual limits for textile products, defined in a very specific manner so as to prevent circumvention of the restraints.

These limitations are sanctioned by a multilateral agreement known as the Multi-Fiber Agreement (MFA), which was concluded under the auspices of the GATT, and to which nearly all major textile importing and exporting countries are signatory. The MFA includes not only cotton textiles but also manmade fiber and wool textile products. The Agreement has been extended in various forms since the inception of the bilateral agreements in 1961.

These restraints were literally imposed on many of the developing countries by the U.S. government under threat of extensive and prohibitive import quotas, which the Kennedy administration did not want to employ. The agreements therefore maintained the charade that the U.S. government is "in principle" in favor of freer trade and does not itself impose barriers to that trade.

The entire process of protection was stimulated by the depressed condition of the textile industry in the late 1950s and early 1960s, and the campaign promise made by President Kennedy to "do something for the textile industry," in the hopes of garnering the support of Southern states. He was later reluctant to provide extensive support or protection to the industry, but a package of assistance was developed, whose major feature was the restraint of imports. There was no feeling inside top circles of the administration that the textile industry ought to be maintained in any given volume or structure; rather, it was considered that it should "die a little," but the administration did not know how to encourage that and still maintain the support of the South. The government has not prevented marginal firms from closing or being acquired by others, and there has been a shift in the composition of U.S. production. However, the adjustment has not been as fast as foreign supplier nations would have hoped or as free-market decisions would have elicited.

Footwear

Since the mid-1960s the footwear industry in the United States has been in decline, as evidenced by a reduction of the number of plants, declining production, and reduced employment, accelerated by an increase in imports from about 13 percent in mid-1960 to nearly 50 percent of total consumption in recent years. In the early 1960s, the source of imports was Italy and Japan; in the later part of that decade and in the early 1970s imports surged from South Korea and Taiwan, followed later by Brazil.

After the surge in 1977 from the Far East, the International Trade Commission determined that "serious injury" had occurred as a result of the imports and recommended application of a tariff quota. President Carter chose instead to negotiate an "orderly marketing arrangement" with Taiwan and South Korea on rubber footwear. Each supplier nation agreed to cut back its exports by 15–20 percent, with a growth factor built in for subsequent years. These agreements have not arrested the decline of the U.S. footwear industry, which is faced with increased imports from other suppliers.

Color Television

In 1977, a group of labor unions and some smaller firms in the electronics industry petitioned the International Trade Commission to prevent continued injury from Japanese exports of color televisions to the United States. The ITC recommended multistage tariff relief, over a five-year period, but the President again opted for restraint by the exporting nation. An orderly marketing agreement was negotiated, and Japan agreed to limit its exports to around 60 percent of its most recent level. Despite a drop of over one million sets per year from Japan, imports of color television increased substantially—nine-fold from South Korea and two-fold from Taiwan, plus a dramatic rise in imports of incomplete color TV receivers from Taiwan and Mexico, many produced by subsidiaries of U.S. companies abroad. In addition, Japanese companies established or expanded production facilities in the United States for TV sets and components.

The result has been a concentration of production in fewer manufacturers within the United States and a reduction of worker man-hours due to the import of incomplete TV sets and components.

Consequently, orderly marketing agreements were also negotiated with South Korea and Taiwan in order to maintain U.S. production, which has increasingly been shifted to the control of foreign-owned subsidiaries.

Steel

In the face of rapidly increasing imports in the 1970s from both Europe and Japan, and strong pleas from steel companies for import quotas, the U.S. government devised and imposed a "trigger-price mechanism." Under this arrangement the duties on steel rise if the foreign price falls below the U.S. price by a specified amount. The purpose of the protection was to give the U.S. steel industry the opportunity to begin the modernization of its investment and to institute other programs to raise its productivity. The industry responded that it was, in fact, as productive as foreign companies, but that the latter were subsidized by their governments and were "dumping" in the U.S. markets.

Since the mechanism did not work adequately, in the view of the companies, there has been continued pressure to impose quotas or to obtain voluntary export limitations on the part of the foreign countries—notably Japan and some in Europe. Once again, the onus is placed on the foreigner, thereby keeping the reputation of the United States clean, at least in its own eyes, through maintaining the principle of free, open-market trade.

The lack of an industrial policy for this sector is demonstrated by the fact that, although there has been no significant acceleration of capital investment in the sector, the U.S. government is taking no action to make certain that the sector survives or is competitive. And government aid would probably not have been forthcoming but for the threat of greater unemployment in an area critical to President Carter's electoral strength and at a time of widespread unemployment. Again, the government's action appears to have greater political than economic justification.

Automobiles

The automotive industry is second only to textiles in attention from government received over the past two decades. There have been four phases of government involvement in the sector: the U.S.-Canadian Auto Agreement; the negotiation of an orderly marketing arrangement with Japan; support to Chrysler; and attempts at persuading Japanese companies to establish manufacturing facilities in the United States. All four interventions have been efforts to resolve the question of the location of industrial activity and to maintain high levels of production and employment in the Untied States. They may indicate how the United States is likely to respond to problems of international industrial integration or repartition, when pressed to take some formal action.

The Canada-U.S. Automotive Agreement of 1965 was initiated by the U.S. government, but in response to a threat that Canada would impose barriers to both investment and trade. By shifting production within its borders, Canada hoped to reduce a large balance of payments deficit in automotive trade. The Canadian government had proposed quietly to a number of the U.S. companies that they shift some of their manufacturing facilities into Canada, thereby eliminating the need to import from the United States. It offered encouragements to export through a permission to import at lower duties those components that would continue to be supplied from the United States. The U.S. government responded that the requested action would involve subsidization of Canadian exports and would trigger countervailing duties by the United States.

Consequently, in violation of the GATT (and requiring a waiver) an intergovernmental agreement was negotiated providing for duty-free trade between the two countries in most new vehicles and those parts to be used as original equipment. So that Canada would not become a pass-through for imports of components or automobiles from other countries, imports from Canada required a minimum of 50 percent North American content to be given duty-free treatment. Canada also imposed local-content requirements so as to raise the value-added in vehicles production in Canada.

This Agreement was an attempt to alter the location of production through a requirement of local production-to-sales ratios, which in effect prevented the industry from relocating on the U.S. side if it became more attractive to do so either economically or commercially. Neither the United States or Canada has been wholly satisfied with the operation of the Agreement, and each has sought renegotiation at different times.

One study has concluded that the stimulus to the overall Canadian economy was profound. It is estimated that by 1969 gross national expenditure was nearly 5 percent higher in real terms than it would have been in the absence of the Agreement or of compensatory government actions, exports of total goods and services more than 20 percent higher, and total employment over 2.8 percent higher.[4]

In the late 1970s, when imports from Japan had risen to 30 percent of U.S. automobile sales, the auto industry—both management and labor—turned to the government for import restrictions, specifically requesting quotas. Rather than impose such quantitative limitations, the administration once again turned to an orderly marketing arrangement, requesting the Japanese to undertake "voluntary export restraint." The Japanese government was reluctant to provide evidence of such close ties between the government and industry as would be indicated by a ready acceptance of a governmental request, so the automotive industry itself decided to reduce shipments. This was done company by company under procedures not made public.

The U.S. government had still not made any determination as to the desirable size of U.S. automotive capacity or production, nor as to how the industry should be structured or what ownership pattern would be acceptable. Thus, without any observation pro or con, it had readily permitted American Motors to be bought on a minority basis by Renault (French), and Chrysler, Ford, and General Motors have instituted joint ventures with Japanese counterparts, which include a shipment of components and vehicles into the U.S. market. In the absence of Japanese export restraint, Ford Motor Company threatened to move more of its production facilities overseas and to import back into the United States.

Sectoral Objectives

The experiences in textiles, footwear, steel, and autos demonstrate that the U.S. government assists a sector or company differentially only when it faces difficulties that raise concerns for broader economic policies and objectives of the government. A textile industry in decline would have meant considerable unemployment in the South in a period when President Kennedy was trying to "get the country moving again," and in a region whose political support he required. Little was done to stimulate the industry; rather, a series of signals were given that a readjustment and redirection of its product lines were required if it was to become viable internationally. This was done over a period of several years, and the industry is relatively viable under the present arrangements.

It *appears* that the U.S. government would let the domestic auto companies gradually go out of business if they found a way to do so without damage to U.S. employment and incomes, for example by encouraging foreign companies to come in. If low levels of unemployment in the United States permitted a rapid move of workers out of the auto industry into electronics or other high technology sectors, it *appears* that the U.S. government would let the auto industry itself atrophy somewhat— similiarly for steel, though not necessarily for the national security sectors. However, the government is willing to see some *companies* in these industries fail.

But there is no public evidence that the government has considered the question of how *far* it would let any sector die out before it determined to stop or reverse the situation. That is, there seems to be no policy position that the United States ought to have a given amount of steel production, or of textiles, autos, or any industry within its borders. It appears certain, however, that there is some point at which the Congress if not the administration, would react.

COMPETITION AND/OR COOPERATION?

U.S. policy is predicated on the assumption that the world should be ordered under competitive principles, an assumption it was able to persuade the world to adopt, in principle, after World War II. It was able to obtain this agreement because of its own willingness to cooperate in providing three necessary conditions: (a) sufficient funding to reestablish industrial capabilities in Europe and to bring Japan and some of the developing countries into the industrial orbit; (b) an initiative to reduce its own barriers to imports to permit others to export enough to the United States to repay loans and to purchase needed capital equipment and other goods for their own reconstruction and development; and (c) the maintenance of a sound economy, characterized by continued employment and a strong dollar.

This policy was, therefore, both a cooperative and a competitive one, but the cooperation was in the building of the base and determining the rules of competition. It was assumed that all countries would accept the structure of industrial production and economic activity that would come out of (freer) market decision-making procedures around the world. What the United States did not understand was that hardly any other country had as fully accepted the neoclassical economic principles, and few were willing to let decisions as to the location of economic activity be made wholly under free market signals, especially not for key sectors and not by TNCs, which would not have local national interests in mind.

Further, the U.S. government was permitted to take this policy posture because its industry was dominant, as illustrated by the fact that the U.S. gross national product was about 45 percent of free-world production even into the mid-1960s; its foreign direct investment accounted for half the world total, and its percentage of world trade was over one-third of the total for some years—though all three measures began to decline in the 1970s and are now at about half their 1950s levels.

In principle, the United States was willing to recognize that open trading channels constrain the increase of wages in the United States, help to determine the level of specific product prices, alter product lines through competition, and help to determine the types of technology that are appropriate or required. However, operating in a *relatively* closed national market, some industries were able to raise wages far above international levels and still remain competitive simply because of the weakness of international competition. With the growing competitiveness of other countries, and the interests of governments in shaping industrial structures, U.S. competitiveness has declined, thereby constraining the growth of key U.S. industrial sectors, both at home and abroad.

The necessary industrial adjustments to new international competition and shifts in government policies are more easily accommodated when economies are expanding. But with the retarded growth of the late 1970s and as anticipated in the 1980s, the shifts required are more difficult to accept, and it is more difficult to identify potentially expanding sectors. Given the pressure of all countries to expand their industrial activities so as to continue the increases in standards of living expected by their citizens, there is a particularly excruciating pressure on markets in the United States, which remains a rather open economy—open both to imports and foreign direct investment.

NOTES

1. *The Use of Investment Incentives and Performance Requirements by Foreign Governments,* Office of International Investment, U.S. Department of Commerce, October 1981, p. 7.
2. Morris E. Morkre and David G. Tarr, *Staff Report on Effects of Restrictions of United State Imports: Five Case Studies in Theory* (Washington, D.C.: Federal Trade Commission, June 1980), pp. 196–200.
3. R. Roger Majak, "When All Else Fails, National Industrial Planning?", in Mark B. Winchester (ed.), *The International Essays for Business Decision Makers,* Vol. V (New York: AMACOM, 1980), pp. 7–17.
4. David L. Emerson, *Production, Location, and the Automotive Agreement* (Ottawa: The Economic Council of Canada, 1975). See also Carl E. Beigie, *The Canada-U.S. Automotive Agreement: An Evaluation* (Montreal: Canadian-American Committee, 1970).

Chapter 17

Industrial Policy and International Competitiveness in West Germany

Frank D. Weiss*

During the 1970s the world economy was subjected to several shocks, which demanded a high degree of structural adaptation from the open economies. West Germany was no exception. First, on the basis of policy changes in the less developed countries initiated even earlier, exports of manufactured goods from those countries began to capture increasing shares of markets in which West Germany had long been an entrenched supplier, such as clothing, textiles, and leather goods. Second, Japan emerged as a major supplier of goods in which West Germany had held a decisive competitive edge, such as electrical engineering goods and, more recently, automobiles. Third, sharp major price increases for energy and various raw materials placed profound adjustment pressure on industries in West Germany. In turn, these developments elicited a myriad of policy responses at several levels in West Germany, and also within the European Economic Communities (EEC), which are intended to ameliorate, or help adjust to, those shocks. The diverse measures undertaken can be subsumed under the name of industrial policy.

Although the publicized intentions of industrial policy are usually rather clear, ranging from adjustment assistance to government assistance for potentially profitable investments, such as R&D, but also

*Kiel Institute for World Economics

including some explicitly job-preserving measures, the effectiveness of the measures in achieving the stated aims is controversial. Indeed, the enumeration of all relevant measures, not to mention their quantification, is alone an arduous undertaking. This difficulty may be due to the nature of the phenomenon; one is not dealing with a single well-articulated policy, but with a set of measures, each element of which is intended to deal with some particular aspect of industrial change. This paper briefly outlines the empirical evidence available on government measures affecting the international competitiveness of industry in West Germany, explains the mechanism by which industrial policy is supposed to affect international competitiveness, and analyzes empirically the determinants of industrial policy.

INDUSTRIAL POLICY IN WEST GERMANY

In analyzing industrial policy, it is relevant to consider instruments that enable one industry to compete on factor or product markets at terms different from other industries. Under this wide definition, one would have to include, in the case of West Germany: (a) foreign trade protection carried out at the EEC level; (b) subsidies to industry emanating from the West German federal government, as well as from the various provincial governments; and (c) nonfinancial barriers to trade undertaken at the EEC or national levels.

Systematic quantitative evidence on the magnitude of these policies is scarce. In the case of industries engaging in international trade, the information required is known conceptually—namely, differences in prices confronting domestic and foreign producers in each industry, reflecting the net effects of tariff and nontariff barriers, and differences in factor costs confronting domestic producers. Tracing the actual implementation of these differences is tedious at best. More readily available, in the case of West Germany, are systematic measures of some components, especially tariff and financial activities of industrial policy, classified by the various purposes of industrial policy, as well as by the industry actually benefited.

Tariff policy is the best documented field of industrial policy, but it is generally of declining importance in the total bundle of policy measures undertaken. One reason for the diminished significance of tariffs is the effective multilateralization of tariff setting, which has encouraged the substitution of other financial and nonfinancial instruments for tariffs in industrial policy. The result is a better ability to tailor measures to the individual national, regional, or sectoral problem at hand. Thus, at the same time that one can observe declines in

Table 17.1. Government Transfers to the Business Sector, 1970–1977 (in Millions of Deutsche Marks)

Year	Current and Capital Transfers	Tax Exemption	R&D	Total	Percentage of GNP
1970	15,422.0	10,186.0	503.4	26,111.4	3.8
1971	15,789.0	11,239.0	690.6	27,718.6	3.7
1972	18,738.4	11,952.0	918.7	31,609.1	3.8
1973	22,714.5	12,320.0	1,040.6	36,076.1	3.9
1974	24,378.3	14,321.0	1,307.2	40,006.5	4.1
1975	24,552.4	14,873.0	1,514.4	40,939.8	4.0
1976	30,653.3	15,570.0	1,249.6	47,472.9	4.2
1977	32,727.0	15,933.0	1,605.5	50,265.5	4.3

Source: Calculated from Schwarze (1980); Statistisches Bundesamt (Wiesbaden), Statistisches Jahrbuch für die Bundesrepublik Deutschland (various issues).

Table 17.2. Government Transfer for the Business Sector, 1977 (in Millions of Deutsche Marks)

Industry	Current Transfers	Capital Transfers	Tax Exemption	R&D Support	Total	Percentage of Value Added
Agriculture	6,559.0	885.7	2,766.0	0.4	10,211.1	30.5
Utilities	1,677.7	1,283.2	—	376.2	3,337.1	10.1
Mining	575.1	729.0	249.0	143.4	1,696.5	15.2
Manufacturing	749.0	2,912.6	6,233.0	869.1	10,763.7	2.4
Transportation	7,657.8	4,074.1	1,444.0	—	13,175.9	30.4
Dwellings	1,554.3	839.9	4,828.0	—	7,222.2	11.1
Other	437.1	2,792.5	413.0	216.4	3,859.0	0.7
Total	19,210.0	13,517.8	15,933.0	1,605.5	50,265.5	4.3
Percentage of Total	38.2	26.9	31.7	3.2	100.0	—

Source: Calculated from Schwarze (1980); Statistisches Bundesamt (Wiesbaden), Statistisches Jahrbuch für die Bundesrepublik Deutschland, 1980.

nominal tariff rates, as well as the dispersion of those rates, implemented in the Kennedy and Tokyo Rounds of liberalization, one can also observe an increase in nontariff industrial policy measures in West Germany. This trend is reflected in budgetary transfers of the government to the business sector, as shown in Table 17.1. Transfers rose from 3.8 percent of gross national product (GNP) in 1970 to 4.3 percent of GNP in 1977. The sectoral breakdown in Table 17.2 shows that transfers were most important, as a share of value added, in agriculture and transportation, although manufacturing was the greatest beneficiary of R&D support.

This observation raises the question as to the aims of industrial policy in West Germany, for different support programs apparently have quite different net beneficiaries of financial transfers. For this purpose, it is useful to classify financial transfers to the business sector in terms of the institutional means applied to grant aid. One can distinguish R&D subsidization, regional subsidization, and other industry-specific programs.

R&D subsidization has the express purpose of "maintaining and increasing" the efficiency and (international) competitiveness of the economy (*Bundesbericht Forschung VI, 1979*). Funds are earmarked for specific purposes, and the enumerated purposes are explicitly political decisions. Aside from defense-related projects and basic research, energy research is currently the most important field of activity, though electronics and communications technologies are also promoted heavily in the business sector proper.

Regional subsidization is a uniquely German institution, in the sense that the constitution makes express provision for measures to equalize economic conditions throughout the country. For this purpose, the federal government and the states jointly support business, mostly through tax subsidies to investment, guaranteed credit, and reduced-interest-rate loans. Presumably because of the constitutional stature of the program, aid is distributed to individual regions (rather than to specific industries) on the basis of criteria determined by the federal and state governments jointly in a Planning Commission. The state governments then redistribute these funds to companies through the banking system.

This institution has an idiosyncratic voting procedure: Each state has one vote, but the federal government has votes equal to the sum of the number of states. Furthermore, a three-fourths majority is required to adopt a criterion (*Deutscher Bundestag, 1976*).

Development aid for the area bordering East Germany is channeled through this program as well. The zonal border area and the other regions eligible for joint program aid constitute two-thirds of West Germany's surface and about one-third of its population. In addition, the regional support program to ensure the economic viability of West Berlin uses the same criteria, but is funded separately. The Planning Commission has seen fit to adopt criteria that determine whether a town or city and its environs may be taken up in the program as a potential "pôle de croissance," these having low per capita income but some industrial base (Adlung, Götzinger, Lammers et al. 1979, pp. 171–79).

The remaining group of financial aids is heterogeneous in the sense that the aims of the programs differ—ranging from job preservation to restructuring assistance. But they are almost all industry specific, and generally work by subsidizing investment. The most important of these, in the industrial sector, are for mining, shipbuilding, and the steel industry. They are founded on specific laws passed by the Bundestag and financed out of the annual budget, with funding passed more or less automatically once the initial legal framework has been established.

The aggregate effective rates of domestic subsidization and effective tariff protection granted at the EEC level are shown for manufacturing industries in Table 17.3, which summarizes unique data sets on tariffs and subsidies. Included are all forms of subsidization, such as the grant element in low-interest loans, and tax breaks for various purposes, as well as direct financial transfers on the part of federal and provincial governments. Large variations are observed in both tariff protection and domestic subsidization. In 1974, at least, the bulk of effective financial assistance was channeled through regional aid programs, the main exception being the aircraft industry. Among industries heavily protected, food products leads the list, followed by some raw-material-intensive basic industries, clothing and textiles, and mining.

Even at first glance, the interindustry structure of assistance seems inconsistent with the stated aims of industrial policy and the perceived reasons for its need. One major stated rationale for that policy has been to promote new technology and fast-growing industries. Another major motive, and recently the overriding one, has been to restore a sector's international competitiveness, in turn a cause of the move away from short-term across-the-board assistance for cyclical difficulties toward more or less permanent industry-specific assistance.

DETERMINANTS OF INDUSTRIAL POLICY IN WEST GERMANY

A promising hypothesis to explain the structure of protection actually granted is that differential rates of effective subsidization in Germany have been determined by an underlying economic logic, based on the opportunity costs of the business sector in demanding protection and of the political sector in supplying protection.[1]

In the business or interest-group sector on the demand side, one would expect that lobbying activities aimed at eliciting protection would be the greater (a) the smaller the number of firms in an industry; (b) the smaller the number of employees in an industry; and (c) the greater the regional concentration of an industry. In all three cases the same rationale applies: communication costs are relatively small for a small number of agents, especially when they are physically close together and problems of excludability are substantially avoided. In addition, if

Table 17.3. Effective Rates of Tariff Protection and Domestic Assistance in West Germany (Percentage of Value Added)

Industry	EEC Tariff Protection[a] (1972)	Domestic Subsidization[b] (1974) Total	Domestic Subsidization[b] (1974) Non-regional	Total Protection (1972/74)
Agriculture	(25.0)	–	–	–
Vegetables and grains	(79.8)	–	–	–
Meats	(44.3)	–	–	–
Food and food products[c]	(40.5)	(8.6)	–	(49.1)
Coal mining	– 1.9	27.2	–	25.3
Other mining	– 6.0	12.2	–	6.2
Stone and clay products	3.7	1.1	0.3	4.8
Primary iron and steel	17.0	0.6	0.2	17.6
Casting	12.1	0.7	0.1	12.8
Rolling mills	7.7	0.6	0.1	8.3
Nonferrous metals	22.3	2.4	0.3	24.7
Chemicals	14.4	1.3	0.8	15.7
Petroleum refining	(6.5)	(10.0)	–	(16.5)
Saw mills	13.7	2.2	1.1	15.9
Pulp, paper, paperboard	29.6	0.9	0.2	30.5
Rubber and asbestos	8.7	0.6	0.1	9.3
Structural engineering	1.4	1.4	0.4	2.8
Mechanical engineering	2.5	1.3	0.8	3.8
Road vehicles	5.8	0.8	0.2	6.6
Shipbuilding	– 10.1	(6.0)	–	(– 4.1)
Aircraft	(– 0.9)	23.5	23.4	(22.6)
Electrical engineering	4.5	2.7	0.8	7.2
Precision mechanics, optics, watches	4.9	1.7	0.8	6.6
Fabricated metal products	5.6	1.3	0.2	6.9
Precision ceramics	9.9	1.1	0.2	11.0
Glass and glass products	11.1	0.9	0.3	12.0
Wood products	9.9	0.8	0.0	10.7
Musical instruments, toys etc.	6.9	0.7	0.0	7.6
Paper products	19.9	0.8	0.2	20.7
Printing and publishing	5.3	4.4	3.8	9.7
Plastic products	9.8	1.3	0.2	11.1
Leather, leather goods, shoes	9.4	0.5	0.3	9.9
Textiles	20.8	1.3	0.6	22.1
Clothing	20.7	1.8	0.6	22.5

Source: Donges, Fels, and Neu (1973); Fels (1976); Jüttemeier and Lammers (1979); Rodemer (1980); Dicke (1977).

Note: Figures in parentheses are either rougher, based upon data different from the others, or, in the case of shipbuilding and aircraft, underestimated.

[a] Percentage of value added, net of tariff protection at previous stages of protection.
[b] Percentage of value added.
[c] 1970.

an industry is in decline, the opportunity costs of seeking protection are reduced for both capital and labor (though conglomerates may find it relatively cheap to respecialize).

As for the government, or supply side of protection, declines in an industry's employment are likely to raise protection. Employees in shrinking industries where jobs are endangered are likely to raise protection. Employees in shrinking industries where jobs are endangered are likely to elicit public sympathy, and hence public support and votes for protection, either on altruistic grounds or as a form of insurance. The altruistic argument would also tend to apply to workers in industries where value added per employee, or human capital, and hence wages per employee are low.

In the case of industry employment, the effect on government is opposite to the effect on interest groups. Because of the greater number of votes at stake, large industries are more likely to be helped, leaving the net effect ambiguous. In the case of regional concentration, a subnational region would provide aid to an industry so concentrated; but the response of the national government is by no means clear a priori. Specific institutional conditions have to be taken into account before a hypothesis can be formulated.

German labor unions are highly encompassing groups organized along branch lines.[2] Though union membership varies across industries, in effect unions bargain and lobby for all employees of the industry they have organized.[3] This means that communication costs, even in large industries, are not high. Hence, the propensity to demand protection would not be reduced by increasing size. As a result, employment size is no longer ambiguous in its influence on protection—it is clearly positive.

German industrial unions are associated in the "Deutscher Gewerkschaftsbund" (DGB), which in turn lives in symbiosis with the Social Democratic Party (SPD). Individual industrial unions' policies are formulated at least in part in consensus with these two organizations. Clearly, gains any one industrial union may achieve from government intervention will impose costs on other members of the encompassing organizations. Hence, any single industrial union would be loathe to press special interests very hard.[4] This in turn would mean that, to the extent that protection is positively associated with industry employment, a pure supply response on the part of government is being reflected.

As for the influence of regional concentration on the interindustrial structure of domestic assistance, the salient features of the German subsidization system need to be taken into account. For the industries examined here, almost half (48.6 percent) of the aid received is channeled through various regional development programs. The institutional set-up of the regional aid machinery, as described above, implies that individual states' interests can easily by stymied: while an industry concentrated in one state may lobby at the state level, and that state may very well desire to grant that industry regional aid, it would have to overcome the opposition of all the other states, as well as the federal government. While state votes could surely be traded, a majority could never be achieved that way. Given perfect log-rolling among states on each issue, the federal votes still constitute a blocking coalition. Since the issues to be decided in effect amount to the designation of towns and cities eligible for aid, the states' strategy has been to disaggregate as much as possible and thereby have as many municipalities included in the program as possible. But this provides a rationale for regionally concentrated industries to be discriminated against in the context of this program.[5] Hence, for the particular institutional conditions extant in Germany, the regional concentration hypothesis must be differentiated in order to sharpen it: regional aid would tend to discriminate against regionally concentrated industries; all other aid need not.

Aid granted to industries outside the scope of the joint federal-state program is project or industry specific. Thus, a multitude of individual measures makes up the remaining 51.4 percent of subsidies to the manufacturing industries considered here. These measures consist of project-specific R&D programs and industry-specific job preservation or restructuring programs. They have in common the nature of their distribution, beginning with a general legal framework passed by the Bundestag, which avoids the log-rolling observed in the Planning Commission's administration of regional development aid. Then, administration of these programs is handed over to the ministerial bureaucracy, with funding more or less automatically included in the annual budget. Hence, the distribution of funding is subject to the interaction among bureaucratic interests, government and representatives' interests, and the lobbying efforts of the potential recipients. As a consequence, one would expect the specific hypotheses advanced by the "political economy of protection" approach would apply more unambiguously to these nonregional aids.

Perhaps the most important single hypothesis for the explanation of the structure of protection is that the degree of import penetration is a key determinant of commercial policy (Anderson, 1979). While import penetration is only one of the sources of demand for protection, it may elicit a distinctive response from government in granting protection. Some of the costs of government intervention aimed specifically against imports will fall upon foreigners who have no votes, or little influence, in shaping domestic policy.

In a highly open economy like West Germany, however, exports would have to be treated symmetrically with imports. Any given manufacturing industry, subindustry, product group, or even firm will be likely to export and import at the same time (Kravis and Lipsey 1971; Grubel and Lloyd 1975).[6] To the extent that exports and imports are substitutes in production, an entrepreneur may, in the face of stiffening competition from abroad, find that switching production from product variants under more pressure to those under less pressure is cheaper than investing in lobbying activities. Hence, the structure of competitiveness, or the nature of comparative advantage, rather than import penetration would appear to constitute an important determinant of the structure of protection.

The final major hypothesis to explain protection in Germany also depends on an institutional idiosyncracy, namely the country's membership in the EEC. Subsidies granted by German governments add their allocational impact to that of protection granted in Brussels. Protection at the EEC level should reduce the quantity of protection demanded at various domestic levels: that is, it is hypothesized that protection from the two sources are substitutes, though how well they substitute for one another is an empirical question.

The empirical counterparts to these constructs are relatively straightforward:

Value added per employee (1972), number of firms (1970), number of employees (1970), and change in the number of employees (1964–1970) are directly available.

Human capital intensity (1970) was measured according to a concept introduced by Fels (1972) as the difference between average hourly earning (by industry) and the hourly earnings of an unskilled worker in each industry. This sum constitutes the remuneration to labor over and above the disutility incurred by the unskilled in each industry.

Competitiveness is measured as a variant of "revealed comparative advantage" (export/import ratio) (Balassa, 1967) for the year 1970.

Regional concentration is measured as the coefficient of variation of an industry's share in total industrial employment across eleven states.

Regressions run to explain the structure of domestic subsidization to manufacturing are shown in Table 17.4. Equation 1 assumes that the source of the disturbance, i.e., competitiveness, is not important. Neither Equation 1 nor Equation 2, which eliminates the insignificant variables from Equation 1 and disaggregates value added into human and physical capital, does well in explaining the structure of domestic subsidization as measured by the F-test. Replacing value added or its components with the structure of competitiveness (Equation 3), which is largely deter-

Table 17.4. Determinants of Effective Subsidization to Manufacturing Industries in West Germany, 1974

Regression Equations | $\bar{R}^2$ | F

(1) $\ln$ DOMSUB = 8.19 − 1.67 $\ln$ VAPE + 0.15 $\ln$ NOE − 0.02 $\ln$ DNOE − 0.25 $\ln$ NOF − 0.72 $\ln$ REG − 1.19 $\ln$ TARPRO
(1.28) (−1.42) (−0.78) (−0.10) (2.54)[a] (−2.22)[a] (−2.82)[a,c]
$\bar{R}^2$ = 0.26   F = 2.46

(2) $\ln$ DOMSUB = 5.42 + 0.01 $\ln$ HUM − 0.24 $\ln$ KAP − 0.24 $\ln$ NOF − 0.61 $\ln$ REG − 0.93 in TARPRO
(1.63) (0.01) (−0.59) (−2.23)[a] (−1.92)[a] (−1.49)
$\bar{R}^2$ = 0.24   F = 2.54

(3) $\ln$ DOMSUB = 5.97 − 0.41 $\ln$ RCATOT − 0.17 $\ln$ NOF − 0.62 $\ln$ REG − 1.50 $\ln$ TARPRO
(4.43)(−2.38)[a] (−2.23)[a] (−2.25)[a] (−3.81)[a,c]
$\bar{R}^2$ = 0.41   F = 5.37[a]

(4) $\ln$ DOMSUB = 5.39 − 0.67 $\ln$ RCAEEC − 0.22 $\ln$ NOF − 0.67 $\ln$ REG − 1.22 $\ln$ TARPRO
(3.45)(−0.70) (−2.59)[a] (−2.10)[a] (−2.75)[a,c]
$\bar{R}^2$ = 0.27   F = 3.31[a]

(5) $\ln$ DOMSUB = 5.18 − 0.31 $\ln$ RCANEC − 0.14 $\ln$ NOF − 0.45 $\ln$ REG − 1.37 $\ln$ TARPRO
(4.15)(−2.64)[a] (−1.69)[b] (−1.63)[b] (−3.80)[a,c]
$\bar{R}^2$ = 0.44   F = 5.88[a]

(6) $\ln$ DOMSUB = 7.01 − 0.15 RCALDC − 0.26 $\ln$ NOF − 0.68 $\ln$ REG − 1.59 $\ln$ TARPRO
(4.73)(−2.60)[a] (−3.40)[a] (−2.50)[a] (−4.00)[a,c]
$\bar{R}^2$ = 0.43   F = 5.80[a]

Source: Calculated from Donges, Fels, Neu (1973); Jüttemeier, Lammers (1979); Statistisches Bundesamt, Wiesbaden [Statistisches Jahrbuch für die Bundesrepublik Deutschland, various issues; Fachserie 7, Reihe 7, 1970].

Note: T=Statistics in parentheses. DOMSUB=total effective subsidization from domestic sources; TARPRO=effective rate of tariff protection; NOE=number of employees 1970; DNOE=change in the number of employees, 1964–1970; NOF=number of firms 1970; REG=regional concentration 1970 (variation coefficient of industry *i*'s employment share across eleven "Bundesländer"); HUM=human capital intensity 1970 (average wage per employee minus unskilled worker's wage); KAP=physical capital intensity 1970 (gross fixed capital in 1970 prices); RCA . . . = "revealed comparative advantage" (exports/imports), with TOT=vis-à-vis total world, NEC=vis-à-vis EEC non-members, LDC=vis-à-vis less developed countries.

[a] Significant at 5 percent.
[b] Significant at 10 percent.
[c] Not significantly different from minus unity at 5 percent.

mined by the structure of human capital intensity, considerably improves the results. These results are maintained when competitiveness vis-à-vis non-EEC countries (Equation 5) or competitiveness vis-à-vis LDCs (Equation 6) replaces overall competitiveness.

The individual coefficients show that higher levels of domestic subsidization are associated with (a) lower competitiveness, (b) fewer firms, (c) lower regional concentration, and (d) lower EEC tariff protection. The direction of influence of regional concentration accords with the particular institutional framework used to distribute funds in Germany. However, a key variable, the number of employees in an industry, is not shown to be significant by the test, implying a limited "political economy of protection" in Germany.

This picture changes when the nonregional component of domestic subsidization, i.e., R&D aid and special industry programs, is subject to test (Table 17.5) alone. Following the same testing strategy outlined above for domestic subsidization, the number of employees in each industry does emerge significantly, with the expected sign (Equations 2 and 4), lending support to the existence of a political economy of protection in Germany. Not surprisingly, given the ambiguity introduced by the existence of more than one level of government, regional concentration was never significant in regressions (not shown) explaining nonregional aids.

Regional economic and political forces have been trying to circumvent those institutions and to get aid for industries concentrated in their regions through the annual budgetary (parliamentary) process. For example, programs to help shipbuilding, concentrated in the coastal states, more than doubled between 1974 and 1979 (Jüttemeier and Lammers, p. 46). In addition, the maritime states (Schleswig-Holstein, Hamburg, Lower Saxony, and Bremen) are demanding federal matching funds for a coastal program,[7] and a Ruhr Program initiated on the insistence of North-Rhine Westphalia has passed the Bundestag. But there is reason to suspect that "coastal program" and "Ruhr program" really mean "shipbuilding program" and "steel industry program."

It has been argued that the source of pressure matters in determining the supply of protection i.e., that the political process would more readily grant subsidies to industries suffering from low international competitiveness, all else being equal. Does the geographical source of that foreign competition matter? A comparison of Equations 5 and 6, Table 17.4, with Equations 4 and 5, Table 17.5, testing total domestic subsidization and nonregional domestic subsidization, sheds some light on this issue. Whereas the structure of competitiveness against all non-EEC member countries codetermines the structure of total as well as of nonregional subsidization, the same is not true of competitiveness

Table 17.5. Determinants of Effective Domestic Nonregional Assistance to Manufacturing Industries in West Germany, 1974 (n=26)

Regression Equations	R^2	F
(1) ln NONREG = 0.00 + 0.17 ln HUM −0.22 ln KAP −0.32 ln NOF +0.45 ln NOE −1.24 ln RESTAID (0.00) (0.12) (−0.28) (−1.19) (1.07) (−0.95)	0.04	1.26
(2) ln NONREG = −0.34 − 0.83 ln RCATOT + 0.75 ln NOE −0.32 ln NOF −2.33 ln RESTAID (−0.08)(−2.26)[a] (2.19)[a] (−1.96)[a] (−2.92)[a]	0.27	3.30[a]
(3) ln NONREG = 0.50 − 0.06 ln RCAEC + 0.47 ln NOE −0.33 ln NOF −1.52 ln RESTAID (0.11)(−0.17) (1.25) (−1.81)[a] (−1.74)[a]	0.09	1.67
(4) ln NONREG = −1.10 − 0.57 ln RCANEC + 0.69 ln NOE −0.27 ln NOF −2.08 ln RESTAID (−0.28)(−2.40)[a] (2.13)[a] (−1.71)[a] (−2.83)[a]	0.29	3.52[a]
(5) ln NONREG = 1.47 − 0.16 ln RCALDC + 0.58 ln NOE −0.40 ln NOF −2.02 ln RESTAID (0.34)(−1.29) (1.65)[b] (−2.19)[a] (−2.33)[a]	0.16	2.18

Source: Calculated from Donges, Fels, Neu (1973); Jüttemeier, Lammers (1979); Statistisches Bundesamt, Wiesbaden [Statistisches Jahrbuch für die Bundesrepublik Deutschland, various issues; Fachserie 7, Reihe 7, 1970].

Note: T = Statistics in parentheses. NONREG = effective rate of domestic assistance not attributed to regional aid programs; RESTAID = effective rate of assistance attributable to regional aid programs plus effective tariff protection; NOE = number of employees, 1970; DNOE = change in the number of employees, 1964–1970; NOF = number of firms, 1970; REG = regional concentration 1970 (variation coefficient of industry 1's employment share across eleven "Bundesländer"); HUM = human capital intensity, 1970 (average wage per employee minus unskilled worker's wage); KAP = physical capital intensity, 1970 (gross fixed capital in 1970 prices); RCA . . . = "revealed comparative advantage" (exports/imports), with TOT = vis-à-vis total world, NEC = vis-à-vis EEC non-members, LDC = vis-à-vis less developed countries.

[a] Significant at 5 percent.
[b] Significant at 10 percent.

vis-à-vis the LDCs alone. That variable has explanatory power only when regional subsidies are included.

Apparently, regional aid is channeled to regions that have production structures similar to that of LDCs and that hence suffer most from new competitors abroad.[8] The same cannot be said for nonregional subsidization; here overall competitiveness of the industry is crucial. Demands for new regional aid programs outside of regular channels in Germany therefore have major implications for LDC exporters. While heretofore German producers threatened by LDC competition could count on aid only if they were not concentrated regionally, if demands for new protection are met they will receive aid even if they are concentrated regionally. This, in turn, implies that the aid will be more concentrated on individual branches than heretofore. And, the fact that the number of employees has a positive influence on this type of aid means that the large, old, established industries suffering from LDC competition can be expected to get above-average support from domestic sources in the future.

It should be borne in mind that these conclusions hold for domestic assistance, which supplements EEC tariff protection. An analysis of EEC tariff setting along the lines pursued for Germany would surpass the bounds of this chapter. Nevertheless some useful observations can be made about the determinants of EEC tariff policy, since some of the variables used to explain the German case are unambiguously related to the same determinants in other EEC countries.

This would be true of human and physical capital intensity across industries in the absence of factor reversals.

This may be true of the cross-industry structure of the number of firms, because technological considerations play a key role in determining industrial concentration.

This may also be true of the cross-industry structure of the change in the number of employees, but of course not in the absolute number of employees.

On this rationale, a regression to explain the interindustry structure of EEC effective tariffs was run. The approach was equivalent to that chosen by Riedel (1977) for the explanation of changes in tariff structure:

$$\ln \text{TAR} = 4.21 + 0.01 \ln \text{DNOE} -0.06 \ln \text{NOF} -0.74 \ln \text{HUM} + 0.43 \ln \text{KAP}$$
$$(4.71) \ (0.10) \qquad (-1.73) \qquad (-4.22) \qquad (3.97)$$
$$\bar{R}^2 = 0.53 \qquad F = 8.00$$

where t-statistics are in parentheses and notation is as in Table 17.5. The equation as a whole significantly explains the EEC tariff structure and lends support to the hypothesis that a political market was operative during the harmonization process upon founding of the EEC. At the community level, it appears that the interests of unskilled labor, physical capital, and concentrated industries prevail. Of particular interest to LDC exporters is the size of influence of human capital intensity: labor-intensive industries are heavily discriminated against, a phenomenon not observable in this form for German domestic protection, especially not for nonregional aid.

These results for the structure of EEC tariff protection are largely consistent with those of Riedel (1977), who found that reductions in effective total protection were associated with greater employment in the industry, lower human capital intensity, and lower previous industry growth rates.

In summary, the empirical evidence supports the hypothesis that the political process in Germany responds to demands for protection on the part of interest groups on the basis of vote maximizing; that interest groups' demand for protection is heavily influenced by excludability considerations; that the source of the disturbance (domestic vs. foreign) matters in granting assistance; and that domestic protection and tariff protection are substitutes. However, the regional component of subsidization, heavily weighted by the joint federal-state program for improving the regional economic structure, obeys its own laws. At least within this and related regional programs, the expected log-rolling process has been stymied.

BIBLIOGRAPHY

Adlung, Rudolf, Hermann Götzinger, Konrad Lammers et al., (1979). *Konzeption und Instrumente einer potentialorientierten Regionalpolitik,* Institut für Kommunalwissenschaften der Konrad-Adenauer-Stiftung e.V., St. Augusten.

Anderson, Kym, (1979). "The Political Market for Government Assistance to Australia Manufacturing Industries," unpublished manuscript.

Anderson, Kym, (1978). "The Political Market for Government Assistance to Industries," unpublished manuscript.

Balassa, Bela, (1967). *Trade Liberalization among Industrial Countries: Objectives and Alternatives,* New York.

Buchanan, James, and Gordon Tullock, (1962). *The Calculus of Consent,* Ann Arbor.

Bundesbericht Forschung, VI, (1979), Deutscher Bundestag, 8. Wahlperiode, Unterrichtung durch die Bundesregierung, Drucksache 8/3024, Bonn.

Cheh, John, (1974). "United States Concession in the Kennedy Round and Short-run Labor Adjustment Costs," *Journal of International Economics.*

Deutscher Bundestag, (1976), 7. Wahlperiode, Unterrichtung durch die

Bundesregierung: Fünfter Rahmenplan der Gemeinschaftsaufgabe. "Verbesserung der regionalen Wirtschaftsstruktur," Drucksache 7/4742, Bonn.

Dicke, Hugo, (1977). *"Die Wirkungen strukturpolitischer Maßnahmen in der Ernährungsindustrie,"* Kieler Studien No. 144.

Donges, Jürgen, Gerhard Fels, Axel D. Neu, et al. (1973). *Protektion und Branchenstruktur in der westdeutschen Wirtschaft,* Kieler Studien 123.

Fels, Gerhard, (1976). "Overall Assistance to German Industry," in Max Corden and Gerhard Fels (eds.), *Public Assistance to Industries,* London.

Glismann, Hans H., and Frank Weiss (1980). "On the Political Economy of Protection in Germany," World Bank Working Paper No. 427, Washington, D.C.

Grubel, Herbert, and Peter B. Lloyd (1975). *Intra-Industry Trade.* London.

Jüttemeier, Karl-Heinz, and Konrad Lammers, (1979). *Subventionen in der Bundesrepublik,* Kiel Discussion Paper 63/64.

Kravis, Irving B. and Robert E. Lipsey, (1971). *Price Competitiveness in World Trade,* New York.

Krengel, Rolf, et al., Produktionsvolumen und -potential, Produktionsfaktoren auf dem Gebiet der Bundesrepublik Deutschland und Berlin (West), Berlin, various issues.

Krueger, Anne O., (1974). "The Political Economy of a Rent-Seeking Society," *American Economic Review.*

Neu, Axel D., (1976). "Protection of the German Textile Industry," in Max Corden and Gerhard Fels (eds), *Public Assistances to Industry,* London.

Olson, Mancur, (1965). *The Logic of Collective Action,* Cambridge, Mass.

Olson, Mancur, (1978). "The Political Economy of Comparative Growth Rates," unpublished manuscript.

Pincus, J. J., (1975). "Pressure Groups and the Pattern of Tariffs," *Journal of Political Economy.*

Riedel, James, (1977). "Tariff Concessions in the Kennedy Round and the Structure of Protection in West Germany," *Journal of International Economics.*

Rodemer, Horst, (1980). *Die EG-Agrarpolitik,* Kieler Studien No. 164, Tübingen.

Schwarze, Ulla, (1980). "Subventionen-spürbare Beeinflussung des Wirtschaftsgefüges?", Mitteilungen des Rheinisch-Westfälischen Instituts für Wirtschaftsforschung.

Statistisches Bundesamt (Wiesbaden): Facheserie 7/Reihe 7, *Außenhandel nach dem Warenverzeichnis für die Industriestatistik,* annual. *Statistisches Jahrbuch für die Bundesrepublik Deutschland,* annual.

Wolter, Frank, (1976). "Adjusting to Imports from Developing Countries," in H. Giersch (ed.), *Reshaping the World Economic Order,* Tübingen.

NOTES

1. See Downs (1957), Buchanan and Tullock (1962), and Olson (1965) for underlying considerations of the economics of politics; and for applications to international trade, see especially Cheh (1974), Krueger (1974), Pincus (1975), Riedel (1977), and Anderson (1978, 1979).

2. The encompassingness of interest groups is a point emphasized by Mancur Olson (1978) for determining the kinds of policies they will pursue.
3. This institutional feature of the West German economy helps explain the absence of explicit minimum wage laws. From the point of view of the unions, they are not required.
4. It must be admitted, however, that there are signs of a breakdown of such consensus. For example, the labor unions have walked out of joint labor-management "Concerted Action," where incomes policies were negotiated. These agreements, however, were not binding.
5. The second major regional aid program aims at maintaining the economic viability of West Berlin. The subsidy base is similar to that of the joint federal-state development program, namely investment. But this program does not really promote regionally concentrated industry, as West Berlin's economic structure still corresponds quite well to that of the dozen or so major German cities.
6. Firms may export their products at the same time that they act as importers (wholesalers) of products with which to complement their assortment.
7. A program opposed by mountainous, landlocked Bavaria, even though two of the coastal states are governed by the CDU, sister party of the Bavarian CSU.
8. This is also consistent with Wolter's (1976) finding that industries concentrated in low-income regions in West Germany are most exposed to LDC competition.

About the Editors

ROBERT E. DRISCOLL is Executive Vice President and Chief Operating Officer of the Fund for Multinational Management Education, a New York based not-for-profit educational, training and research organization. Mr. Driscoll has been with the Fund since 1973. He has been a consultant to a number of major U.S. corporations on issues affecting international investments in the developing countries. He served as project coordinator for a major study examining U.S. business perspectives toward technology transfer and development, a study undertaken for the U.S. Department of State. He has also served as an advisor to the National Academy of Sciences. Mr. Driscoll holds an M.A. degree from the University of Texas at Austin. He is author/editor of a number of books and articles, including *The Social and Economic Impacts of Transnational Corporations: Case Studies of the U.S. Paper Industry in Brazil* (1976); *Foreign Investment in Egypt* (1978); *Technology Transfer and Development: Viewpoints of U.S. Business* (1979); and *The Private Sector in Brazilian Development: Investment and Technology for the 1980's.* (1980).

JACK N. BEHRMAN is Luther Hodges Distinguished Professor at the University of North Carolina Graduate School of Business Administration. He has held faculty appointments at Davidson College, Washington and Lee University, and the University of Delaware, and visiting professorships at George Washington University and the Harvard Business School. In addition, Dr. Behrman is a frequent member of research panels for the National Academy of Sciences and the National Academy of Engineering; and advisor the the U.S. Department of State and the U.N. Centre on Transnational Corporations; and Senior Research Advisor to the Fund for Multinational Management Education in New

York. From 1961 to 1964, he was Assistant Secretary of Commerce for Domestic and International Business. Dr. Behrman is the author of numerous articles, books, and monographs, including *Some Patterns in the Rise of the Multinational Enterprise* (1969), *National Interests and the Multinational Enterprise* (1970), *U.S. International Business and Governments* (1971), *The Role of International Companies in Latin American Integration* (1972), and *Industry Ties with Science and Technology Policies in Developing Countries* (1980); he is coauthor of *International Business-Government Communications* (1975), *Transfers of Manufacturing Technology Within Multinational Enterprises* (1976), and *Science and Technology for Development* (1980).

Index